SANDY STOTT

< CRITICAL HOURS >

SEARCH AND RESCUE

IN THE WHITE MOUNTAINS

University Press of New England   *Hanover and London*

University Press of New England

www.upne.com

© 2018 University Press of New England

All rights reserved

Manufactured in the United States of America

Designed by Mindy Basinger Hill

Typeset in Minion Pro

Library of Congress Cataloging-in-Publication Data

Names: Stott, Sandy, author.

Title: Critical hours: search and rescue in the White Mountains /
Sandy Stott.

Description: Hanover, NH: University Press of New England, 2018.
| Includes bibliographical references and index.

Identifiers: LCCN 2017036433 (print) | LCCN 2017058341 (ebook) |
ISBN 9781512601763 (epub, mobi, & pdf) | ISBN 9781512600407
(pbk.: alk. paper)

Subjects: LCSH: Mountaineering—Search and rescue operations—
White Mountains (N.H. and Me.)—History. | White Mountains
(N.H. and Me.)—History.

Classification: LCC GV200.183 (ebook) | LCC GV200.183 .S74 2018
(print) | DDC 796.5220974—dc23

LC record available at https://lccn.loc.gov/2017036433

5   4   3   2   1

For my father,

FRED "MAC" STOTT,

who took me

to the trails,

and for

LUCILLE,

who goes out

with me every day

CONTENTS

ACKNOWLEDGMENTS

Because this is a nonfiction book, it is built on the stories of the past. I am grateful to the storytellers who have published accounts of those stories. Without them, there would be no foundation for my work, nor would there be a perch from which to survey the current scene and wonder about its future. Books central to my understanding of how White Mountain search and rescue developed are *Forest and Crag*, by Laura and Guy Waterman; *Not without Peril*, by Nick Howe; *Joe Dodge: One New Hampshire Institution*, by William Lowell Putnam; and *Mountain Voices*, by Doug Mayer and Rebecca Oreskes. These volumes gave me the sense of White Mountain history and its inflection points that allowed me to choose stories that carried within them the evolution of search and rescue and its modern structure and practices. I also drew heavily on the accumulated history in *Appalachia*, the AMC's semiannual journal. *Appalachia* offers a record going back to 1877, and in such incidents as that of Curtis and Ormsbee, it provided extensive description and commentary.

Other works and writers that brought me memorable stories and excellent questions are listed in the bibliography.

Just as they provide an extraordinary service to adventurers in the White Mountains, so too were searchers, rescuers, and those they sought generous with their time and stories when I spoke with them. In particular, interviews with these participants in our searches and rescues were invaluable: Bill and Barbara Arnold, Matt Bowman, Alain Comeau, Brad Ray, Rebecca Orsekes, Chris Joosen, Paul Cormier, Steve Larson, James Wrigley, Paul Cunha, Mike Pelchat, Paul Neubauer, Rick Wilcox, Allan Clark, Steve Smith, Steve Dupuis, Justin Preisendorfer, Kevin Jordan, Heidi Murphy, Wayne Saunders, Mark Ober, Jim Kneeland, Crispin Battles, Iain Hamilton, Dan Jacques, Greg Gerbig, Kyle Madigan, Adam DeWolfe, Greg Reck, Lelia Vann, Julie Horgan, Pat Grimm.

Writers work with words and have a fondness for them. Images sometimes present more of an unknown. I was fortunate to have people who gave me good advice and excellent images for illustration. Thanks to the photographers credited, and to AMC archivist Becky Fullerton and to Ty Gagne, both of whom helped me find images that supported the stories of the book.

I talk often about risk with two friends who work at managing risk for a living. Geoff Smith and Ty Gagne both offered keen insights and questions, and each showed the sort of interest that keeps a writer going. Other friends joined in conversation over e-mail, and those conversations brought paragraphs and pages to this book—thanks to Patty Hager, Chris Woodside, and Sally Manikian. Thanks also to people in the Cardigan writing group, who asked questions when we gathered in October 2016, and so let me know that others might be interested.

In the midst of all this thinking and writing, a visit with the "croo" of AMC's Galehead Hut gave me insight into the present and hope for the future. Thanks to Scott Berkley, Erica Lehner, Anna Ready-Campbell, Annie Schide, and Greg Konar.

Around three-quarters of the way into this book, I got the gift of two first readers: David Dunbar and Scott Berkley sent back observations that improved the work and encouraged me.

A special thanks to Doug Mayer, who not only put up with my constant questions, but also put me up at his Randolph home on many occasions. Doug also gave me good insight into the rescue scene in Chamonix, France, where he works and lives part of the year.

I am also grateful to University Press of New England for supporting this project: to my acquiring editor, Richard Pult, for believing in it throughout, to Susan Abel for managing the whole march to production, and to copyeditor Cannon Labrie for his close and careful work with my words. Such clear-eyed readers are the rarest of gifts.

Any errors in these pages are mine and mine alone.

I am lucky to have a partner who joins and encourages me on various trails, and who is a most sure-footed guide along the sentence-trails of my writing. First companion and first editor, without Lucille there would be no book.

ABBREVIATIONS

This book is full of abbreviations that avoid the need to spell out the lengthy names of search and rescue teams and other organizations. For the reader's convenience, here is a list of groups that appear often and their abbreviations.

AMC	Appalachian Mountain Club
AVSAR	Androscoggin Valley Search and Rescue
CO	New Hampshire Fish and Game conservation officer
DHART	Dartmouth-Hitchcock Advanced Rescue Team
MRS	Mountain Rescue Service
NEK9	New England K9 Search and Rescue
NHANG	New Hampshire Army National Guard
NHFG	New Hampshire Fish and Game
NHOC	New Hampshire Outdoor Council
PVSART	Pemigewasset Valley Search and Rescue Team
RMC	Randolph Mountain Club
SOLO	Stonehearth Outdoor Learning Opportunities
USFS	United States Forest Service
UVWRT	Upper Valley Wilderness Rescue Team
WMSRT	White Mountain Swiftwater Rescue Team

A NOTE ON NAMES

A note about people's names: In discussing incidents that have been highly publicized, I have used full names. In other instances, where the incident was little reported, I have used the convention we use in the Appalachian Mountain Club's semiannual journal *Appalachia*, where I write a column on White Mountain accidents and their lessons. There, we offer a degree of anonymity by using only a first name and last initial.

< CRITICAL HOURS >

INTRODUCTION

"It's not as hard as you think . . .
most mountain travelers want to help,
and the more experienced they are,
the more willing to help. I just ask people,
and damned few ever turn me down. . . .
That's the way it is with most of the people
that work and hike around these hills.
If someone is in trouble, they all want to help."

WILLIAM LOWELL PUTNAM
Joe Dodge: "One New Hampshire Institution"

A Moment

High on the ridges above Pinkham Notch, the sun slips down, and the fog thickens; the rocks glisten wanly. You are late. What had seemed a friendly upland world now offers faint menace. Time to hurry. You look up, away from the trail, into the future; that's when it happens. You miss the small shelf of rock by an inch, your toe slips down, and you follow. The landing, emphasized by your thirty-pound pack, jars. You hear the twig-snapping sound, and, even before you roll to test it, even before pain's announcement, you know you've broken your ankle.

You look up, then around . . . into absence. The hut you left a couple of hours ago is now numbingly distant; even the relative shelter of the woods is far away over this jumbled rock. Reluctantly (or, perhaps, hurriedly) you pull your pack around in front and dig into its pocket for your phone. You press 911, and—happiness—you get a voice. "How can we help?" you hear. "I've broken my ankle," you say. "I'm on Mount Washington. It's getting dark." You draw a breath and wait. Nothing. You look at your screen; it reads, *Call dropped.* "No," you say aloud. "No!" You try again—nothing—and again. No service. "No!"

Did they get what you said? Are they coming? Will they find you?

You pull clothes from your pack and begin to wait. Meanwhile, down below, the 911 operator has received enough information from your call to make the next call. She contacts the state police, and they in turn call New Hampshire Fish and Game, where their dispatcher records what little they know: the time of your call, your reported injury, your phone number, the coordinates of your call (which may or may not be spot on). The next call goes to Conservation Officer Mark Ober. Ober is on his way home after a day of providing directions for and, on occasion, managing the accidents of ATV drivers from Jericho State Park; he's tired and ready for day's end. "Really?" he says aloud to his phone's ringtone. "Really?"

Yes, really. Ober sighs, answers, notes down what's known of you and your plight. He tries your phone, gets nothing. Then he begins a series of further calls. He calls Mount Washington State Park atop the mountain and asks if they can send someone down to check the area of your reported coordinates. Maybe, he thinks, I'll get lucky and Mike Pelchat will still be up there. It sounds like a carryout, so he'll need at least twelve people, preferably eighteen or more, so folks can rotate their carrying time as they negotiate the unevenness and obstacles beside the trail. Soon, he's got two more conservation officers (COs) and eight volunteers from Androscoggin Valley Search and Rescue (AVSAR), all headed for the Auto Road, where they can be driven in vans to a point closest to your coordinates. He calls the Appalachian Mountain Club (AMC), where he'll set up his command post and, he hopes, get more volunteers. He calls Mountain Rescue Service (MRS) and asks that they stand by. The coordinates he has from the phone call suggest you may have fallen in Tuckerman Ravine; maybe he'll need high-angle help from their technical climbers. A cold front has been forecast. The ridges above 4,000 feet may see a first dusting of snow. The cold will make time a factor, with the night stretching out before him.

And you? No one's come along the trail in this foggy dusk. You've tried crawling—no go—and so you've pulled out all your clothes and packed yourself down as much as possible in the rocks. The cold seems denser. Still no service. You will have to wait in night's room, amid its absences and visions. You hope with an urgency near prayer that they will find you.

> Every walk, run, or climb takes you near such an edge. And every mountain wanderer who is lucid about that upland life knows that it is lived conditionally. That, whatever your age, even as you have always returned from upland trails, there is the chance you will not. That each time you step away from the everyday into the mountains, you are bound for the edge of elsewhere.

One August Day: It Could Be You— This Time It's Me

I've never been rescued. But that doesn't mean I haven't been close, lying in my imagination by a trail, hoping for a string of bobbing headlamps. Or moored to a tree, hoping to see a rope drop into view, followed by the scrabbling sound of descending feet. I have a number of instances to choose among. And each time I write about another's troubles along this edge, I imagine myself there, take up residence with that other. Here, then, in the spirit of going out, is one day from a life of walking and climbing mountains. Perhaps you can imagine your way into this day and match it with one of your own.

I'm a cautious sort when it comes to lightning and cloudbursts in general, and a good measure of that caution comes from a lifelong fascination with all things weather. Well before the advent of easy access to weather radar, I'd tuned my reading of clouds and wind to become an accurate short-term forecaster and okay at twenty-four-hour predictions. Wherever our family happened to be, my father and I competed in reading the sky. "That cloud's all show," he'd say of a gray ridge-grazer, and then we'd see. I learned to look to the sky as often as I looked to the ground. In my preferred landscape, the mountains, I kept close tabs on whatever slice of sky I could see and counted on surprise from behind peaks and ridges. I didn't get caught out often when hail battered a ridge or some divinity began to play with electricity. And when I did get caught, I knew how to minimize the chances of ending up in various accident reports.

Still, on August 2, 2011, I got surprised during a traverse of New Hampshire's narrow and windswept Franconia Ridge, when a thunderstorm appeared, hugged an imaginary curve in its track over Cannon Mountain, and turned my way.

The day began as good mountain days do: early with coffee in a half-tone darkness. My first glance at the lightening sky and our home mountain's profile joined the cool air to say, "This could be a good ridge day." One of thousands for whom the Franconia Ridge is a version of a best mountain day, I'd been away from its weathered crest for nearly five years, the longest absence since I'd first climbed over its primary peak, Mount Lafayette, as an eleven-year-old. The caffeine-jazzed drive north from Alexandria took a little over an hour, and pulling into the trailhead parking for Liberty Spring while raindrops slapped my windshield offered only mild annoyance. The forecast was good, and the blue to the west didn't look like a "sucker hole." I was walking by 7:00 a.m.

The forest canopy shook off its drops like a dog after a swim, and I went up in the cool early air. One of the ridge's attractions is its one big climb that earns a whole day of easier walking sprinkled with short ups and downs; work early, wander late, could be its motto. I cruised by Liberty Spring campsite, nodding to those about their breakfasts, and reached the ridge, opting to skip the oft-visited eyetooth of Mount Liberty in favor of the high ground to the north. Sun tiger-striped the woods, and the mosses gave them a velvet appeal. A cloud brought back the earlier gray morning, but it left for the deeper Pemigewasset Wilderness to my east, and I ambled north in the little trees.

The uptick before Little Haystack got me sweating again, and it offered the first views of the two southern pyramids, Flume and Liberty. At that point, I noted some haze in the air between us. Then, I popped up above tree line, pausing to look east to the Bonds and Carrigain and at the blue ridges beyond. "Yes," I said aloud, "there's more water in the air than I thought there'd be." A glance west ratified this: a lid of clouds lay over the flattish country northwest of Cannon Mountain, and a few skirts of rain trailed beneath. "Okay, I'll watch those guys," I said to myself and the white-throated sparrow whose song has always meant mountains to me.

For nearly two miles between Little Haystack and the ridge's big dog, Mount Lafayette, the Franconia Ridge is a mountain ambler's paradise. From the south the terrain trends upward, but there are no extended climbs, and there are a number of level stretches where the flat-rocked path let's you saunter along in the sky. At an average elevation of 5,000 feet, the ridge rises

The Franconia Ridge as seen from Mount Moosilauke on a best day. Photo by author.

a steep 2,000 or more feet above the surrounding territory, and the winds and fierce climate permit only a few patches of scrub trees on the east side near the ridgeline. Called in some guides a knife-edge, the ridge is a dull blade, with only a handful of spots where it narrows to a body's length. Still, its walkers are of equal parts air and earth, and the whole rumpled quilt of the White Mountains is clear and wild to the east.

And so on a fine August day, I knew I'd have lots of company, and moments of passing fellow walkers would yield a pleasing set of micronarratives. Take, for example, the couple stalled on a sharp pitch just below Little Haystack: he is standing atop the pitch, reaching down and offering advice on foot placement; she is worrying aloud about falling, and the soft expanse of her calf suggests she may have climbed already above her fitness. I wait for a minute below this bottleneck as he cajoles and she worries, clearing finally the last long step up. Both are carrying overnight packs; time surely will stretch out over this day, these days. I wonder about backpacking as relational litmus test.

I stop atop Little Haystack to compare cloud notes with an overnight hiker who already has his rainproof pack cover on. As we talk I note that his speech comes one word at a time, and I ask if he's been "out" long. "Yes, three weeks," he says and then rests from that wordy exertion. We agree that the western cloud deck is moving this way, albeit at the pace of his speech. "Any thunder?" I ask. "No," he says, "not yet."

I set out north at a good clip, perhaps a little more than two miles per hour, reveling in the easy footing and my sense of rising effortlessly; I am one part sky-creature, looking down with the long view of a raptor. What are all the little people doing in their various valleys today? Altitude is a sort of exceptionalism; I am heady with height.

On Lincoln's summit, I meet a French Canadian with an overnight pack; he's headed south for Liberty Spring. "Rain coming, yes," he says, his strong accent raising the vowels of "rain" toward a long *e*. "By zen I will be in my tent reading my book, yes?" he says. He smiles; a silver tooth winks. "You go up zere?" he asks, nodding north. I try to read his amused smile and get mild skepticism. This makes me think: in the Whites, male French Canadians are legendary for their moments of bravado and folly, getting lost or injured with a frequency that sets search and rescue tongues and heads wagging. Should I be swimming against a French Canadian current?

I measure the mile ahead, with its dip and then rise up Lafayette: it's all open ridge. I scan the storm to my west: it's filled in and its fringe of rain is now a trailing curtain. Thunder, absent from discussion till now, punctuates my thinking. Surely this is the point where accumulated weather wisdom and common sense turn me around, sending me south toward the sheltering trees and off the ridge. Surely.

Not so much. Along the ridge to the north, I can see at least fifteen people still climbing, including what appears to be a camp group of eight ducklings vanishing into the cloud a few hundred yards up from the small saddle beneath Lafayette. I join them, waving goodbye to my French Canadian canary, setting out with quick steps. The lure of going up is stronger than thought. On over Lincoln. "I can be on top of Lafayette in twenty minutes," I say to the clouds to my left; they rumble.

It takes the advent of rain, continued cloud grumbling, and a final sharp report of thunder for me to reassess. I'm near the saddle between the peaks and it's as dark as it was when I awoke this morning. "Whoa," I say, my long habit of self-address intact, "Whoa." The cloud answers. I can't see its limits; it is the whole sky.

> A moment for some mountain thunderstorm basics: compress all the advice available, some of it contradictory or vague, and you get this—don't be attractive. Here, we might channel the ancient Greeks, who had enough experience with lightning on their mountainous peninsula to attribute it to their pantheon's big guy, Zeus. Just as it wasn't a happiness to be too beautiful, thereby drawing Zeus's eye and lust, it also didn't pay to be prominent, especially if your prominence contained a whiff of arrogance. The gods, and Zeus in particular, were alert for humans who aspired to join or even replace them. We belonged down here; the gods belonged up there. And when you think about it, isn't ascension part of what we're after when we climb, when we traipse along the bony ridge that bears us up into the sky?

Prominence, being the tallest or near the tallest object in an area, draws lightning's eye, and when that eye turns your way, the best advice is to get small. Get down off the ridgeline; stay away from taller trees or rocks; leave your metal poles where you can find them later. Then, in humble fashion, crouch down with your feet together in the egg of "lightning position" and wait out the storm. If your pack's not a metal frame one, it's also a good idea to crouch on it, thereby insulating yourself from the ground. What about that favorite shelter along a rocky ridge, the cave or dry space under an overhang? Not a good idea. Zeus's high heat striking the rock above such a cave can get conducted there efficiently; the cave can become a microwave oven, and you can become a toasted offering.

> "Get small," flashes repeatedly in my mind, and I consider the saddle a hundred feet below. A thick scrub crawls to it from the east, and I know there's no threading my way through it and down; going down to the west

is a dicey plunge into Walker Ravine and toward the storm's face on rain-slicked slab and loose scree. The cloud, though everywhere, seems slow, its main action still a few miles west. I turn back, poles clicking out a quick cadence, my heart rate jumping to max, and begin the race back up Lincoln. Once over its top, I will look for my place to get small.

The next fifteen minutes seem a dreamscape made odder still by the contrast between my urgency and the placid faces I pass on my way south. I scoot by a couple on an exposed hump of rock; they are putting on rain gear in a deliberate manner. Below the hump, I find a man sitting under an overhang and smiling. "Plenty of room in here," he says patting the stone bench. "Not the greatest place for a lightning storm," I say, and his reply is lost in the quick distance between us. Everyone seems to have gone stoic, planning to plod or sit through this storm, I think, as I run over Lincoln, which is, I guess, another sort of Greek response to the situation.

Everyone, that is, except for a red rain slicker moving rapidly down in front of me, though I am gaining on it. I am, I reflect as I gauge the many landings of my descent, the fastest human on this ridge and, given my age, that's borderline funny. I catch the slicker, step out over some stones to pass and, as I drop away, I hear, "Not so good up zere, eh?"

A mile into my flight, I reach some scrub with an opening and a hint of path heading east and down. I thread my way fifty yards in, leaving my poles leaning against a dwarf spruce partway down, and in a little clearing I put on a jacket, squat down, and let the baptism of rain and roar pour over me. The wind whirls over the ridge from the west, and I cool quickly, but here among the little trees, I am a little man, too puny, I hope, for the eye of god.

Postscript

The storm blew over, with five or six sharp shots of thunder that boomed as if I were in some cloudatorium with surround-sound speakers set on high. Then the sun returned, and I dried myself on a flat rock, watching the storm cell's backside as it obscured the Hancocks and its wispy hangers-on flew over my head and down the slope, wind made visible. And—you knew this—I then went back up the ridge, reaching Lafayette's summit in a thunderless rain before dropping down its western face to a sunny sojourn on

The Franconia Ridge, just after the thunderstorm. Photo by author.

Greenleaf Hut's porch, a sort of halfway house to the world below. Then back to the valley and its everyday life.

No one got zapped along the ridge that day. Perhaps they prayed. Perhaps Zeus, an ADHD sort of god for sure, was distracted. But surely many were courting the sort of electric attention that no one wants. And surely a few wondered at the white-haired guy who passed them tearing along the ridge as if pursued, gone by in a breath.

And On

Readers and writers seek out such stories. We tell and retell them to our friends, sometimes even to those we've only recently met. Probably that's some of why you've begun this book. But I hope there's further reason: I am drawn equally to the stories and motivations of those who put down their usual lives and go out and up to find and rescue us when we fall or falter. Had I been zapped and survived on that August day, or fallen in my flight, I'd have needed tending and likely a hauling out. Who would have done that? Who are these rescuers, and what do they hope for when they search for and rescue us?

As part of my long affiliation with the Appalachian Mountain Club's semi-annual *Appalachia Journal*, I've read story after story that has come down from the White Mountains—climbers stilled by storm; children who've wandered off; walkers who've stumbled into fractured bones. Ringed around these stories have been the rescuers, many of whom are now familiar to me. Again and again I've read their names, a list of guides and conveyors back to the everyday, saviors really. And slowly I've come to realize that, even as I've never joined a search and rescue group, or been gathered back by one, I see my better self in these men and women who would help us when we fall.

This book gives voice to some of their stories.

WHERE WE COME FROM

- - - -

Thinly Settled to Thickly Surrounded

For millennia, people have been getting lost or getting hurt in the woods and hills. For the most part, getting found over those millennia has been a local phenomenon: your family or your tribe checked the angle of the sun and (you hoped) said, "Where's Li, or Axatumel, or Zorba, or Son Loongoo, or Painted Stick, or Bradford? Anyone seen him?" Then, (you hoped further), people set out to find you. It was a roomy planet, and finding food and exploring—the two primary reasons for going out—often took people into its vastness, where the way might be lost.

That vast wild territory, though often revered as a home to spirits, was just as often feared, and so avoided. Wilderness was said to howl, and most people had an aversion to getting close to its teeth and claws. Topography's high points also housed ornery divinities, like Katahdin's Pamola, said to be large, easily irked, with eagle-like tendencies. Few who knew the legends wanted a piece of Pamola. And surely the European culture that became dominant in northern New England through its early settlers had little use for the heights. Not much of edible value grew or wandered there. Colonists were too busy trying to coax a living from the immediate, bony lowlands and figuring out their relations with natives and each other to seek out added difficulty by going uphill. Such a drive to climb would have to wait until the idea of recreation took root.

For most of us, "recreation" is another word for play, which serves as a counter to work. Various religions also admit and enforce the idea of a break from work's routine to worship or contemplate the god or spirit said to be at the center of creation. The Judeo-Christian God famously rested on the seventh day after the exertions of all that creation. All creation and no recreation makes Yahweh a dull god, after all. And surely the idea that spirit and understanding are often found at some distance from the humdrum of work is also found in Buddhism and Hinduism, while Muslims are asked to break from whatever they are doing to pray five times a day. Beyond these usual breaks, there are other stretches of time when routines change: Passover, Christmas, Ramadan, to name a few. Still, finding such time free from work can be tough when survival is a daily struggle. Some breathing room, some surplus of necessities, some unspoken-for times are needed before recreation arrives as part of a culture. But once those are found, recreation takes hold deeply.

The word "recreation" provokes. It contains, of course, the idea of origin, and it also offers a whiff of hubris: the original won't quite suffice, so let's try again; let's re-create our lives. That charge may account for the seriousness with which some of us pursue our play, even to the point of courting deep trouble or death in the mountains. It's not unusual to hear someone say, "I am most alive when I climb," or, "when I'm out there." When such seekers get lost or hurt, that is where we look for them. Out there.

In New England, outdoor recreation, especially wandering and climbing in the uplands, began to draw people from the towns and cities in the early nineteenth century. The idea had migrated, like many of us, from Europe, where the 1786 first ascent of the continent's highest peak, Mont Blanc, is often cited as the advent of recreational climbing. By 1830, the mix of leisure time with an outward and upward gaze had New Englanders looking at the White Mountains and other northeastern ranges with new eyes. It wasn't long before a significant number of people were following that gaze up into a seemingly limitless wild of rock, sky and wind. What was once seen as "daunting and terrible" began to entice people toward exploration and discovery, of terrain and of self.

Over the last two centuries, our growing numbers have shrunk both the planet and region. A 2008 search for the spot most remote from a road in the lower forty-eight states found it to be a mere twenty miles removed. In the Whites, that figure drops to around four miles, and those four miles are likely to be crisscrossed with trails bearing other walkers. Yet there is still ample room to go missing. And if you do fail to return, or vanish, someone is likely to set out to find you.

But the people who set out to look for you and the manner of their search have changed dramatically from the outset of mountain wandering for pleasure. Wilderness has come under the wing of government agencies, and volunteer search and rescue groups have organized themselves in hierarchies of certification. Mix in the advent of spot-on (or not) technology and flying machines, and you have unprecedented capability for response to those who find themselves in trouble in the wild. What this means for our behavior and what this means for the wild itself are subjects I discuss in this book, as are the stories of those who go missing and, especially, those who go after them.

<2>

FINDING KATE

Searchers' Stories

Every so often, a story emerges, comes down from the Whites, and sets everyone to talking . . . and speculating. In the valleys and across various platforms, the story gets told and retold, and where it intersects with personal stories—"I was just there last week"—it broadens and deepens. It becomes, finally, metaphor for much. So it was in February 2015, when Kate Matrosova went up into the northern Whites and did not return.

Usually, such a story appears as personal tragedy, with its center being a narrative of loss for the victim and her relations. As readers, we learn a lot about the steps that carried the person into trouble. Far less often, we find another view of the same story, told from the points of view of some of those who have gone out looking for that person. And yet, in learning their stories and hearing their voices, we can gain a fuller sense of both the story and of our humanity. Perhaps, in casting back to February 15, 2015, we can penetrate a bit into that so-cold night and the wind-wracked morning that followed, and perhaps we can see a bit more into what it's like to seek . . . and not find. And then to find, finally, what's feared, what's lost. Perhaps then we can see also into the heart of search and rescue, which is lodged finally in the hearts of its people. When the ringtone sounds, they will put down their lives and come find you.

The Call

At 8:30 p.m. on February 15, climber, guide, and Androscoggin Valley Search and Rescue (AVSAR) veteran Matt Bowman and his wife Jenna, also a climber, were sitting by the fire. "It was a school night; the kids were in bed," he recalled. When his phone buzzed, Bowman glanced at the screen and saw the incoming call was from AVSAR, where he is a member of the Winter Above Tree Line Team. Outside, the racketing wind and subzero temperatures made this a memorable night, the year's coldest. As he does with all AVSAR summons, Bowman let the call go to voicemail "so I have the details on record." Then, Bowman retrieved the message and switched to speaker phone so he and Jenna could listen together:

"This is an AVSAR call," said the recording. "This is Bill Arnold calling from AVSAR, at about 8:30 p.m. on Sunday, February 15. We have an overdue hiker, who apparently has set off her personal beacon somewhere on the north slope of either Mount Madison or Mount Adams. . . . Fish and Game is having a hard time figuring that out. They have sent up a group from Fish and Game and one from MRS to try to locate this woman, but they're putting together groups to go out tomorrow morning, Monday, to search for her. The plan is to meet at Appalachia at 8:00 a.m. If you're available, please give me a call."

Bowman's recollection of the next moment follows:

Not that we could see it at 8:30 at night in February, but our house is situated with a view of Madison and Adams. We see it every day, and I'm always pointing out the peaks, changes in weather, and seasons to my kids. Anyway, I remember listening to the wind outside. I recall listening to the message a couple of times, and Jenna and me looking at each other. She usually asks if I want to go, or I'll ask if she thinks (with business and kids) I can go. From what I recall, Jenna just knew I was going. I called Bill to let him know I'd be there at 8:00 a.m.

Earlier that day, Bowman and his friend Dave Salisbury and Bowman's nine-year-old son had gone backcountry skiing. Bowman, a soft-spoken Gorham café owner and all-around mountain sort keeps close tabs on the weather, and he knew extreme cold was on its way. So he and his son dressed carefully and planned to stay down low. As the wind built during the day, the roar above them grew more deep throated, and beneath a few gusts, Bowman's son looked to his dad for reassurance that the wind wouldn't suddenly swoop down and carry them away, that they were okay. Along the sheltered drainage of Avalanche Brook near Pinkham Notch, they were okay. Even in that weather, it was a day to be out . . . for a while.

But up on the ridges, the wind and cold were writing another story. The rumbling sound when a strong cold front blows in has often been likened to a freight train, and rightly so. But there's another sound, one more elemental, that such heavy wind calls up—that of a big wave. Anyone who's spent time at ocean's edge when the storm-spawned large rollers arrive has heard their long, turbulent growl, punctuated by explosive breaking roars and, involuntarily, stepped back. Then, just as the sound thins a bit, making you think you might step forward for a closer look, another wave arrives. The din is constant and serial, the very air choked with spray. Just so the pour of arctic air during a front like that of February 15. When it arrived, it brought huge breaking waves of wind.

At 5:00 a.m. that day, when New York City resident and aspiring mountaineer Kate Matrosova climbed away from the Appalachia parking lot, headed first for the summit of Mount Madison and then on over Mounts Adams, Jefferson, Clay, and Washington, the wind was light and the cold usual. Nearby Mount Washington, routinely the windiest of White Mountain places, had a thirty-five-mile-per-hour wind and −4°F temperature at 4:49 a.m. Yes, the big wind was on its way. The forecasts were clear about the extremes in the offing, and she had read them. But those would happen later, and Matrosova was confident that she could get up and down before the wind waves broke.

Late that morning, Bowman and his son wrapped up their skiing and went home to warm up and enjoy some indoor time. Up high the wind and cold had begun to intensify, and Kate Matrosova found herself behind schedule, down off Madison, with Adams above to the south, and the rest of her planned route probably unreachable. Well dressed for mountain winter, but not carrying any overnight equipment, she had some decisions to make.

Her tragic story, with its reportage of her decisions and speculation about those impossible to report, has been amply written (see, for example, "Too Cold," an essay about Matrosova's tragedy in the winter 2015–16 edition of *Appalachia*, and a January 2016 piece on New Hampshire Public Radio). But there is also this less-chronicled narrative of the search for her that became finally a recovery. To know this search, we must first know a little more about the woman that searchers hoped to find and the terrain where she went missing.

When BNP Parisbas trader Kate Matrosova froze to death near Star Lake between Mounts Madison and Adams sometime on February 15 or 16, 2015, it was all over the news; its starkness drew the eye, engaged the heart. At age thirty-two, she was, by all reports, mountain experienced, though that experience was concentrated within the previous few years, and she was fit and equipped for winter that day. But not, it turned out, for what blew through the Whites during her final forty-eight hours. Can one be "equipped" for winds near eighty miles per hour and temperatures of −30°F? The estimated wind chill on nearby Washington had dropped to nearly −80°F; the ground blizzard of snow must have been impenetrable. A YouTube clip of searchers crossing the slopes of Mount Adams on February 16 shows two of them simply blown over like cutout figures at an amusement park shooting gallery.

Why, so many wondered, walk up into such extremes? All of us who press out into the mountains' elemental world know its lure. There, at distance from the channeled forces that heat and light our houses and apartments, that drive our devices and their synthesized worlds, we find our old selves brought forward from a million years of evolution, which is another name for experience. "Are you experienced?" asked Jimi Hendrix in his short life. "Yes," say our ancient selves, "yes, we are." Or we want to be.

Twinned with this drive is our need for recognition—from others, yes, but often most centrally from ourselves. In Western culture this need often takes on a solo cast; we want to be seen and see ourselves as singular, as distinct and distinctive, and achievement seems the best route. "Whoa," we like to hear, "did you hear that? Who is she? How did he do that?" It begins early in the home or on the playground and rarely goes away. Who doesn't want to be "badass," if only for a short time?

Mix in the mountains, even the ground-down molars of our New England Appalachians, and the weather they breed. For the past three hundred years, after our highlands shifted finally from being home to the gods to being no one's home at all, mountain-drawn folk have found a sort of distinction there. First, there was the challenge of peaks unclimbed; once they'd been climbed, it became routes deemed unclimbable or weather judged too severe. See, for example, the media flurry around January 2015's "free climb" of El Capitan's Dawn Wall, the generally acknowledged "hardest rock climb in the world." Supported by years of practice and planning and liberal rope-hauled supplies, Tommy Caldwell and Kevin Jorgeson's exploit was filmed and blogged and, yes, tweeted throughout its nineteen days. The climb drew long eyes—the thicket of cameras in the meadow below pointed aloft like cannons. Can they do it? Will they break the wall, or will it break them? Will they stay together? Will one fly and the other fall? Caldwell and Jorgeson were "out there," remarkable. They were climbing free of what holds the rest of us in our chairs and jobs and various forms of predictable inertia.

Before that, we riveted our attention on and sometimes glorified the young Alexander Supertramp, aka Chris McCandless, of *Into the Wild* fame. Until his mysterious death, he too wanted to "free climb" through life, defy its gravity.

That, I think, is part of the appeal. You pack up the little town that goes on your back; you step from the lot where people park their cars and their usual lives; you slip between two trees, free for some elemental time in this oldest world. You go up, where divinity once lived, where your hoped-for new self can emerge.

Kate Matrosova was part of that tribe. She would go up—in a grueling daily training regimen on the steps of NYC buildings and to the summits of Kilimanjaro, Elbrus, Aconcagua, and Denali. She hoped eventually to reach the summits of all seven continents. Over the years that stretched ahead, who knows how many other mountains she would have climbed? Ferociously fit and able to endure what many cannot, Matrosova was in the first flush of a passion for the hills.

As Chip Brown's sharp-eyed April 2015 essay for *Bloomberg News* makes clear, Matrosova's capacity for passion drove her training—she trained at levels most can't reach—and kept leading up. Tragically, on those two February days, her passion met weather more turbulent, more driven than it could master. But before we think more about this unhappy meeting, we need to climb the essential details to it, to arrive at the meeting of climber and storm.

By the time she reached the Whites that weekend, Kate Matrosova had already compressed a lifetime of movement into her thirty-two years. Born into meager circumstances in Omsk, Siberia, she showed drive throughout her childhood and gained entrance to Omsk State Transport University, where she studied finance. At age twenty, Matrosova secured a student work visa and flew to the United States where, over the next decade, she transformed herself into an astute financial analyst and remarkable athlete. With a magna cum laude BA from DePaul University, where she studied finance, marketing, and accounting, and a master's from Berkeley in financial engineering, Matrosova climbed quickly to levels of accomplishment most see only from a distance. Those she met and those she worked with were drawn to her zest for life and awed by her abilities and drive. In his *Bloomberg* article, Brown cited a research partner, Li Sun, a PhD physicist who now works for Morgan Stanley: "[Kate] was an adventurer, but I don't think she was a risk-seeker," said Li. "She wanted to know different things, achieve different things, get to different places. It wasn't about risk. It was about achievement."

And so, as part of her upward training, Matrosova and her husband, Charlie Farhoodi, arrived in the winter Whites in mid-February. On the fifteenth, she planned to climb over and through a northern Presidential traverse in alpine style—quick and light over its four summits and sixteen miles, beginning on Mount Madison before dawn, climbing then over Adams and Jefferson, and dropping down from Washington along the Ammonoosuc Ravine Trail as dusk came on. It was an ambitious itinerary. In the face of an extreme forecast, speed would be essential; Matrosova expected to be up and down before it got too tough.

Still, that day's forecast continues to give many pause. Surely the nearby Mount Washington Observatory was explicit in its predictions for punishing cold and wind, as were other forecasters: the coming weather would be the toughest of an already notable winter. Digesting the observatory forecast, the Mount Washington Avalanche Center's snow ranger Jeff Lane put it this way in his February 15 comment:

> Mount Washington will truly be putting on a show today and tomorrow. Its well-earned reputation for harsh winter weather will be on display, and I'd recommend taking a seat away from the action for this show. . . . Temperatures will be falling today, reaching −35°F (−37°C) on the summit overnight. During this time, wind speeds will be rising quickly up to the 100 mph (161 kph) mark, with gusts possibly reaching 125 mph (201 kph). These conditions are not to be taken lightly. I encourage you to be judicious in your choice of adventure today.

Even if your plan is to stay well below tree line today, bring plenty of warm clothes and extra food and water.

There is a measured, laconic quality to Lane's sentences, even as its figures are eye-catchingly extreme. But Lane, deeply experienced, writes from the point of view of someone who has seen all of this before and knows what to make of it.

As veteran mountaineer and rescuer Rick Wilcox pointed out in an interview after the tragedy, there are two ways to approach the mountains: heavy and slow or light and fast. The first is a geared-up, full-pack style reminiscent of the siege method of early high climbing. The second is a stripped-down, bare-essentials quickness close in spirit to trail running. When fully equipped, you carry civilization's core with you—shelter, fire in some form, fuel, clothing—all in service of providing and protecting your elemental heat. The quick-footed climber leaves some of those behind and so depends on not being stopped.

Well below tree line, Mount Madison's Valley Way eases into the woods over gentle contours for its early mile, and Matrosova must have made rapid headway from her 5:00 a.m. departure. After training on stairs and in stairwells, at times with a sixty-pound pack, the liberation of real trails and light weight must have felt grand. And the boot track of this usual way into the northern Presidentials would have made for good walking.

Matrosova was alone in two ways: she and her husband had agreed he would stay in the valley and be the day's driver. While Charlie Farhoodi enjoyed "being drawn along in her wake," he was not an aspiring mountaineer; that was *her* goal. In addition, the day's cold forecast made it unlikely that she'd meet others on these north-, or cold-weather-facing slopes. Still, I'm guessing Matrosova did not feel lonely as she climbed. There is a snug economy to being outfitted for and moving at the right speed through intense cold, where the little engine of your body is kicking out heat and your layered clothes are managing that heat efficiently. From such economy comes pleasure and confidence, a sort of mental fuel and companionship of self.

> For reasons unknown and unknowable, Matrosova's ascent slowed as the morning wore on and she summited Madison, then dropped down to the col

between it and Adams a little before 10:00 a.m. GPS records show that she later climbed another mile from there to the top of Adams and then turned back into the gathering gale, returning, finally and fatally, to a point near the col by Star Lake, where she pressed the button on her locator beacon at 3:30 p.m.

By the time Matrosova summoned help, the morning's heat and confidence had been drawn from her by the ceaseless cold and wind. It's likely that these two administered a final blow as she neared the col, where Mounts Madison and Adams rising above would channel and accelerate that wind through a narrow gap. Androscoggin Valley Search and Rescue team member and then Mount Washington State Park manager Mike Pelchat noted that most of us don't understand the effects of high winds on simple body motions because we haven't experienced them:

> It wasn't a bad day [early on], but you could hear the wind beginning to build like a freight train bringing in the cold air. The front came in really quickly, sooner than forecast. One thing people often don't understand is that every 10-mile-per-hour gain in wind speed increases the force much more than 10 percent. When the winds are 80 or 90 or 100 miles an hour, you can't walk or stay on your feet; you're on your hands and knees waiting for a lull. You can't lift your goggles up; the wind blows your arms behind you. If the temperature is 20 below and a zipper breaks or you drop a glove, you can get into trouble quickly. Hypothermia sneaks up on you, and you start making poor choices. (Chip Brown, "The Trader in the Wild," *Bloomberg News*, April 15, 2015)

Take a look at the progression of the wind and cold recorded on nearby Mount Washington: a steady decline in temperature as the morning wears on, and a corresponding increase in wind speed as the day deepens. A 4:49 a.m. reading of −4°F with thirty-five mile-per-hour winds becomes a 3:51 p.m. reading of −20°F, with seventy-seven mile-per-hour winds.

By 3:30 p.m. Matrosova was achingly close to the point where the trail to the valley scoots through the col and then begins to descend toward the shelter of the woods below. But the wind must have formed a wall she couldn't walk or crawl through. Add to that the effects of prolonged cold and oncoming hypothermia, which also robs one of coordination, and you come to Matrosova's final resting place.

Searchers on the back side of Mount Adams not far from where Kate Matrosova was found on February 16, 2015. Photo by Matt Bowman.

> Some twenty-four hours after skiing with his son, Matt Bowman was bracing himself against hurricane-force winds and −30°F temperatures near Star Lake and the col between Mounts Madison and Adams. There, before him, was a strange sight, a shed pack. Vision limited by goggles, Bowman endured a moment of confusion: had one of his nine fellow rescuers dropped the pack? Then he looked over. Twenty feet away lay Kate Matrosova's body. Bowman felt the air go out of him.

We Will Find You

The phones began playing their ringtones around 4:00 p.m. on the fifteenth. Some thirty minutes earlier a locator beacon had sent its signal skyward from New Hampshire's northern Presidential range, and these chirps, jingles, and snatches of song were its spawn. "Not now," must have been each phone owner's silent prayer. Outside, the light was fading in a day that had tumbled into some thermal abyss; the valley temperatures huddled beneath zero, and the heavy wind probed every shelter. Up high, a howling gale shoved the −20°F temperature down to a −80°F windchill; both were in free fall. And according to the beacon's signal, someone named Kate Matrosova was up there above tree line and in trouble.

In New Hampshire, when such a call comes in from the backcountry, it goes to the state's Fish and Game agency (NHFG), and within that agency, it's the province of the law enforcement division. NHFG conservation officers are responsible for conducting and coordinating search and rescue (SAR), and, while such work isn't the primary focus of a conservation officer's job, it is certainly a high-profile responsibility. And with the advent of easy summons from various devices, it is now a more prevalent one.

On the fifteenth, NHFG sgt. Mark Ober received a call from the state police, in response to a 911 call they had received, reporting the locator beacon's being turned on. Ober's standard ringtone played, just as he was in nearby Twin Mountain wrapping up an investigation of a snowmobile accident. He switched quickly to the calls demanded by this new emergency. He first phoned Matrosova's husband, Charlie Farhoodi, who had placed the 911 call after hearing from the U.S. Air Force Rescue Coordination Center (AFRCC) at Tyndall Air Force Base in Panama City, Florida, that his wife's beacon had been activated. Farhoodi gave Ober a summary of his wife's intended route, her phone number, her preparedness, and her character. As Ober wrote in his incident summary, "He [Farhoodi] said that she was a determined individual and would not activate her beacon unless something was really wrong."

During a January 2016 conversation at Gorham's White Mountain Café, Ober recalled his first thoughts as he gathered information about Matrosova: "I hoped it was a mistake, an incidental activation by chance, because I knew where [the signal] was would be near impossible to get to today, tonight. I've had pretty good cell coverage there, so I thought perhaps I could call and get in touch and find out."

But when he got no response to his call, and as it became apparent that this was no mistaken activation, Ober began a practiced routine. He now had a sketch of a climber crossing exposed terrain made fearsome by the day's gale and cold, and he had more calls to make, many more calls. When an NHFG officer determines that a rescue may be needed, he can activate a whole network of professionals and volunteers. The professionals are NHFG conservation officers, local fire and police departments, and, at times, National Guardsmen and members of the Civil Air Patrol. The volunteers come from a fullness of acronyms—AVSAR, MRS (Mountain Rescue Service), PVSART (Pemigewasset Valley Search and Rescue Team), AMC, SOLO (Stonehearth Outdoor Learning Opportunities), to name some. There is, in short, a lot of talent willing to come to your aid if you encounter trouble in the White Mountains. But here's the catch: that talent is not in some display case at each trailhead, behind a note saying Break Glass in Case of Emergency. Rescuers are instead dispersed throughout the region's various towns and hamlets. Or, if they are conservation officers, they may be attending to some other problem, as Sgt. Ober was when called.

When asked about the most challenging part of search and rescue, Ober, who has conducted and coordinated his share, said, "It's the calling. Getting a rescue together takes a lot of calling. And that calling takes a lot of time." Here we bump up against a common frustration for all SAR folks: when a beacon goes off or a call for help comes in, the person in need on the other end has been in touch instantly; his or her expectation of help soars at what seems the near possibility of help. But then, as he or she settles in to wait and time passes, hope may flag; life may be leaking away. Asked what he would most want the public to know about search and rescue, AVSAR veteran Mike Cherim, who was part of the team that found Kate Matrosova on the sixteenth, said via e-mail, "It takes a LONG time for help to come. Be prepared to help yourself. Expecting or anticipating a timely rescue when the need arises is foolhardy." Instant connection does not mean immediate rescue.

Of course, everyone associated with SAR knows that time is often critical, and as a coldest night came in on the fifteenth, Ober and those receiving his calls knew this was going to be true. They hurried to respond. Ober paged fellow conservation officers Matt Holmes, Glen Lucas, and Bob Mancini, all of whom were initially at work in places where they couldn't call out. He checked with the State Police Troop F dispatcher, who had been trying unsuccessfully to connect with Matrosova's cell and satellite phones, and asked for a call back immediately if the dispatcher could give him a "ping" from either phone. Ober's next call went to the top of NHFG command's chain, Colonel Martin Garabedian, who would make the final decision about search efforts that night. Advised of all Ober knew, including the last known beacon ping, Garabedian, himself a veteran of many searches, said, "We have to try. Let's see if we can go get her." Ober went back to the phone.

The next call went to Rick Wilcox, president of Mountain Rescue Service. Wilcox, a veteran of Everest and other Himalayan climbs, is also a longtime leader in White Mountain climbing culture, and in 1976, he became the first (and, until winter 2016, only) president of MRS. When the slant of terrain or exposure to above tree line and other extremes complicates a search or rescue, MRS gets the call. As Ober said to me, "We defer to MRS in situations like this, more than some people think. We ask for their advice and opinions on the safest way to conduct a rescue that is a life-or-death situation. They are the technical experts and are above tree line in the winter way more than we are." Wilcox began his own set of calls, and as he did, Ober set up his command post at the Appalachia trailhead Matrosova had left twelve hours earlier. There, he noted, "the wind was gusting, and I showed a temperature of −10 degrees." On top of nearby Washington, it was now −37°F, with wind gusts topping a hundred miles per hour.

While waiting for callbacks and results, Ober "made and received a steady flow of calls." Someone hovering over the northern Whites might have detected a convergence of lights from all directions, homing in on Ober's lone light in the Appalachia parking lot. Perhaps, hoped Ober, another lone light was struggling toward that lot from high above in the col near Star Lake, site of the first beacon signal. He had reason for hope: a 5:00 p.m. update from AFRCC gave a new beacon location that Ober plotted as six-tenths of a mile northeast of the first signal, between the Watson Path and the Valley Way. Off trail and in thick snow, yes, but perhaps Matrosova was slowly making her way toward them.

Up into the Maelstrom

At 6:30 p.m., the three conservation officers, Matt Holmes, Glen Lucas, and Bob Mancini, climbed up the Valley Way. Mancini's GPS held the coordinates of the 5:00 p.m. beacon signal, and the three COs had instructions to go up to the point on the trail closest to those coordinates, and then wait for the MRS team that would soon follow. The three COs also had "explicit directions to take no unnecessary risks, and if they felt their lives were in danger, to turn around." From those first steps toward Kate Matrosova, the COs were in charge of their own safety, and indeed, in midclimb, Lucas began to feel ill, and he turned back. Such a decision is both difficult and essential. Rescuer safety must come first, and incident commanders worry constantly about rescuers who are out there.

That worry also explains the decision that the COs would await the MRS team before anyone tried to thread the off-trail woods to the beacon signal coordinates. As is often common on popular trails in winter, the Valley Way was packed out by previous hikers, but on either side of the trail, the snow was deep and unconsolidated. As part of her plan to travel fast and light, Matrosova had not taken snowshoes. Searchers carried and would need snowshoes to go off-trail to look for her. Searching off-trail in rough, steep, snow-masked terrain holds many risks, and those risks were multiplied by darkness and the extreme weather. There would be no buffer of safety in two; there would be some in six.

A little after 7:30 p.m. the four-person MRS team—Geoff Wilson, Scott Lee, Steve Larson, and Steve Dupuis (team leader, and, as of winter 2016, MRS president)—was ready to go. But at this point, an updated beacon signal complicated the rescue: its coordinates now placed the beacon in the middle of King Ravine, over a half-mile northwest of the second signal, and an even greater span when one looked at the precipitous slopes someone would have to navigate to get there from either of the first two beacon signals. Also, King Ravine held dangerous avalanche risks, which could not be assessed at night, and Ober and Dupuis agreed that no one was going in there. Ober's confidence that Matrosova was moving their way was shaken. Still, the second position seemed the closest, most logical bet, and the MRS team aimed up at their meeting with the COs. If hit number two didn't pan out, perhaps the team could go on to the first beacon hit.

The MRS rescuers climbed as quickly as they could while still managing body temperature to minimize sweating. In extreme cold, sweat can be lethal, its cooling qualities taking hold when a climber stops, so they tried to be both prudent and hurried. Around 11:30 p.m. MRS rescuers joined the two COS at the site on the Valley Way from which they would launch their search of the second beacon-signal location. COS Mancini and Holmes, already cold from their wait, would stay at the site on the trail and provide backup support for the MRS team. Dupuis recalled some of what they hoped for:

> The initial plan was to go to the [second beacon] waypoint, which was just below the Pine Link, roughly at tree line. My thought was to get there and search the area in a grid out 60 meters from that spot, and hopefully find her. If not, then we'd reevaluate the weather, our team, and see if we could go on to the next [first beacon] location at Star Lake. Honestly, I had very little confidence that we would be able to venture much above tree line that night with the forecast. The wind was steady in the ninety-plus mile-per-hour range and temps were off my thermometer, well below −25°F when we were at the first waypoint; and I could hear the "freight train" just above us, actually the loudest roar I have ever heard. It was after midnight.

While this first search was unfolding near tree line, Ober was still working his phone in the parking lot. He called Wilcox again, asking for a second MRS team to carry a litter up in support of the rescuers; he stayed in constant touch with the teams on the mountain; he called the Civil Air Patrol to see if they had aircraft that could fly over and try to pinpoint the locator beacon. Then he turned to the possibilities of the morning, calling Bill Arnold at AVSAR, asking for a team on standby. If the teams up high didn't find Matrosova, Ober knew they'd need new teams ready to try again at first light. Meanwhile, the temperature at the Mount Washington Observatory continued its free fall.

All the while, technological complexity morphed into perplexity: at 8:39 p.m. AFRCC reported the beacon in the Great Gulf Wilderness near the Osgood Trail (over a mile southeast from the King Ravine hit); at 9:26 p.m. AFRCC showed this same location; then, at 10:19 p.m. AFRCC reported the beacon back in King Ravine. Later, after the searchers had retreated from the mountain, Ober got a 6:00 a.m. update saying that a series of beacon hits at 2:17 a.m., 3:42 a.m., 4:35 a.m., and 5:27 a.m. had given a consistent reading of coordinates. Frustratingly for Ober and everyone else, these coordinates matched the first set that had placed Matrosova near Star Lake late the prior afternoon.

> Here is a moment of cautionary pause. Many of us now devise a net of knowing and safety with our devices; precise marking of location seems, at times, a miracle brought to us by an unseen but all-seeing satellite eye above. But before we assign our devices a divine infallibility, it's good to consider how and when they may err. As use of locator technology has grown more prevalent in the Whites, so too have stories of its sometimes wild variability. Not long ago, I recall writing up a rescue on Madison (*Appalachia*, Summer 2014), not far from where Matrosova's story unfolded: an October cold front blew in with hurricane force winds and dropping temperatures, trapping a Vermont couple, who sheltered in sleeping bags and wrapped themselves in a tent behind rocks above tree line. They called for help, and when rescuers checked the coordinates of the ping from their phone, the numbers placed them over in King Ravine. Fortunately for everyone, the couple knew the names of the trails they'd walked, and knew that they were on the Pine Link near Madison Spring and not in the ravine; rescuers climbed right to them instead of chasing a ping into absence.

Specifically, the ACR ResQLink locator beacon Matrosova carried is characterized as, "small and mighty, the ResQLink+, a buoyant, GPS-enabled rescue beacon designed for anglers, pilots and backcountry adventurers." ARTEX, the outfit that makes this beacon, has, of course, a "Survivors Club," which you can tap into on their website; there you can find stories from those rescued at their broadcast coordinates. You can even see photos of all the survivors. It's a very effective collage of people still alive.

For the most part, my research suggests that much of this hype is true, that much of the time, this is a "small and mighty" device that is spot on. But then there is the variability that Sgt. Ober experienced as he received multiple coordinates in the extreme weather during which Kate Matrosova perished.

In the aftermath of the search, NHFG and the Civil Air Patrol (CAP) conducted some tests to better understand this variability. NHFG lt. Wayne Saunders explained to me that when CAP flew a plane over the same model beacon Matrosova carried, it got an accurate location as long as the beacon and antenna were upright. When, however, they placed the beacon on its side, as it was when Matrosova was found, the locations transmitted varied. And of course violent weather could easily affect how one deploys a beacon. Saunders also said that this review by both agencies had helped AFRCC gain a better sense for being able to offer a best probability when receiving beacon hits that show a number of possible locations.

All of this is no reason to eschew responsible use of such beacons. It's simply a reminder that we cannot always be located and plucked reliably from trouble by the eyes that look down on us.

> Back on the mountain, MRS 1 reached the two COS at 11:30 p.m., and after a consult, the four MRS rescuers forged through the scrub and snow toward the second set of coordinates, where they didn't find Matrosova or any sign of her. Now what? Dupuis looked back at the moment: "My biggest concern about going any higher was not being able to return to tree line, as the wind would then be in our faces. Also, the cold was really sapping our energy at that point. We were in snow at times waist deep and other times fighting through thick scrub which grabbed us at every step. As a team [after not finding Matrosova near the coordinates] we had a quick huddle and decided it was time to go down."

MRS 2 (Bayard Russell, Max Lurie, Nick Aiello, and Janet Wilkerson) had started up with the litter at 10:53 p.m., and by 1:00 a.m. they were 2.5 miles up the trail, where they stashed the litter for possible later use. MRS 1 was then working its way back to the trail. Ober and his three teams agreed by radio that it was time for everyone to come out: MRS 2 got back at 2:00 a.m.; COS Holmes and Mancini got there at 2:18 a.m.; MRS 1 reached Appalachia at 3:00 a.m. "You could see they were all exhausted. Their neck warmers and faces were crusted with ice. They looked like zombies," recalled Ober. After debriefing with Ober, they all left to get some rest. Ober then drove to a series of trailheads where Matrosova just might appear if she had made it down off the ridge into the Great Gulf, a slim hope, but one worth checking. Finding no sign of recent activity at those points, he "returned to Appalachia and maintained the command post."

A Brief Compendium on Cold

It's hard to describe the kind of cold rescuers found and endured during this search; to do so, you would have to go, literally, to the ends of the earth. Even as most of us have felt really cold at times, it is also hard to describe deep cold's effects. Words simply can't capture the way cold skews then stills life. But by pausing here for brief meditation, we at least genuflect in the direction of winter's lethal element.

In an e-mail, MRS 2 climber Janet Wilkerson recalled that night's cold:

> I remember the dark, cold, windy parking lot, getting our team packed up and the litter prepped (the role of our team was to follow the lead teams with a litter in case she was found that night). Her husband approached us. He was gentle and kind and appreciative of our being there. I was surprised he didn't seem more panicked. I started the hike with my warmest gloves and outermost puffy jacket layer on, and thirty minutes up the trail I was still not warm enough to de-layer, despite having a forty-plus-pound pack on and hiking uphill at a good clip with the team. That was surprising and showed just how cold it was. And when we took brief breaks to switch out the litter hauler, get a drink, or check in with the radio, my fingers, even in large gloves, were cold within moments.

Dupuis added this:

> I thought about the cold and wind, and how to be sure I would not get frostbite. I double-checked my gear so as to not forget anything. I had been out guiding on the previous two days (Friday up the Valley Way up to Madison Hut, and Saturday to the summit of Mount Washington) so my stuff was a bit scattered and drying out. I thought that there was absolutely NO room for any mistakes of any kind that night. I thought about all the possible exits off of Adams out of the wind and how I would handle it if I was in her shoes. And I said a prayer asking God for protection through that night, and the strength to get there and BACK.

Cold works on us from the outside in. First our extremities—fingers, toes, nose—feel its bite, then, as cold takes hold, not much at all. Our body, ever alert to threat, pools its warmth at our core, where vital organs are. Our brain, working best when well bathed by blood, gets its share too, at least at first. But trouble can begin easily at the ends of fingers and toes, where fine motor skills and motion can suffer. We drop things, can't grip them; we slow down. Cold then conspires to make us stupid. The body, intent on its core, thins the brain's ration. We decide slowly, wrongly, not at all. What looks simple to the warm observer may be a chalkboard full of physics to the cold person. Then the wind blows in, the chalk dust flies, and even the board is a blank. Hypothermia literature is full of odd decisions and absence of decisions. It is, for example, not uncommon to find a hypothermia victim partially undressed in response to the delusion of being hot. Cold, finally, undoes reality.

When thinking of that cold, we recall Matt Bowman's son's instinctive worry about wind, cold's conveyor, and we recall Steve Dupuis's earlier comment that, as they tried to reach Matrosova's coordinates, "the cold was really sapping us." And perhaps we recall our own moments, when cold made it impossible to manipulate a zipper, tie a lace, or even press a button. As the blood withdraws from our limbs and head to protect the body's core, soon there's not much left of the capability and expression we call life.

Day Two: Up and then Down

As the early morning light found Sgt. Ober still in the Appalachia parking lot, the cold had only intensified. Light often heralds a lifting of spirit, but, looking up, Ober could find little to be optimistic about. The recent beacon signals had collected back near Star Lake and, if Matrosova were there, Ober saw little hope that she could have weathered such a night, or the day that was howling overhead now. Still, possibility prodded: there was a rescue to continue.

Ober's relief would be Lt. Wayne Saunders. When they met at Appalachia at 7:00 a.m., the two decided to move the command post to the Randolph Fire Station. The parking lot was simply too cold to muster the various teams. Ober gave Saunders and his partner, Lt. Goss, all of the beacon coordinates and a summary of the night's actions. With the beacon hits located on a map, they planned the day's searches. Four teams were assembling; three would go to the more likely coordinates, while the fourth would be held in reserve to support any one of the three search teams, or to respond to any new hope.

Searchers near Star Lake on February 16, 2015. Temperature at −20°F; winds gusting to one hundred miles per hour. Photo by Matt Bowman.

Team 1, composed of ten AVSAR and MRS volunteers and conservation officers, would go up to Madison Spring Hut, and from there, weather permitting, search the area near Star Lake, site of the initial and later beacon hits. Team 2, all MRS volunteers, would search in the tricky terrain of King Ravine. Team 3, made up of AVSAR volunteers and conservation officers, would search the area of the beacon hits in the Great Gulf. The spread of these locations meant that each team would search via a different route. The teams headed out from Randolph a little after 8:30 a.m.

Ober's night of calls had also activated the possibility of helicopter help, and a New Hampshire Army National Guard Blackhawk helicopter, piloted by Iain Hamilton, with crew chief Greg Gerbig, flew north from Concord at 9:00 a.m., arriving in the area forty-five minutes later. There, they hoped to employ a FLIR (forward looking infrared) device to search for a heat signal that might be Matrosova. But the high winds created an impenetrable whiteout up on the ridges, and, after fifteen minutes, the helicopter, running low on fuel from battling the winds, had to leave. The Civil Air Patrol also flew a fixed-wing plane over in an attempt to zero in further on the beacon location, but the winds forced them to stay at 10,000 feet, and they were unable to narrow the search area.

By late morning, further work with AFRCC and CAP suggested that the Star Lake coordinates were the most likely ones, and team 3 was called back from the Great Gulf. Then, at around 2:00 p.m., close to their agreed-upon turnaround time, Team 1 called down: Bowman had found Matrosova. The search was now a recovery.

Getting Close

Some of what rescuers have said to me in outlining the actions and emotions of searching for someone describes a sort of intimacy. The possibility of rescue—no matter how long the odds—sustains them. Hope brings searchers close, then keeps them close, to the person being sought.

This intimacy can start to take root as a searcher begins the gathering of equipment, personnel, and resolve and steps toward the person lost or injured; it's always there, potentially. Justin Preisendorfer, a MRS veteran and spokesperson and former Tuckerman Ravine snow ranger, offered this example in the 2008 story of a fellow climber, Peter Roux:

> There are so many stories of folks rescued where a context sets up so that your heartstrings are being tugged even before you're out there. It could be a missing elderly person, a lost Boy Scout. One recent avalanche fatality affected me that way: Peter Roux was a climber who had cut his teeth in the Northeast, then moved away, and he had just come back to these roots for a visit and to climb with friends. On the day before they were to climb, Roux went out into Huntington Ravine on his own. Put yourself in his shoes—someone coming home to a familiar area; you want to make the most of your time. He went up into Huntington during elevated avalanche danger; he went up from excitement. On his descent, he was avalanched and died. We were in the Fan [a jumble of boulders near the base of Huntington Ravine] when the sun came up, hoping still to find him. When we located his body in the avalanche debris, we felt deflated; hope was lost.

Such connection can take on added urgency and specificity as a search lengthens, odds decline, and the sketch of the victim's story comes clear. Working against extremes—wind, cold, time lost, odds—sharpens urgency, which heightens expectation. Then, if the victim is not found, or if she is found dead, it feels like a sudden fall from the height of hope.

Such a fall happened twice during the Matrosova search: first on the night of the fifteenth, when MRS 1 reached the second beacon hit, and found nothing. Imagine the expectation as, after hours of climbing through tumult, they near the coordinates, struggling through deep snow, arctic cold, and wiry krummholz. We're here, they think . . . and then, headlamps spiking this way and that, they set to a grid search as best they can manage in the screaming wind. She could, she should, be right here; we are that close. But as they finish their wallowing trample, no . . . no one's here. Possibility flies off on the wind. Their spirits sink.

Then, there was the next day. In the broad light, but blanketed often by ground blizzard, team 1's ten searchers are in the area of the initial beacon hit, the one that has been replicated four times early that morning; they may be near. Possibility retains its 1 percent of hope; she could be alive. As he works through "waves of wind," having often to kneel and wait out the waves, Matt Bowman comes upon an anomaly—here's a pack, sitting on the surface; what's that doing here? Bowman's first thought: Did one of us take off his pack? Then, twenty feet away, he sees Matrosova, unmoving, fully clothed, leg extended. "She looked flash frozen," he recalled. Bowman, hunched against the wind, hurries over; her eyes are open—he will remember this—unseeing. Ohhh . . . it is an outrush of hope.

During a January 2016 conversation, Justin Preisendorfer reflected a bit on how searchers focus on hope rather than grim likelihood when a search stretches on in unfavorable conditions: "We all prepare differently. But there is a common thread: we try to look at possibility, not likelihood; the possibility of finding her [Matrosova] alive was still there, even if unlikely. That's also why the images of finding someone dead stay with us, because they occur at the point where we realize what we'd hoped for is no longer. It's difficult because we've searched for and found all sorts of people. You want to believe they'll live through it and they'll learn."

Coda: A Walk to Low's Bald Spot

Not long after my January 2016 conversations and exchanges with Sgt. Ober, Matt Bowman, and others, an afternoon opened up. A little earlier, I'd stopped by the Appalachia parking area just to look at this story's beginning. A cold front had blown in, and its north wind harried a dusting of snow, chasing it in arcs across the tarmac like a dropped scarf. I sat for a few minutes in my warmed car, looking at the signage that marks the start of the Valley Way; a gust rocked the car gently with reminder.

A bit later, from Route 2, I looked up into the whitened col between Madison and Adams; the side of the Adams spur, John Quincy, glowed in the slanted sun. The col seemed almost a cliché, a place near and far, but not quite; really it was another world above.

> Why not sort this story through by taking a walk, I thought as I drove? The day was bright and average, temps a notch or so above zero, winds moderate for a mountain. I pushed off on the Old Jackson Road around 1:00 p.m. with a pack full of layers, snacks, and water (even down low, winter asks that we carry a lot); the new inch or so of snow, already foot-beaten by morning walkers, squeaked a little underfoot.

As I walked, I thought back to the SAR people I'd spoken with, and I felt warmed by their commitment, and warmed also by the absence of bluster and ego. The wind may roar announcement of self in the Whites, but its SAR people do not. So I'd heard no pontificating, seen no finger-pointing or head wagging. When I'd heard quiet criticism, it tended toward lament: if only people would turn back sooner when conditions deteriorate.

I'd aimed the few miles out and up to Low's Bald Spot, where I'd be able to peek into the beginning of the Great Gulf and look up again at Adams and Madison. An hour later, I watched two plumes of snow unfurl from these mountains; even on this low spot, there was enough wind to give the 8°F temperature some teeth. I was, I realized, on the other side of the mountain, which is where this particular story ends.

‹ 3 ›

SEVEN CALLS

— — — —

Help Me Who's Coming What Took You So Long?

To someone injured or lost within them, New Hampshire's White Mountains seem vast, a nearly infinite stretch of knuckled uplands and thick forests, where even a hundred yards from a trail, people have disappeared. But the Whites are, in truth, a road-and-people-girt set of low peaks, contained mostly within the 800,000-acre White Mountain National Forest. Seen from the air at night, they are a few compact dark spaces surrounded by winking lights, and they are trisected by three major, north-south roads (Routes 16, 302, and 93) along which the coned probes of headlights pass all night. So even given the major "if" of navigable weather, if you are lost or injured, help is only a ridge or two away. But who is coming over that ridge? The answer varies and is best given by example. Here, then, are seven recent search and rescue stories, each one set in a different region of the Whites. They will also constitute a census of available help. Here—when you've tumbled to trouble and made your trouble known—is who's coming after you.

To Begin at the Top: Two Stories

Mount Washington is the tent pole around which the whole circus of White Mountain climbing, sliding, and wandering takes place, and its eastern slope has some of the region's most famous terrain. Three great, glacial gouges mark that slope, and the central one is the Whites' high-angle mecca for those who would climb and slide in the snow season, and for all who would stand in awe in any season. On a warming spring day, when the snow softens and the sky is an upside-down bluebird, Tuckerman Ravine may have as many as four thousand pilgrims in the cup of its massive hand. And those pilgrims will people a spectrum that runs from daredevil to spectator, and from expert to flop footed, with its bell curve skewed toward the risky, if not the accomplished, end of the line. "Tucks," or "Tuck's," depending on how possessive you feel about it, can be a place crying out for both freedom to flail and fall and rescue's restored order when accident occurs.

Above these ravines, lies the summit cone of Washington, and it too exercises a magnetic draw on climbers in all seasons and sliders in the snow. It is, at 6,293 feet, a low peak, but it is also the Northeast's sprawling highpoint, and above 4,800 feet, its terrain becomes an other-scape of lichen and broken stone that endures some of the world's worst weather. Climbers training for the world's hardest climates—Denali, the high Himalayas, the Antarctic—often condition themselves on Washington's winter slopes. Mix in the many ways up this mountain—a web of trails, an auto road, a cog railway—and the summit presence of a museum and snack bar, both open during the summer and early fall, and you get guarantee of more crowds. The Mount Washington State Park staffs these buildings, and there is also the year-round Mount Washington weather observatory, but both sets of buildings are closed to the public during the extended winter season. All this traffic and a "settled" summit make for frequent misunderstandings. People may arrive on top and expect shelter and/or transportation down and find themselves marooned instead on one of the world's harshest weather makers. So Washington can be both a peopled and a lethal mountain in all seasons. Its body count stretches back to the mid-nineteenth century and now exceeds 150, with the threat of addition an annual concern.

Who, you might wonder, is responsible for this big top of recreation when someone climbs or slides into difficulty? "That depends" is the beginning of an intricate answer that highlights the composite nature of search and rescue in New Hampshire. From December 1 until May 31, "Tucks" and the close, eastern-slope surroundings of the Cutler River Drainage are under the supervision of the U.S. Forest Service, and the USFS's feet on the ground are its wonderfully named snow rangers. These rangers work in, and predict the shape and slippage of, the slopes of the ravine, and when an accident happens there, they take charge. For the other six months, when trouble finds a hiker or climber in this drainage, New Hampshire Fish and Game's aforementioned law enforcement division bears legal responsibility

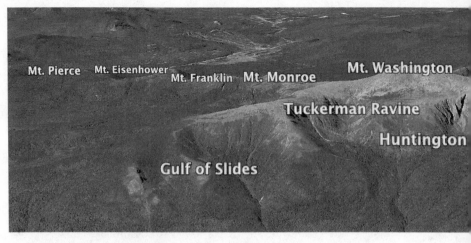

The Presidential Range. Many of the incidents in this book, including the first four in chapter 3, can be placed on this map and in its famous terrain. Map created by Daniel Hynds.

for bringing help. Its officers turn then to the host of nearby nonprofits and volunteer groups, who adhere to and sometimes even live on the Northeast's biggest, most famous peak. NHFG, USFS, AMC, AVSAR, MRS, MWVSP, MWSP, MWOBS, SOLO, RMC, DHART, NHANG are some of the prominent acronyms we've met in chapter 2, or with which we'll become familiar on this first father of mountains.

Quest in the Heart of Winter

The winter of 2013–14's major incident occurred during a tempest above tree line on Mount Washington on January 19. But at 4:16 a.m. the summit temperature was a (relatively) mild 9°F, and the winds whispered from the west at a coincident nine miles per hour; light snow drifted in the air. The Mount Washington Observatory's forecast, however, might have given anyone planning to climb the mountain pause: "increasing winds . . . kicked up snow . . . ground blizzards at times with whiteout conditions likely; in addition to high winds, cold arctic air will start to make a return today. A windchill advisory will go into effect at sunset today." This forecast echoed that of the previous day.

Mt. Clay Mt. Jefferson Mt. Adams Mt. Madison Ravine

Pause was not taken, however. At 4:30 a.m. a group of fifteen hikers of varied experience from Pennsylvania's Bloomsburg State College's Quest Program set out from Pinkham Notch for Washington's summit. As they climbed, they divided into three groups, and at 5,000 feet, atop Lion Head, one group of five elected to turn back; the remaining two groups of six and four kept on, reaching the summit at 12:30 p.m. There, they took summit photos and turned to descend.

The smaller of the two groups, made up of Andrew S., Rhea M., Kelly S., and Wayne E., which included two of the overall group's four leaders, made very slow progress, in large measure because Wayne was struggling. A hiker of limited experience with no winter-climbing background, Wayne was exhausted and unsteady; he fell often as the foursome climbed down the summit cone. Meanwhile, the morning forecast was coming true: the winds rose, picking up the loose snow, and vision and route finding became difficult. Amid the blown snow, the group missed the turn for Lion Head, and not long after that, one leader, Andrew, realized that they were heading for the lip of Tuckerman Ravine. From previous climbs on Washington, he knew this was not a descent they wanted to make—its steep slopes and technical demands were beyond the group's experience and capabilities. At around

4:00 p.m., with Wayne struggling still, darkness coming and the conditions making route finding nearly impossible, Andrew punched the emergency button on his SPOT locator beacon. He followed that with a 911 call that got through. But then the link went dead. The group hunkered down to shelter as best they could and await a hoped-for rescue. The temperature at the nearby summit was now −5°F with sustained winds between seventy and eighty miles per hour.

U.S. Forest Service snow ranger Chris Joosen took charge of coordinating the effort, gathering rescuers from the Forest Service, Mountain Rescue Service, and New Hampshire Fish and Game. Because the prevailing conditions and the forecast suggested that a night out could be lethal, Joosen launched a night rescue. He sent a party of four on snowmobiles to the head of the winter Lion Head trail, where they would then climb toward the stranded party. Thirteen more rescuers boarded New Hampshire State Park and Mount Washington Observatory snowcats and were driven up to the six-mile post on the Mount Washington Auto Road; from there, the rescuers would follow the Alpine Garden Trail toward the GPS coordinates provided by Andrew's SPOT beacon.

Though travel and coordination were exceedingly difficult, by around 9:30 p.m., rescuers from both groups had reached their target coordinates. With winds still at or near hurricane force and vision limited by darkness and snow to the smallest perimeter of a headlamp's beam, they began a grid search. Such a search intensifies difficulty further, because searchers must maintain a search line and contact with each other despite the boulders and crevices in front of them. As veteran rescuer Mike Pelchat (AVSAR and MWSP) noted in chapter 1, most of us simply don't understand the force of wind when it reaches sixty or seventy miles per hour.

Approximately forty-five minutes later, they found the four hikers. Wayne needed help moving; the other three were still mobile. By 10:50 p.m. the group had begun the roughly two-mile, north and so wind-facing trek across the Alpine Garden to the waiting snowcats. A rotation of rescuers assisted Wayne, with one at each elbow throughout the crossing. A litter was ready should Wayne be unable to keep going. The group's progress was slow, but by 1:30 a.m. they had arrived at the safety of the snowcats. From there, they were driven to the mountain's base.

> My work as a columnist for *Appalachia* asks that I sift such stories for their lessons, and, in doing so, help readers reflect on their mountain adventures, and, perhaps, mishaps. In theory, we can learn from others' mistakes. In practice that may be true, though doing so asks also much of our imaginations. It asks us to conjure weather and circumstances that live out on or beyond the edge of experience, even as we nest in a favorite chair. Here, then, are some thoughts in response to this rescue, offered with the hope that they summon your own.

It is abundantly clear that the Quest group got itself into a predicament that could have killed some or all of the four left on the mountain at day's end. As is often true, it took a series of misjudgments and mistakes to arrive at the point where Andrew set off his SPOT beacon. Primary among them was bringing a group with mixed experience and competence to Mount Washington in winter. Upper Washington is not a mountain to begin on; it's a mountain to bring your best knowledge and experience to. Add to this not monitoring the weather forecast—there's a reason that experienced climbers are among the weather obsessed—which offered consistent warning of tough stuff ahead. Here, there's a line of inference from the program's name to its behavior: quests often require suspension of usual caution, a stepping beyond; they summon the inner hero, who, in retrospect, often does silly things, and, once these things are decided upon, they develop a momentum of their own. Not many people call off quests. That attitude is reflected also in the group's planned turnaround time of 12:45 p.m. Though they reached the summit at 12:30 p.m., their eight-hour allotment of climbing time seems far too generous, leaving only half that time to descend before winter's early darkness arrives. An earlier turnaround time might have kept them from reaching the summit, but it might also have helped Wayne's group begin to climb down before trouble took over.

The group was reasonably well equipped, but much of the gear was rented and so unfamiliar to the hikers. Again, this is not the mountain on which to be learning one's gear. In a roaring whiteout or in darkness, every piece of gear should be familiar to the touch, its functions tested by repeated use. Finally, as underlining contrast to this commentary, here is the lead paragraph to Quest's notice for this trip: "Join Quest on their most thrilling adventure of the year. An ascent up Mount Washington in New Hampshire 'home of the world's worst weather." Four-day trip includes transportation to and from New Hampshire, motel rooms, and mountaineer training. *Most gear is included and no experience is necessary*" (their emphasis).

Once meteorological mayhem descended and the foursome was stuck, they endured well. Their decision to stick together probably helped save Wayne's life, and it made them easier to find. Also, they probably bolstered each other's spirits during the roughly six hours they waited for rescue. That six-hour interval between call and rescue occasions a thought about summoning rescue: even the deeply experienced climbers who rescued the foursome were at the limits of possibility in these conditions. As incident commander Chris Joosen's commentary on the invaluable Mount Washington Avalanche Center's website makes clear, "had conditions deteriorated much further, rescue that night may not have been possible."

During postrescue interviews with rescuers, it also became clear that the group of six that preceded the later-rescued foursome down the mountain had also missed the turn for the Lion Head Trail. Luckily, they had happened upon a climber who warned them away from the Tuckerman Ravine Trail and set them back on the Lion Head route. Had they not met this climber, these six would have descended into the steeps of the ravine on a day when the USFS had rated the avalanche danger as high. (The USFS publishes a daily avalanche forecast for Tuckerman and nearby Huntington ravines throughout the winter. It is essential reading for anyone venturing onto Washington during that season.)

On occasion, I check back on the aftermath of an incident to see what results or lessons it may have imparted to those involved. The Quest group returned in 2015, aiming up at Washington in mid-January. But according to Brett Simpson, Quest's executive director, they were a different group.

Simpson's first change was to return to leading the climb himself. With fifteen ascents of Washington, high-altitude mountaineering experience, and avalanche 1 and 2 certifications, Simpson brought the sort of training Washington can ask for. Chief among other changes for that next year's climb were better screening of participants and training for them. The 2015 party of seven (two guides and five participants) spent a full day training at the base of Crawford Notch's Willey Slide before climbing Washington. They trained and climbed with upgraded equipment as well. Their training also included practice with feeding and watering on the go to avoid stops, and it gave close consideration to pacing. Simpson also set checkpoints for the day; at these points the climbers checked time, pace, and fitness, ready to turn back if they were too slow, or if someone was faltering. Also, the two guides carried full packs with shelter and stoves and back-up batteries for both GPS and phone. The climb, undertaken on a cold, windy day, went well; all seven reached the top and returned together. Over the phone, Simpson said that 2014's incident, the harshest in the Quest program's forty-three-year history, had been a good teacher, and that they were a better program for the experience. Their return in 2015 supported his assessment.

Organizations involved with the January 2014 search and rescue mission: USFS, Mountain Rescue Service (MRS), NHFG, AMC, Mount Washington State Park (MWSP), Mount Washington Observatory (MWObs).

The Other Season: Trouble on the Headwall

On September 19, 2013, Luc P., age twenty-five, and four friends drove from Montreal, Quebec, to Pinkham Notch and set out to climb Mount Washington via the Tuckerman Ravine and Lion Head trails. It was a clear day with light winds and temperatures forecast to be near fifty. Reaching the summit in early afternoon, the group celebrated with lunch and a bottle of wine split among them; then, they headed down the summit cone to the Tuckerman Ravine Trail. Around a quarter of the way down the headwall, Luc and two of the group followed a worn side trail to take a look at the waterfall that drops through this area. One of Luc's friends, Gabriel L., said that Luc edged out to refill his water bottle in the stream, slipped, and dropped feet first over the ledge. Luc fell approximately 150 feet, coming to a stop on a small ledge of the steep slope. Three of the group stayed put on the trail and called 911, while the fourth, David P., descended the difficult terrain to where Luc lay. Gorham Police received the 911 call and, in turn, called New Hampshire Fish and Game. Conservation Officer Mark Ober got the call from Fish and Game's dispatcher at about 5:15 p.m.

Sgt. Ober set the gathering and dispatching of rescuers in motion. Those nearest included AMC's caretaker at Hermit Lake and personnel from the Mount Washington State Park and the Mount Washington Observatory. By around 6:15 p.m., two rescuers—the AMC caretaker and a nearby hiker, who was also a registered nurse—had joined Luc and Luc's friend on the small ledge. They were soon joined by Mike Pelchat and Brian Fitzgerald, from the state park and the observatory, respectively. This group's assessment of Luc's dire condition—he was still conscious and speaking—relayed via radio led Officer Ober, who was by now located a few miles to the north at a command post on the Mount Washington Auto Road, to call the New Hampshire Army National Guard and ask for a Blackhawk helicopter to attempt to airlift Luc from the ledge and fly him to a hospital. The sun was slated to set that evening at 6:50 p.m.

A little before 7:00 p.m. the helicopter lifted off from Concord, New Hampshire, and, at 7:27 p.m. the crew reported being above Luc and his rescuers. In his official incident report, Sgt. Ober described the next thirty minutes as a "harrowing display of flying and coordination between the Blackhawk's crew and the ground crew with the victim." The sharp angle of the headwall meant that the helicopter needed to fly higher than normal to lower the litter to the crew on the ledge and keep its rotor clear of the high-angled rock; that angle also meant the helicopter was working with little margin for error. Blessedly, though it was now twilight, the winds were calm. At 7:37 p.m. the helicopter crew lowered the litter and "tag line" and then backed away from the site as the rescuers on the ground worked to secure Luc into the litter. At 7:49 p.m. Luc was in the litter and ready to be hoisted to the helicopter. At this point, the added height of the helicopter meant that the "tag line" to the litter, held by the ground crew, was difficult to control as they strove to keep the litter from spinning while it was hoisted to the helicopter. All of this was being attempted in deepening darkness. By 7:56 p.m. the helicopter with Luc in it was on its way to Memorial Hospital in Conway, where, despite doctors' best efforts, Luc P. was pronounced dead.

> The quick response to Luc's fall is eye-catching: a 5:15 p.m. call to NHFG becomes a 7:56 p.m. lift-off by NHANG's helicopter. Everything except the body trauma from his fall worked in Luc's favor. Still, he became Mount Washington's next of more than 150 deaths. As happens in tragedy's aftermath, people wanted to know what happened, and the experienced rescuers who went to Luc's aid offered some thoughts and speculations.

Rick Wilcox, longtime head of the Mountain Rescue Service, which also responded to this incident, noted that in 2011 the Tuckerman Ravine Trail had been relocated in this area to take it away from the waterfall, which had been the site of recurring accidents. Still, the official incident report cites a "well-worn path to the waterfall." Such stepping away from the approved trail is common as hikers look for views and fresh perspectives. Also, there is the lure of water, both to refill water bottles and refresh selves. What a review of accidents over the years also makes clear is the peril to be found at the tops of waterfalls. Something draws people to inch out to where they may peer down or out, and that inching often takes place on wet ground or rock. When trouble occurs, it is usually slippage of some sort, and that, according to eyewitness Gabriel L., is what happened to Luc. The steep, angled terrain led to a long fall and, as Wilcox noted for an article in the *Conway Daily Sun*, such long falls often end in death.

What also draws attention is the remarkable convergence of rescuers at this accident. From below and above, and finally from the air, skilled rescuers hastened into difficult terrain and coordinated a remarkable airlift as night came on. So often, rescuers in the Whites work on the edge of the day and into the night. Many hikers and climbers start uphill as Luc's group did, after a drive in late morning. But in mid-September that left little cushion of time should something unusual happen, and, while an early start wouldn't have prevented this accident, it might have made the rescuers' response to it a little less harrowing.

Then, there is the lure of side trails, especially when we are on the way down. It seems that a sort of ease takes us over as we walk down. The day's goal has been met; our store of energy has proved adequate; we have had our peak experience. The wiring of descent doesn't run as hot; its flow is lulled by gravity's assistance. It can feel like a time to digress a bit, to amble along a sidetrack to see a new view, to extend the glad day for a few more moments.

New Hampshire Fish and Game's report noted also that Mount Washington was unfamiliar terrain for this group; it was their first visit. That summons thoughts about our own first approaches to various ranges and the way ease of access may misrepresent what rises before us. The White Mountains are famously within a day's drive for millions of people, and the incoming tide of visitors carries up walkers of widely various experience. While there are many entry points to our hills, replete with guidance and good information, it is also true that visitors can simply pull up to any trailhead, slip between two trees, and be away on their own. At that point, guidance narrows to the trail each is on.

White Mountain trails are, for the most part, beautiful, easily followed constructions. Their signage and steps encourage confidence. So the White Mountain neophytes, especially those who are young and fit, may feel a surge of capability to accompany the happiness that flows from going uphill. What is less evident, unless one reads and hews to a good topo map, is the way that our trails sometimes arrive in dangerous terrain. That terrain must be read well, without explicit signage. As Mount Washington State Park manager and White Mountain SAR veteran Pelchat noted in an e-mail about the terrain of this accident: "The trail in the area is much wider from recent work, but if you leave the trail look out!" Our mountains are refreshingly clear of tacked-up warning signs (save for my lifelong favorites, the yellow enamel signs warning of the potential for exposure in our alpine zones: the worst weather in the world!) So each of us must read the ground and the weather we encounter.

Is there a mountain "spider sense?" Yes, I think there is, but mostly it develops only as miles accrue. Might this group new to Tuckerman Ravine have felt that sense's "tingle" as they stepped onto its steepness? Perhaps. All new territory should elicit it.

Search and Rescue Organizations involved in this incident: NHFG, AMC, MWSP, MWobs, MRS, NHNG.

A Gulfside Story

September 20, a pivot point for seasons in the valleys, and the often early onslaught of cold up high. On this day in 2014, the Mount Washington Observatory reported temperatures in the low forties, with sustained winds of fifty to sixty miles per hour and very low visibility. Also on this day Suzanne C., age forty-six, and her friend Julie L. were crossing the Gulfside Trail between Mounts Adams and Jefferson on their way toward AMC's Lakes of the Clouds Hut, when, at around 11:15 a.m. Suzanne C. slipped on wet rocks and fell, twisting her knee. She felt injured enough to need aid. Julie L. left to return to Madison Hut for help. Soon after a hiker from a nearby party arrived and, following quick assessment, he advised Suzanne not to walk. This hiker then set out in search of a cell phone, finally coming across another hiker with a phone three-quarters of a mile later. He then called 911, and at 12:30 p.m. New Hampshire Fish and Game was notified that a hiker was injured and needed aid.

Sgt. Mark Ober took charge of the rescue, and in his later report, he said that the initial call for rescue made Suzanne C.'s injuries out to be "a possible life-threatening emergency." So Ober responded accordingly, first exploring the possibility of helicopter rescue (weather wouldn't permit it), and then summoning a wealth of rescuers (Appalachian Mountain Club (AMC), Randolph Mountain Club (RMC), Androscoggin Valley Search and Rescue (AVSAR), Stonehearth Open Learning Opportunities (SOLO), and three more NHFG conservation officers) for what promised to be a challenging and time-sensitive carryout from a location above tree line and five miles from a road. Also a factor in what became a large and, finally, puzzling effort, were sequential appearances, over time, of two doctors. Each doctor stopped to assess Suzanne C. and advised against walking . . . and then, after doing so, moved on.

By 2:15 p.m. initial rescuers from AMC and RMC (both have nearby huts or shelters staffed at that time of year: AMC's Madison Hut and RMC's Gray Knob and Crag Camp) reported they had arrived at the scene near the junction of the Israel Ridge and Gulfside Trails. They provided added gear and clothing to keep Suzanne C. warm until other rescuers arrived.

At 4:52 p.m. Conservation Officers Glen Lucas and Bob Mancini arrived, and, after assessing Suzanne C.'s injuries, they radioed Ober that they would try to help Suzanne walk down via the Lowe's Path. Meanwhile, many more rescuers were converging on the area. Ober, who was also working with "spotty communication," as he directed the rescue from a command post at the weather observatory atop Washington, called an AVSAR volunteer and had him hike down to the twenty-three volunteers from SOLO, who were climbing the Lowe's Path. They agreed to wait in support at the Log Cabin, which is at around 3,000 feet. AVSAR volunteers who had ascended the Caps Ridge Trail soon joined the rescue. By then more than thirty rescuers were active on the mountain.

At 5:30 p.m. three conservation officers and volunteers from AVSAR, AMC, and RMC began to walk Suzanne C. out. From Thunderstorm Junction, they turned down the Lowe's Path, and, once they reached tree line, the conservation officers were confident that Suzanne C. could complete her walk out. Ober then released the SOLO volunteers and others from AVSAR, who all headed back down the mountain in the fading light. At 12:30 a.m. (some twelve hours after the initial call) the party escorting Suzanne C. arrived at the base, where they were met by an ambulance she had requested.

Officer Ober interviewed Suzanne C. at this point and got the full oddness of her story. After her slip and fall, while she waited as her friend Julie went to Madison Hut for help, Suzanne said that, some minutes apart, two doctors passed by, one reporting to be an ER doctor, the other an anesthesiologist. Each checked on her, and each recommended she stay put and wait for rescue. Then, as noted earlier, each walked away, his back vanishing quickly in the fog. Suzanne also said that she had a cell phone, but chose not to use it to call for rescue.

Officer Ober's written, public report on this rescue was professionally worded, but a sense of exasperation emanated from it, too: "Unfortunately, this was another case of over-exaggeration of the extent of injuries. I'm not sure why the calls that came in via 911 reported such severe injuries, but the bottom line is that the victim was never in any medical emergency. . . . Another interesting part of this scenario is the fact that two medical personnel, who came across [Suzanne C.] and assessed her injuries and determined she shouldn't move, didn't feel it necessary to stay and assist in her rescue."

On first reading Ober's report, I too was puzzled: first by the initial call, launched by a passerby, who hiked three quarters of a mile to find another hiker with a phone, when, by her report, Suzanne C was carrying a phone; then by the chimeric appearance of doctors, who offered opinion and then walked off into the fog. So much seemed to be missing in this account. Without reassembling the whole cast of volunteers and passersby, which, given their anonymity was impossible, it was also impossible to know all the reasons for the eventual scope of this rescue. What became clear was that Fish and Game officers, who bear legal leadership responsibility for such rescues, had to err on the side of overcommitment when the call about trouble on the ridge came in. That cautious approach was emphasized because the temperatures in the forties added the threat of hypothermia.

The fog that enveloped the ridge that day seems an apt symbol of the way information often emerges during the course of a rescue. Rescuers often receive and see part of the pictured problem, which may or may not stay intact as new rumors or facts show up. Or vanish. Soldiers comment often on the unreliable nature of perception in combat as "the fog of war," and it seems possible to extend that fog to search and rescue.

If one places oneself in Suzanne C.'s boots, uncertain about an injury, then being advised by doctors against walking, it's easy to see why she needed the support and confidence supplied by Officers Lucas and Mancini before she attempted to walk down from her accident instead of being carried.

What recommends this incident to story are its confusions. Just as it takes place in a fog bank, where only the near rocks of the immediate are visible, so too does the story unfold amid a swirl of rumor and misinformation, where only Suzanne C.'s location is securely known.

Given the remoteness of that location and the possibility of threat to life, tens of people—four professionals and more than thirty volunteers—dropped whatever was at hand and climbed into the northern Presidentials to help. Full appreciation of this incident asks that each of us inhabit the thinking of a number of the people involved. Easiest, perhaps, is the role of Suzanne C.; we summon times we've needed help, been enfogged too, and cold, and the story develops. By all reports, she was restrained and conservative in her attempt to get help. But what about the passing hiker who ran and summoned rescue, and then, like a walk-on character, walked off? Or two doctors, who also appeared from the fog, reassumed doctor identity, and then shed it and walked on, too? Or one of twenty-three possible litter carriers from SOLO, who, part way to the scene, are holed up in a shelter wondering if they'll go up, organize in crews of six, carry until their arms burn, and then switch in the next six? Or, with his scratchy radio and a responsibility for keeping track of all these people converging on this spot, Sgt. Ober? Imagine all these stories in their particulars, and then ask: What would I have done there?

Search and Rescue organizations engaged in this rescue: NHFG, AMC, RMC, AVSAR, SOLO, MWOBS.

In a Flash

August 11, 2015, hurled some heavy weather at the Whites, and a morning thunderstorm that blew in on Mount Madison scattered a party of five hikers to the point where a significant search had to be launched for one as the day waned. At around 9:00 a.m. on the second day of a section hike along the Appalachian Trail (AT), five Michiganders (with some AT experience, but all new to the Whites) arrived at Madison Spring Hut, where they took a short break. They then turned up toward the summit, and as they climbed, they spread out. A sudden storm surprised the hikers; one described it as worse than any weather he'd ever seen, and it drove them from the barren heights in search of shelter, each fleeing, as it turned out, on a different trail.

On nearby Mount Washington that day, the observatory saw 1.11 inches of rain and a peak gust of seventy-one miles per hour. Jeff S., who later called for help finding his nephew, Jason S., said he hid behind a cairn at the storm's height and saw his nephew go by, but couldn't get his attention. One of the group reportedly shucked off his pack and ran to escape the storm. By late afternoon, four of the hikers had emerged on their various trails; Jason S., age thirty-two, was unaccounted for.

The search that ensued sent searchers from AVSAR, AMC, RMC, and NHFG out onto the nighttime trails and eventually located Jason S. camped at the same Osgood Tent sites that his group of five had been aiming at when they left Madison Spring. It became one of the season's larger efforts, and its narrative, while interesting, is familiar to searchers. When found, Jason S. was also in a spot where his phone didn't get a signal, and so his attempts to contact his four friends, and their attempts to call him, had failed. Such events are both commonplace and complicated. The sheer number of moving variables meant that it was late in the day before the four who fled the summit could register that their fifth was missing.

Weather and the ability to read it lie at the heart of this episode. Madison is an exposed summit, where it pays to be weather wary. The advantage of all that exposure is a hiker's being able to see what clouds are coming, and so, anticipate storms. If there's no fog. But a scan of the weather on nearby Mount Washington during that morning (see the table) shows visibility dropping quickly from ninety miles to a tenth of a mile in an hour; it also

TIME	TEMP	VISIBILITY	WIND	GUST	SKY
6:49 AM	41.0 °F	90.0 mi	South, 43.7 mph	54.1 mph	Overcast
7:48 AM	44.6 °F	0.1 mi	South, 42.6 mph	62.1 mph	Fog
9:48 AM	48.2 °F	0.0 mi	SSE, 41.4 mph	54.1 mph	Fog, Rain
10:47 AM	48.2 °F	0.0 mi	SSE, 49.5 mph	58.7 mph	Fog, Rain

shows a strong wind from the south and rain arriving midmorning. Madison would be directly in the path of this weather, and once it clapped down on the summit area, hikers would be both pummeled and unsighted. If, as reported, lightning and thunder were also embedded in that cloud cap, the effect and nearness of danger would be daunting. Perhaps that explains the scattering of the Michiganders, and some of the panic that ensued.

Reading weather in today's mountains has old and new roots. The old roots—being aware of the day's and days' forecasts; watching clouds; reading wind direction and strength; listening; scanning memory for similarities—vary with each person who climbs. Being weather rooted requires experience. The new roots—tech-enabled forecasts and condition reports (including radar)—require tech that works wherever one is. The Whites are rife with spots where tech signals don't roam, so there are a number of places where the old ways of knowing trump the new.

Then there are the phones with which we increasingly track each other; when they don't or can't connect, our callers think that we are lost. The summons then goes out to searchers. Finding Jason, who was where all five Michiganders had planned to be that evening, took over twenty volunteers.

Search and rescue organizations involved in this incident: NHFG, AMC, RMC, AVSAR.

Going Up There, Eh?—The Franconia Ridge

On Sunday, December 30, 2012, at approximately 7:00 in the evening, New Hampshire State Police notified New Hampshire Fish and Game that they had received notice that an emergency locator beacon was issuing a signal from the Mount Lafayette area in Franconia Notch. Bruno B., age twenty-six, of Sherbrooke, Quebec, and Danny D., also of Sherbrooke, had left home at 6:00 a.m. that day with the goal of climbing Lafayette. The beacon was registered to Bruno B. A search that eventually included rescuers from five groups gathered and got under way.

The weather forecast for December 30 from the Mount Washington Observatory read as follows:

An extremely brisk and therefore dangerous forecast period is on tap for the higher summits, with very strong winds and cold temperatures taking hold. Low pressure that provided another round of snowfall yesterday will depart into the Canadian Maritimes today and bomb out, keeping enough instability over New England for scattered upslope snow showers. In the meantime, a strong high-pressure ridge will push in from the southwest, creating a tremendous pressure gradient over the region. The result will be rapidly accelerating wind speeds today, which will become sustained over 100 mph for a solid 12-hour period beginning late this afternoon, and gusting in excess of 140 mph early tonight. To accompany these formidable winds, temperatures will tumble into the negative numbers, warranting a Wind Chill Advisory beginning noon today, which will be upgraded to a Wind Chill Warning at sunset. . . . A dangerous situation is shaping up on the higher summits later today and tonight. . . . ANY ACTIVITIES ABOVE TREE LINE OVER THE FORECAST PERIOD WILL BE SEVERELY IMPACTED BY THE INCOMING WEATHER. With the anticipated wind chills later today and tonight, frostbite can occur on exposed skin in as little as ten minutes. Be prepared for extremely hazardous conditions.

Okay, that's eye-catching. Enough, you and I might think from our respective chairs, to get potential climbers to back away from a day up high. But clearly, the 7:00 p.m. call said, someone had gone up.

The initial reading from the beacon located the pair of climbers approximately 1,000 feet off the Skookumchuck Trail, high on the western slope of Lafayette. By 3:20 a.m. searchers had reached this point on the Skookumchuck Trail, but deep snow and thick spruce made it too dangerous to traverse those 1,000 feet. The searchers persevered, and their next effort was to climb to the crest and the Garfield Ridge Trail and descend in B's and D's footsteps, but the winds along the ridge made this impossible. By 5:00 a.m. it was clear that a larger daytime effort would be needed.

On Monday morning additional rescue teams joined them, eventually including a Blackhawk helicopter and crew from the New Hampshire Army National Guard. By 8:00 a.m. searchers were again climbing. At 10:00 a.m. new data from the locator beacon showed that the two climbers had descended roughly a half-mile west of their original location. This sent a team up the Greenleaf Trail to try to intercept the two men in that sector of the Lafayette Brook drainage. Not long after noon, the helicopter team arrived, and at 12:50 p.m. they spotted the two men. They were then hoisted to safety by a cable and rescuer deployed from the helicopter. Conservation Officer Lt. James Goss, who later interviewed the two men, noted that the men were well equipped but that, in the severe winds and blowing snow, they had lost the trail before descending into the Lafayette Brook drainage, where they had decided to activate their beacon.

New Hampshire Fish and Game reported use of thirteen of their personnel, who put in 54 hours of work and 111.25 hours of overtime. They also recorded the efforts of eight volunteers, who averaged 10 hours apiece. And finally, there was the National Guard helicopter.

In thinking about this rescue, let's begin with the obvious: this was a bad stretch of weather in which to climb into the alpine zone of Mount Lafayette and its ridge. I make the assumption that, if climbers are tech savvy enough to carry locator beacon warning systems, they are tech savvy enough to monitor the weather forecast. Yes, it was the weekend, with its window of free time, and yes, the wild weather can be a lure after days in the climate-controlled rooms of modern life, but . . . really.

What draws further attention is the rescue and those drawn into it. In that same heavy weather, through the night and morning, rescuers worked and wallowed to reach these men. There's ample risk in that. Finally, the rescue was accomplished via Blackhawk helicopter. There's both risk and a lot of money spent in that. It's no sure thing to bring a helicopter close enough to airlift someone out of a forest at the same time the wind is coursing over the mountain ridges and furling into up- and downdrafts. Typically, the National Guard's helicopter pilots like to hover between 70 and 130 feet off the ground when they are performing what they call a "pick." But downdrafts make them wary of getting too close, even as they will tell you that a

Blackhawk has excellent lifting and climbing power. Of course, there is also the ongoing question of who pays for all those hours of work and overtime, and finally, for the use of the aircraft.

Let's go back to the moment when these hikers decided to fire up their locator device. They had been driven off the Garfield Ridge Trail by the winds and snow and down into the untracked Lafayette Brook drainage. Certainly they were in tough terrain. And yes, the weather was very tough. But they were also well equipped with overnight gear. Might they have chosen instead to bivouac for the night and then, at first light, see if they could fight their way down the next day? Such a decision to live with their earlier decisions and attempt self-rescue would have spared the searchers a night of risk and discomfort, and it would have kept the helicopter safely at home port. I have nothing against carrying locator technology, but doing so adds a burden of restraint to one's actions. If you are going to fire off your locator beacon at the first sign of trouble, you shouldn't be there in the first place.

Search and rescue organizations involved in this incident: NHFG, PVSART, MRS, AVSAR, NHANG.

Heartland: Hard Times in the Pemigewasset

On October 16, 2015, after a significant search of the Pemigewasset Wilderness area by land and air on the fifteenth, searchers followed a social media tip and found Clairemarie C.'s body washed up along the North Branch of the Gale River. NHFG conservation officers speculated that on September 30, after heavy rains, while descending the Gale River Trail, Clairemarie, age sixty-four, had tried to cross a swollen Garfield Brook and been caught in its current and carried nearly a half-mile downstream to where she was found.

This search, unusual in the Whites for the lag time between accident and discovery, unfurled across one of the largest dark spots of the night map of these mountains. The Pemigewasset Wilderness, known universally as the Pemi, has become, after a late nineteenth- and early twentieth-century devastation from logging, a brook- and bear-rich stretch of wild that lies at the heart of the Whites. From its center, on Bondcliff, a walker sees only mountains and valleys, and it is easy to imagine oneself far from the usual world.

Clairemarie had planned an early October, five-day, solo hike from the Garfield Trail parking lot out to Bondcliff and back, with stays at the Garfield Ridge and Guyot campsites. It was a twenty-six-mile itinerary that suggested ample time for diversions, for walking and nosing about. Such hikes were an annual tradition for her, and she took her two weeks of vacation at that time to make them possible. Clairemarie was an experienced hiker and longtime AMC member, and it was clear that she had the experience to go solo. It was also likely that she would have met plenty of people during this popular hiking period. Once she was reported missing by her brother on October 14, after he was alerted that she had not shown up for work at vacation's end on the thirteenth, authorities began looking for her. It then became clear that she had come to the mountains a week earlier than planned. Her brother later said that she often altered plans to match the forecasted weather.

After an unsuccessful search on the fifteenth, posts asking for help on social media elicited from two hikers a sighting of someone fitting Clairemarie's description at AMC's Galehead Hut on the night of September 29. That tip, confirmed by her signature on the hut's register, and the heavy rains of the thirtieth, led NHFG to shift from searching Clairemarie's planned route and instead look at the possibility that she had descended the Gale River Trail. Such a descent would have reached the road only a mile and a half from her car. And there, in the brook along that trail, they found her.

As tragedies do, especially well-publicized ones, Clairemarie's story drew considerable comment. When we go out alone, our plans can be rewritten by what we encounter or by our whims, and, as they change, whatever trip-tik we've left behind goes out of date. So if we go missing, that summary provides only a starting point for those looking for us. In talking with rescuers about this incident, I heard no condemnation; they were simply noting that finding us when we stray is sometimes, even in this era of technology and aerial searches, guesswork. That social media has become part of that guesswork is a recent expansion of searching.

Although precipices and other slanted heights often draw the lion's share of attention, when mountain walkers consider danger, water is probably the Whites' most dangerous element. When it rains, the narrow drainages feed the steep streams rapidly, and what is usually a benign rock hop across a low brook can become a risky step above or into fast water. Even a half foot of

The upper Pemigewasset Valley as seen from Galehead Hut. Photo by author.

quick water can drive a foot to a bad landing, and, if you fall into the water, the pressure piles up quickly on however much of you is submerged. Being swept away becomes easy, suddenly.

Here, in the spirit of White Mountain rescuers' favorite type of rescue—none at all—are a few thoughts about crossing rivers alone. Even at the edge of mild streams and rivers, I follow the advice of Steve Smith, my favorite White Mountain blogger (Mountain Wandering link: http://mountainwandering. blogspot.com/) and a PVSART member, and always pause for a moment to look both up and downstream. We both want a sense of the terrain and the river's flow, where it goes and what it might mean to go/be taken there.

Once I decide to cross, there are other steps to take: unclip my waist belt and shoulder strap to make shucking my pack easy if I fall; pick a route and then examine its surfaces; decide if staying dry is possible (for me, it is only if the rocks I'll cross on look stable, have good traction, and don't demand leaps). If I know I will wade, I take off my socks and leave my boots/shoes on; take small steps; face partially upstream. If the water is swift and above knee-level, I consider finding another crossing . . . or waiting, even if it adds a day. I've scouted up or downstream for a half hour to find a better crossing. Also, I hike and run now with poles most of the time, and they can be a great help with balance in water. If I'm not carrying poles, I'll often choose a solid stick for a third point of balance. River crossing is such a complex and fraught subject that a National Outdoor Leadership School (NOLS) guide offers more than six pages of advice on the subject.

An added consideration from this story: once full fall arrives and trees and other plants stop drawing much water from the ground, the cooling air tightens it, and water runs more freely into rivers. Summer's sponging effect goes away. So rivers rise even more quickly when it rains heavily, which would have been true of the time when Clairemarie was out. As example, the two hikers who reported seeing Clairemarie at Galehead on the twenty-ninth, descended on the Twin Brook Trail the next day; the heavy rains made their river crossing dangerous, and they were forced to spend a night in the woods.

By coincidence Clairemarie was reported missing on the same day that Appalachian Trail thru-hiker Geraldine Largay's remains were discovered less than two miles from the trail in Maine's Hundred-Mile Wilderness. Largay had been missing for over two years. The two incidents are joined by how little is known about each solo hiker's steps that led to her disappearance and by the rarity of such incidents. SAR people in the Whites say that the vast majority of their missions aim at reaching someone whose location is known or easily approximated.

Organizations involved in this search: NHFG, AMC, PVSART, AVSAR, . . . and social media

Outlands and Outliers: Kilkenny Night

Attached to the central Whites by trails, even as they are separated out by roads, passes, and valleys, are what I'll call the outlands. They are mountains of a little less loft, but often of a wilder disposition. While they don't usually draw the crowds that cluster on the Presidentials and the Franconias, they appeal in their wildness to some walkers in all seasons. Some of those hikers, of course, turn up late, go missing, or don't turn up at all. Here is the story of one such night in the northern Kilkenny Range; it typifies the partial information that can trickle back from these mountains, especially in this era of instant communication, and it features also the sudden appearance of a rogue searcher, an X factor from outside the usual cast.

On the morning of January 10, 2014, Thomas R. and his black Lab (no name in NHFG's official report, alas) left the Bunnell Notch trailhead to traverse part of the Kilkenny Range and return via the Unknown Pond Trail. The weather was temperate for January, with warming in the forecast. At 7:00 p.m. Thomas's girlfriend, Teri H., called New Hampshire State Police to say he was overdue and that she had not heard from him since an early-morning text message. State Police in turn notified Fish and Game; Conservation Officer Mark Ober called Teri and got Thomas's detailed route plan and learned also that he was fully equipped for winter hiking.

At 9:30 p.m. Ober and fellow conservation officer Glen Lucas set off up the Unknown Pond Trail to find Thomas. Two hours into their search, Ober and Lucas heard a voice calling out, "Tom," and they answered. This brought them to Jason B., a hiker from Maine, who also had received a call from Teri H. while he was on his way to climb elsewhere. Jason had revamped his plans and come to look for his friend, Thomas. Jason reported that he knew the terrain well, and it became clear that he was very fit and fast. As CO Ober put it in his report, Jason "soon outpaced" the two officers.

Three hours into their search, just below Unknown Pond, the two officers came upon a set of snowshoe and dog tracks that veered off trail and downhill. They followed these tracks for about a half-mile to where the walker turned around to return to the trail. Then, they continued up along the Kilkenny Ridge Trail, over the Horn and the Bulge. At 1:30 a.m., as he entered an area with cell phone reception, Ober responded to a missed call from Teri H. and learned that Jason had located Thomas and that they were descending the Bunnell Notch Trail. Later that morning, the officers received confirmation that Thomas had reached the trailhead. At that point, nearly equidistant from their own starting point and this destination, Ober and Lucas slogged on, emerging from the woods at 7:00 a.m.

In a later statement to Fish and Game, Thomas R. said he had lost the trail near Unknown Pond and, after searching for it, decided to backtrack. Absence of cell phone coverage meant that he couldn't inform Teri H. of his change in plans, and the long walk and work of retracing his steps had made him late. In his report, Officer Ober also noted that "it was apparent that the trail system in the Kilkenny Range has not been blazed in quite a while," so "it was easy to see where someone could get lost . . . especially when [the trail] is snow-covered and hasn't been opened up by other hikers." Ober went on to recommend fresh blazing of the trail and sign at the point where Thomas lost the trail.

A few other details catch a reader's attention: Yes, Thomas R. set off alone in unfamiliar territory in winter. But he was experienced and he was well equipped should he have to spend more time out than anticipated. Once Thomas determined that he couldn't find the trail, he exercised good sense in backtracking, even though doing so meant climbing back over the day's three peaks and ensuring that he would be out well into the night. Jason B. appears in this story like a bolt from the blue. He alters plans for a night hike and, eventually, locates Thomas and walks out to the trailhead with him. In midsearch, he meets the two conservation officers, but soon he has blazed on ahead, and he provides a question mark in this incident: Was it good that he went on ahead on his own, or might he have tempered his speed and stayed with the two officers, thereby ensuring that only one person was missing in the night? Doing that can be difficult when one is fit and fast, but perhaps it's more prudent.

Other than that consideration, there's no fault to find in this incident. It's here mostly as a note of appreciation for the uncomplaining, matter-of-fact report from CO Ober, an attitude that typifies much of the Whites' SAR community. He and CO Lucas are out all night, and, at the time Jason finds Thomas, Ober writes, "Looking at the map, CO Lucas and I saw we were 5.7 miles from the parking lot if we kept going south or 5.4 miles if we turned around and went back." The officers slogged on; this is the work they've chosen, and they simply do it.

NHFG was the only organization involved in this search.

> That, then, is a smattering of modern search and rescue stories as an introduction to some of the Whites' rescuers and the types of incidents that summon them. It is a sort of call-and-response catalogue. A reader will also note a few recurring characters—Sgt. Ober, Mike Pelchat, Rick Wilcox, and others—and in those recurrences lies another truth of White Mountain SAR: the same professionals and volunteers go out time after time to save us. To a person, they live where they look; they see these mountains as their community.

4

IN THE BEGINNING

On tops of mountains,
as everywhere to hopeful souls,
it is always morning.
HENRY DAVID THOREAU

Many of our oldest stories chase their subjects out into the wilderness, where all manner of trial takes place. The Judeo-Christian God kicks inquisitive Eve and gullible Adam out of Eden for a spell of wandering and woe (which, some say, goes on still); the Buddha leaves his family and the comfort of the compound to find the light; many Native Americans insist that to arrive at your adult self, you have to go out alone where the core spirit and vision of that self can find you.

When each culture's famous folk come back, their stories of what they searched for and what they found help shape that culture. As you would expect, however, some who set out on these quests never return. Such stories feature the lost, whose first steps are known, but whose endings are only imagined. These narratives of lost venturers also shape cultures, surrounding them with a forest or mountain or sea or sky of risk and trouble. At least that's how these wildernesses looked to people at first.

This ages-old venturing spirit applies to New Hampshire's White Mountains. Though they may not be as lofty or legendary as others of the planet's high places, they are storied enough to serve as symbols of going out and coming back changed, and of faltering sometimes along the way, never to return. Equally symbolic is the tribe of rescuers, who, over time, have gathered to go out and help their era's explorers.

The territory that became New Hampshire was threaded with trails long before Europeans arrived along the coast and began their stuttering press inland. Early seventeenth-century New England was home to as many as

100,000 Native Americans, with perhaps 80 percent of that population concentrated in the south, where agriculture played an important role in food supply. From Maine's Kennebec River northward, growing seasons were too short and plantings largely absent, so inhabitants got their food from seasonal hunting and gathering. Even the southern Indians realized much of their food from wild resources. All of this rooting about for and chasing of food relied on mobility, with northern Indians tending toward the coast in the warmer months and to the sheltered river valleys and woods in the colder ones. Such movement followed waterways and lowland trails, some of which persist today as routes for our highways. The old Indian tracks through major White Mountain notches, for example, all carry roads today.

Indian trails didn't climb mountains, other than traversing some lower ridges for hunting, because . . . why would you? All that was up there were stones and spirits, who could be provoked by human presence; climbing was a form of arrogance and wasted energy.

The early colonists, who moved uncertainly north into its hard landscapes and uneasy relationship with its natives, kept largely to the valleys, too. There, they found pockets of arable land, potable water, and the rushing energy of rivers and streams; there they could try to build a life in one place. Because European colonists came from and would replicate a tradition of fixed dwellings and towns in contrast to the mobile, seasonal lives of the Indians, they would depend upon exchange with others to get whatever they couldn't produce on their own. That exchange would take place over roads and trails, and later, rails—all lowland ways. Hunting, which might take a colonist into the upper backcountry, would also shift over time from a mostly subsistence calling to a leisure pursuit. Nature in its wild forms was seen as an opponent, something to be battled and subdued, and, like any powerful opponent, something to be feared. So for the most part, early settlers among the mountains were rarely lost or searched for in the wild uplands; it would take the advent of leisure time and a new view of nature to send people up into the hills.

Along the River and Beyond the Pond

As the former Europeans settled into the villages and their dug-in homes, set down roots and, finally, had time to look up from their labors, they discovered new ways to see nature and its terrain where people had not settled. The European ideal of the sublime also crossed the Atlantic, and in the early 1800s, a few New Englanders began to report their visions of the formerly "daunting and terrible" mountains differently. In 1784, Jeremy Belknap, looking at Mount Washington from Pinkham Notch, had this to say: "Almost everything in nature, which can be supposed capable of inspiring ideas of the sublime and beautiful, is here realized. Aged mountains, stupendous elevations, rolling clouds, impending rocks, verdant woods, crystal streams, the gentle rill and the roaring torrent, all conspire to amaze, to soothe and to enrapture" (*Forest and Crag*, 71).

But Belknap was only a word-based forerunner for the visualizations of the sublime that would sweep over the region when the Hudson River School artists (also sometimes called The White Mountain School) began painting. Starting in 1825, Thomas Cole, and then second-generation painters like Frederick Church and Albert Bierstadt, offered everyone who saw their works (and they became deeply popular) visions of colorful, soaring peaks juxtaposed with a pastoral idealization of attractive agriculture. When they appeared at all, people were tiny in these vast canvases of nature. Even as the painted peaks soared and the clouds roiled, harmony and beauty prevailed. A new vision of America was on offer, and people wanted to visit this land. They began to travel to do so.

Increasingly, towns and cities grew denser, and so thicker with fumes and, sometimes, the fury that rises from tightly packed living. Also, as the drive to subsist gave way to the goal of making a profit, people sought escape, if only for a short time before they went back to aspiring, or simply persisting. Lives of "quiet desperation" were coming to the fore. At least that's how one writer and social critic, born in 1817, saw it. Henry David Thoreau went first to a pond and later to press to offer the most piercing social critique ever written of his evolving country and its kin. Walden Pond and its local terrain became the site of Thoreau's "experiment" in how to live, and his way of learning that life offered example too: every day he was able, Thoreau set out for a long walk to see what the land and nature had to say. Four hours on foot was Thoreau's preferred minimum and, even as he walked often off road or trail, he covered his miles. Thoreau thought nothing of a twenty-mile "saunter." That such a mobile man was also a most precise and astute observer of little moments along the way—a bird's nest, an unfurling flower, the track of a tiny insect—speaks of a new awareness. His is perhaps the clearest and most poetic expression of a transcendent ideal that took shape amid an improbable gathering of notable minds in Thoreau's native Concord, Massachusetts, in the mid-nineteenth century.

For the Transcendentalists, walking was a way out. And up. Even the word itself prompts one to look out and up. Where might I go? it asks. It may seem an odd extension, but Transcendentalism can be seen as a spiritual form of search and rescue; in its walkings and contemplation of nature, in its hope of connecting for short stretches with the world spirit of the "oversoul," its object is to save the self.

Had he been born in New England's North Country, given his walking habit, Thoreau would have been one of the early mountaineers, and his name might now carry the White Mountain ring of Crawford. But even hailing from flatland Concord, where he made much of its little prominences, Thoreau made much of mountains. In particular, he gave early voice to New England's two most lionized peaks, Washington (Agiocochook) in 1839 and 1858, and Katahdin (Ktaadn) in 1846. The two ascents of Washington, in particular, offer a clear picture of how the approach to mountains was changing in the mid-nineteenth century. Thoreau was a new sort of hunter-gatherer: his quarry was experience, knowledge, and story; his hunting ground was nature that we had left untouched, nature that surrounded us still. The uplands held an abundance of that nature.

In 1839, at age twenty-two, Thoreau approached the White Mountains with his older brother John in time-honored fashion. The brothers set off for their first mountain camping trip via the Sudbury River, rowing and drifting downstream to the Concord and on to the Merrimack, where they turned upstream toward New Hampshire and its hills. They would climb first a river and then, after a carriage-ride north, their region's tallest mountain, replicating in their two-week journey both the course of European settlement of the north lands and the classic hero's journey. As river travelers, the Thoreaus were usual, even a little behind the times as the railroad had begun to eclipse the waterways; as climbers they were in a vanguard. People had just begun to climb mountains, often on horseback by the bridle paths that were being constructed at that time, and not many descriptions of such journeys existed. Even Henry Thoreau, of the expressive two-million-word journal, seemed uncertain what to make of ascending Washington; his entry for the day contains a clipped sentence: "September 10th ascended the mountain and rode to Conway," whereas his river voyage with his brother grew into the thicketed prose of his first book, *A Week on the Concord and Merrimack Rivers*.

By the time Thoreau returned to the White Mountains in 1858, this time with his friend Edward Hoar, he was part of a wave of tourers, and, in this now popular landscape he, like other White Mountain hikers, had a lot to say. His journal entries are effusive and detailed, stretching to sixty pages rife with observations of plants, rocks, and people. A modern walker can follow his routes easily, as J. Parker Huber has done in his pleasing compendium *Elevating Ourselves*, which traces Thoreau's journeys on mountains. Thoreau was also middlingly well known by then—*Walden* had been published to good reviews and mild public enthusiasm in 1854—and, in the heated, pre–Civil War political scene, he was known as an effective, radical speaker for the cause of abolition.

The mountains Hoar and Thoreau approached now had hotels (to which Thoreau objected) on some of the prominent summits and bridle and nascent carriage paths to them. Though few risks were taken on these genteel climbs, in part because they were confined to the summer season, the first of what would become a catalogue of weather-driven mishaps had already happened. In October of 1849, Frederick Strickland, a young Englishman on an American tour and infused with the era's expansiveness, arrived at Thomas Crawford's place, the Notch House, in soon-to-be-called Crawford Notch. There, he announced he would like to climb Mount Washington via the Crawford Path. While the valley weather still passed for fall, a storm had already buried the high ridges with snow, and another was coming on. But only the native Crawford understood how altitude could shift the seasons, and though he warned against climbing, Strickland would not be deterred. So on October 19, he set out with an English friend, a guide, and two horses. A little beyond the summit of Mount Clinton, three miles in, the snow deepened to the point where the horses could not continue, and the guide recommended turning back; Strickland argued for onward and the summit five miles away.

There they parted company. The guide, horses and unnamed English companion retreated down the Crawford Path, and Strickland set out in his usual clothes and overcoat for Washington. That he made the summit is testament to his resolve, because his ascent plowed through snow and into winter. On top, he located the shorter Fabayan's bridle path and began his descent along what would become the cog railway's line. Searchers, who found him dead in Clay Brook two days later, saw in his meandering tracks that Strickland had lost the trail in the woods and wandered looking for a way down. They found also that he was badly bruised and cut from his various falls and had shed his pants finally not far from where he was found, cold-addled behaviors that read like a classic modern hypothermia story. Strickland's was the first of more than 150 deaths on these slopes, and the first to be analyzed by his searchers.

But Strickland's story paled before the press given to Lizzie Bourne in 1855, just three years before Thoreau and Hoar traveled north to Washington's summit. Bourne's September story begins as many mountain tragedies do—late. On the thirteenth, the day broke rainy, so Lizzie, her uncle, and his daughter postponed their planned trip for an overnight at the Summit Hotel until the next day, when they would ride horses there. But then the weather cleared, and Lizzie, an irrepressible twenty-year-old excited by the prospect of a night on the summit, prevailed upon her uncle to walk up the carriage road. The threesome set out at 2:00 p.m., and along the mild, leveled grades of the first four miles, they made good time, reaching the Halfway House at 4:00 p.m. From there, the rougher bridle path rose from the trees over ridge after bare ridge and, as the wind increased, the party slowed. It also grew colder.

They reached what's called the Cow Pasture, a level area below the summit cone, at sunset, and paused to admire the sun's westering. As the clouds clapped down, they climbed on, expecting to reach the top soon. Finally, in absolute darkness, amid sharp stone and pummeled by what was now a gale, they could go no farther. Bourne's uncle had the two young women lie down. He then labored to build a windbreak of stones for some protection, stopping at times, then lying down to rest and try to warm the girls.

Sometime around 10:00 p.m., as he dropped back to rest and warm, the uncle found Lizzie's hand cold, unresponsive. When morning light filtered in, Bourne's uncle and cousin found themselves mere yards from the hotel, which they reached in a few strides.

Strickland's and especially Bourne's deaths had joined the Hudson River School's paintings in capturing the public's imagination, and the reports flowing from the incidents and the stories sent out by those living on summer mountaintops added a frisson of danger to the romantic idea of climbing. They also added to mountain lore the stories of those who searched for the fallen. Mountain search—and its progeny, the expectation of rescue—had been born.

> Perhaps all this narrative and mountain bustle is part of what's behind the volume of Thoreau's commentary on his second White Mountain trip, but what also catches the modern eye is his July 8 description of leaving Mount Washington's summit in the fog, bound for Tuckerman Ravine:

About 8:15 a.m., being still in dense fog, restarted direct for Tuckerman Ravine, I having taken the bearing of it before the fog. But Spaulding (Summit hotelier) also went some ten rods with us and pointed toward the head of the ravine, which was about S 15 degrees W. Hoar tried to hire Page to go with us, carrying part of our baggage,—as he had already brought it up from the shanty [part way up along the carriage road where they had spent the prior night]—and he professed to be acquainted with the mountain; but his brother, who lived at the summit, warned him not to go, lest he should not be able to find his way back again, and he declined. The landlords were rather anxious about us. I looked at my compass every four or five rods and then walked toward some rock in our course, but frequently after taking three or four steps, though the fog was no more dense, I would lose the rock I steered for. The fog was very bewildering. You would think that the rock you steered for was some large boulder twenty rods off, or perchance it looked like the bow of a distant spur, but a dozen steps would take you to it, and it would suddenly have sunk into the ground. I discovered this illusion. I said to my companions, "You see that boulder of peculiar form, slanting over another. Well, that is in our course. How large do you think it is, and how far?" To my surprise, one answered three rods, but the other said nine. I guessed four, and we all thought it about eight feet high. We could not see beyond it, and it looked like the highest part of a ridge before us. At the end of twenty-one paces, or three and a half rods, I stepped upon it,—less than two feet high—and I could not have distinguished it from the hundred similar ones around it, if I had not kept my eye on it all the while.

Thoreau, who was a quick study, then offered comment that reads as kin to the sort of advice a reader can find in a modern guidebook about hiking, or in the lesson-drawing comments of mountain-accident analyses:

> It is unwise for one to ramble over these mountains at any time, unless he is prepared to move with as much certainty as if he were solving a geometrical problem. A cloud may at any moment settle around him, and unless he has a compass and knows which way to go, he will be lost at once. . . . To travel there with security, a person must know his bearings at every step, be it fair weather or foul. An ordinary rock in a fog, being in the apparent horizon, is exaggerated to, perhaps, at least ten times its size and stance. You will think you have gone further than you have to get to it. (*Journal*, vol. 11, July 8, 1858)

There is, in Thoreau's description, the hint of menace that fog and unsight-edness can carry on an exposed mountain. You can quickly lose your way and become wrapped in illusion, which carries you farther afield. All the while, the very rocks on which you walk seem to change size, shift shapes, reminding you that nothing is certain up here, that life's supports are far below, and that you must get back there to live on. Because he was an inveterate walker, had good facility with a compass, and had learned good footing and measurement skills in his work as a surveyor, Thoreau could lead the way precisely. He, Hoar, and a companion go down unerringly to Tuckerman Ravine. Thoreau, characteristically, "know[s] his bearings at every step." But Thoreau also seems aware that they have reached an edge, a place where accident and trouble are close by, a place visited often by modern search and rescue and its narratives of loss. These mountains, he senses, even in the high summer of early July, can be trouble.

To Climb and Find:
The Appalachian Mountain Club Forms

To find the roots of search and rescue in the White Mountains, you have to examine the routes of people's early explorations. Few people get lost until a lot of people go looking at scenery in hidden folds and on high ridges. Those who did go looking, the mid- and late-nineteenth-century explorers and adventurers, sought the sublime, the transcendent, and the beauty of nature on the summits and in the cleft ravines. Like their modern descendants, they sought also themselves. But to get to these ideals and places, they needed paths, and so they sought also the way up.

The early innkeepers, hoteliers, and guides, like the Crawfords and Fabayans and Spauldings, had cut their way through the forests and scrub spruce, fashioning a few foot and bridle paths that would bolster their enterprises. But they were in the business of creating and serving tourists. It would take people of another bent to attend to the exploration, mapping, and trail making that would open up the Whites and bring people into all their corners. Such work would also lead to the need to search those corners when people went missing. The bent of mind needed was that of the questioner: What's over there? What's that open ledge like? Where did these rocks come from? What's that plant? How do you get over there? The first of those questioners were the Churches and Thoreaus just mentioned, and the answers they gathered excited more interest. As the twentieth-century's preeminent White Mountain historians Guy and Laura Waterman point out, these tourists' primary interest lay in "being among the mountains," rather than in exploring them. A leisurely uphill day on a horse's back with the views arrayed before them would suffice for most pre–Civil War tourists.

The Civil War's convulsions diminished the swell of tourists and sent those who might have explored to another edge of life, the battlefield. A stretch of quiet years ensued in the Whites. But that dormancy waned with the war decade, and soon harbingers of a new age appeared across the country and in the Whites: "Unabashed joy in the pleasures of pure pedestrianism exploded all over the national scene right after the Civil War. City dwellers strolled the avenues. Vacationers paced the country lanes. Well-known national figures extolled the virtues of the vigorous constitutional. . . . The growing national interest in walking during the 1860s, 1870s and 1880s may be compared to the national interest in running almost exactly one hundred years later" (Waterman, *Forest and Crag*, 151).

Among the next wave drawn north from the cities to the White Mountains was a richness of professional questioners. These professors and teachers asked questions for a living; now they asked them so they could learn their way deeper into the mountains, and so into their lives.

Used to the way their schools shaped communities of inquiry, a group of teachers formed a club community around their shared love of mountains. The seed school was the Massachusetts Institute of Technology, and the group founded was the Appalachian Mountain Club. One hundred and forty years later, both organizations are central to their areas of interest. MIT is a premier research institution, a gold standard for universities, and AMC is the Northeast region's most influential outdoor club, with over 100,000 members and a reach that stretches south, down the Appalachian chain from which it takes it name. But in 1876, the AMC's founders were drawn toward the parts of the White Mountains that the first wave of tourists and path builders had ignored. Their interest was exploration.

The early Appalachians (as they soon became known) had two avatars as fore-walkers—professors who inquired before their time. In 1849, Swiss national and recent émigré and later Princeton professor Arnold Guyot launched a lifelong inquiry into the Appalachian Mountains with forays into the trailless region of Mount Carrigain. Over the next decades, he would explore countless untracked and unmapped regions of the chain, from Maine to Georgia, leaving his name on more than a half dozen U.S. peaks. Following Guyot's tracks today would be a long, exhausting quest, even on established trails. That Guyot did most of his walking and climbing by bushwhacking is stunning. Did Guyot ever need rescue? I can find no record of it. But perhaps someone who began many of his mountain explorations with the expectation of being in unknown territory, and so, intentionally lost, was simply immune to the feeling and experience.

The other walking avatar was Charles Hitchcock, prominent geologist and the first mapmaker of consequence in the White Mountains. Hitchcock brought the grid, our way of knowing the land and transmitting that knowledge to others, a way of knowing that prefigures today's within-an-inch-of-where-you-are GPS readings. With his teams of students, Hitchcock began to pin down the mountains, even as they remained mostly trackless, and so impenetrable to most walkers.

We are, famously, social animals, and while the solitaries among us may show the way sometimes, when we hit on an activity we like, we look about for like and likable souls. So it was that Professor Edward C. Pickering and his friend John B. Henck Jr., new summer converts to White Mountain rambles, invited twenty-plus similarly enthused men to a meeting on January 8, 1876. Pickering and Henck had designs for forming a mountain club devoted to exploring, measuring, mapping, and building trails on peaks that were still wilderness. They took their example and, at times, their people from the Alpine Club of Williamstown and the Portland, Maine, White Mountain Club. Both of these nascent clubs soon faded, but the Appalachian Mountain Club, founded on that January day, took off.

Part of that taking off lay in the founders' two foci—exploration and improvement—impulses and goals that do not always move easily together (Waterman, *Forest and Crag*, 192). Explorers press out into the unknown; they seek out edges of terrain and experience. By definition, they are dependent upon that unknown; there is no exploration, in the common sense of the word, if the terrain is known, measured, and walked or climbed by many. Improvers, on the other hand, seek to make their discoveries and excitements available to others, to invite others into their experiences and landscapes so that those others may enjoy them, too. Improvers are builders, and builders do not inhabit the unknown; they make it known. It takes little imagination to see how these two types might collaborate at the outset. In the AMC, they stayed together. Though the two sorts of affection created considerable tension, they endured and cohered, held together, perhaps, by their love of the mountains and clear evidence that those mountains were susceptible to threats far larger than being loved variously or differently. A modern reader need only look back at turn-of-the-century photos of swaths of logged and burned-over forest to see that there were others with completely different ideas for exploring and "improving" the White Mountains.

The founders of the AMC were prescient in another important way as well: at their second meeting, they voted to admit women to full membership, thereby setting in motion an expansion of the club and a line of remarkable women associated with both the club and the mountains. Whereas Lizzie Bourne's unfortunate death in 1855 might have cautioned women against pressing into the Whites in that era, AMC trips filled quickly with women walkers, and the club was enlivened by the stories they brought back. The mountain stage was being set for serious women climbers of the twentieth century, like Marian Pychowska and Miriam Underhill. In fact, as we look later at the structure and composition of twenty-first-century search and rescue, the women of the AMC seem again to be in the forefront of what comes next.

The first few waves of AMC leaders and members were vigorous in their questing and questioning and legendary for their efficiency. New England notable Thomas Wentworth Higginson said this about the club: "It seems to me that if anywhere there is a universe in need of administration, it might well be turned over to the Appalachian Mountain Club" (Waterman, *Forest and Crag*, 191). By the turn of the twentieth century, there were over a thousand "Appalachians," and their spirit and works were everywhere evident in the White Mountains.

5

WHITE FINGERS POINTING
TOWARD THE WIND

The Incident That Helped Shape
Our Modern Mountains

At the pivot point of the first year of a new century, two of their era's strongest climbers set out for an Appalachian Mountain Club field meeting on the summit of Mount Washington. The June 30, 1900, meeting had no doubt been scheduled with balmy temperatures, long light, and walks to and views of distant blue ridges in mind. But it drew a different set of cards from weather's deck: cold rain swept the low ridges, and above tree line that rain mixed with sleet and became finally wind-hurled ice rain. Most of those attending the meeting chose the shelter of the cog railway or carriage road as a way up, but "Father Bill" Curtis, age sixty-two, and Allan Ormsbee, age twenty-eight, inclined toward the Crawford Path and its eight-mile southern approach. After a brief foray up Mount Willard, they set out in the forenoon, clothed mostly in their reputations as formidable mountain walkers. Curtis, in particular, was known for covering distance, being inured to cold, and hiking in light clothing; it was a point of pride.

The panes of glass in the Summit House hotel's windows began to shatter on Saturday morning. As the storm intensified, bits of wind-driven ice broke one pane after another, and employees hurried to tack rectangles of wood into each opening. One can imagine a gradual darkening of the room. Still, the Appalachians, as AMC members were called, were undeterred. They read papers and held discussions, and the trains kept carrying new arrivals up. At 2:00 p.m., the Reverend (later to be called Uncle by everyone across the North Country) Harry Nichols staggered through the door with his sixteen-year-old son, Donaldson. The pair and two guides had spent the night before near Mount Isolation on the then trailless Montalban Ridge, and their climb from the exposed expanse of Bigelow Lawn up the cone to the summit had been a near thing.

Nichols's report, and the fact that the Appalachians knew that Curtis and Ormsbee had set out to climb the Crawford Path to this meeting raised anxiety in the room. As the day crept, and outside, howled on, the pair remained absent. Fred Ilgen did appear with Curtis and Ormsbee's luggage, but that deepened the anxiety. Ilgen had been the third member in the group's week-long hiking trip, which had begun at Wonalancet and had seen them up several White Mountain peaks. That day, Ilgen had opted to climb up and down Twin Mountain and then take the train to the summit; he would prove the prudent one.

The Summit House was full of notables, a who's who of White Mountain hiking history. A modern reader of that history or walker of its terrain can't help but bump into reminders of these pioneers: the Edmands Path or Edmands Col recalls the Presidential Range's greatest path builder, Rayner Edmands; an old topo map points to mapmaker Louis Cutter; AMC's long history is embodied by its first president and forty-year editor of *Appalachia* Charles Fay and a cadre of MIT professors. These three men and many others were at the hotel meeting. They were used to solving problems, and their kind of solving meant acting. But as they waited for Curtis and Ormsbee and kept to their meeting schedule, they were also pinned inside by the storm. And that storm went on, only strengthening through Saturday night and into Sunday.

While those doing the waiting were august mountain figures, one of the men walking their way carried an athletic fame few in the country could match. Born in 1837 in Salisbury, Vermont, William Curtis didn't have a childhood that presaged the action-oriented, vigorous man he would become. Early tuberculosis compromised his health and slowed him. But somewhere in that childhood, Curtis also developed a formidable resolve that drove him forward athletically and intellectually. As a boy he formed the dream of attending West Point. When he couldn't achieve that and went instead to college in the Midwest, he mastered the West Point curriculum in his spare time. His mastery of mathematics, in particular, gave him a precise bent of mind and an aura of accomplishment that astounded others.

At the same time, Curtis took up sprinting and weight throwing. For over twenty years, he beat all comers in the one-hundred-yard dash, and he won three AAU national championships in the hammer throw. A founder of the New York Athletic Club and the AAU, Curtis left both organizations in favor of his central focus, the Fresh Air Club, which was devoted to balancing the cramped, interior city life with long, vigorous outings in the country. Some of those outings covered up to thirty road and trail miles on a Saturday, so the pace could be formidable. What most of the club's walkers didn't know was that Curtis had scouted and forged over the entire route, making choices and trying alternatives before the Fresh Air folk got there. Somehow, he was able to test his routes at the same time he held a job as editor of the *Spirit of the Times*, a newspaper devoted to athletics and their promotion.

All of this shepherding of walkers and organizations earned Curtis the name "Father Bill," which acknowledged his seminal position in American athletics. But the quasi-religious tone of the nickname seems on point too. Father Bill, unmarried and childless, was a guide to the spirit of the body in motion.

During the week before their climb into the cold clouds, the twenty-eight-year-old Allan Ormsbee, himself a fit, accomplished athlete, had followed Father Bill up a host of peaks. On this day, they were simply keeping on as they and everyone else would have expected them to do.

On Saturday night, at the urging of others, noted guide Thaddeus Lowe and another man took lanterns and went out for a look-see. If nothing else, the pair hoped their lights might offer guidance to Curtis and Ormsbee should they be out there in the thick dark. Within steps, the wind snuffed their lanterns and in the absolute blackness, Lowe and his companion struggled to cross the iced rocks and regain the hotel. Clearly, the only action was waiting. Against the relentlessly audible roar of hurried air, the Appalachians waited. When they finally emerged on Monday morning, they walked out into a changed mountain world.

The July sun began to melt the accrued ice. Some chunks weighed in at hundreds of pounds as they fell from summit structures, and the rime ice, "white fingers pointing toward the wind," dropped from every post and stone. Across this glassed landscape, the Appalachians looked for Curtis and Ormsbee, finding Curtis first, fallen and glazed on the Crawford Path, not far from the Lakes of the Clouds. Ormsbee took more finding. Eventually, a three-man sweep following the intuition of Ormsbee's friend Herschel Parker (later to gain fame on Mount McKinley), located his body a mere 130 vertical feet below the summit. Battered from recurring slips and collisions with the summit cone's sharp rocks (the coroner would count fifty significant bruises), Ormsbee had almost made it to safety.

The episode shocked the Appalachians and other mountain folk. That two superb athletes could be killed by cold and ice at summer's height pointed to the extremes possible in the White Mountains, extremes that simply don't visit lower mountains to the south. That recognition would cast the Whites as suitable training ground for many of the world's other ranges, and it would suggest to the builders prominent in the AMC that safety on these uplands could be improved.

Such was the fame and effect of Curtis and Ormsbee's deaths that the final words of the story didn't arrive until much later. Fred Ilgen, the party's third walker, who opted not to climb the Crawford Path that day, wrote his own account of the tragedy (*The Fatal Hiking Trip*), but he waited until 1941 to do so. The fifteen-page story wasn't published until 1942, after Ilgen had died. Much of the chronicle depicts a sunny walk north as the three companions summit peaks and revel in views and each other's company. But it is also clear that these steps had replayed in Ilgen's mind throughout the rest of his life. Both Curtis and Ormsbee had suffered knee problems during the week leading up to June 30. Curtis's seemed born of long years of use; Ormsbee's came courtesy of a collision with a rock while scrambling in the underground caverns along the Lost River beneath Mount Moosilauke. Those knee woes seemed resolved by the thirtieth, but they point to the pair as being more vulnerable than they are often seen to be.

On that day, Ilgen later wrote, "the time for the splitting up of our party was now at hand." Ilgen wished to explore the Twin range that morning and then catch the cog railway to the summit of Washington in the afternoon. Curtis, while he would have liked to explore the Twins ("something entirely new for me"), thought it more important that the younger Ormsbee, who was due back in New York on Monday, get two days on the Presidential Range.

During his climb up the Little River Valley and the 4,900-foot South Twin Mountain, Ilgen reports that early bursts of sunlight gave way first to rain and then to sleet. Ilgen pressed on toward North Twin, hoping for a return of sun and "to be rewarded with something of a view," but, when the sleet kept on and the cold sapped him, he turned back, descending South Twin and returning finally to valley weather more redolent of the summer season: "When I reached the spring at the foot of the trail, the sun shone brightly, though the mountaintops were still inclosed in fog." He then went on, as arranged, to Fabayan's Hotel, where he gathered his companions' luggage and took the train to the summit. His anxiety for his friends and the ever-thickening ice of the next thirty-six hours are clear.

After Curtis and Ormsbee are found dead, Ilgen rides a specially arranged night train down with his dead friends. Their bodies are strapped to cots and those cots are secured atop the train's seat. There is no light in the car, writes Ilgen, only the "occasional gleam come in from a lantern which swung on the engine in front." Ilgen watches his friends' bodies, and as he does, he sees that Ormsbee's head is not fully secure; it is lolling this way and that as the train sways. Ilgen moves over, holds his friend's head as they go down: "I stood up in the aisle and kept his head steady with my hands. It was a weird and uncanny ride—one which I can never erase from my memory."

Finally, Ilgen stays with his friends as they are examined by the local undertakers and he records their response: "These men expressed the utmost astonishment at Curtis's chest and muscle development, and declared that, in all their experience, they had never seen anything like it." Ilgen knows his friend, and, even in death and even in writing forty-one years later, he is careful of his pride. Ilgen rescues what is left.

This was a different sort of mountain dying than those that preceded it. Even now, it reads like a modern accident: two superb athletes, confident of self and quick afoot, press against nature's limits—and lose. Modernize their clothes and give them headlamps and beacons, and they could be Kate Matrosova, aiming at Washington from the other side, and finding a place in both White Mountain legend and 2015's accident reports. Or they could be two of the new breed of long-distance runners who sometimes arrive as a surprise behind us on the trails.

The Appalachians who waited and then searched that day would have been anyone's first choice for a rescue party. They were hardy, strong-willed, and mountain savvy. Yet they had been powerless. If the mountain weather at the height of the well-lit summer season could carry away a generation's best climbers and render helpless the rest, something more than human resolve was needed in these hills, even dotted as they were with summit structures. Some way for climbers to rescue themselves when others could not seemed called for. And so in 1901, only months after Father Bill Curtis and Allan Ormsbee perished, a shelter constructed by the AMC appeared near Lakes of the Clouds.

After their brief summary of the Curtis and Ormsbee incident and other early White Mountain tragedies in *Forest and Crag*, Guy and Laura Waterman offer an insightful footnote about the incident's aftermath and effect:

> Response to the Curtis-Ormsbee accident set a pattern that has recurred in subsequent incidents during the twentieth century. In the immediate aftermath of tragedy, responsible officials feel an overwhelming need to respond with action designed to deal directly with the specific events of that accident. This reaction has produced "emergency" buildings on top of Marcy, at Edmands Col in the Northern Presidentials, and at half-mile intervals along Mount Washington's auto road. In each case—as in the pattern-setting Curtis-Ormsbee incident and its resulting "emergency shelter"—the hiking public has soon adopted the building as a regular place to camp, and it has become littered and damaged. In each case mentioned, officials have eventually torn down the shelter, apparently concluding that its possible value in an emergency did not justify the environmental degradation that resulted. (277)

But even as the construction and composition of mountain shelters have changed over the ensuing 125 years, responsible officials continue to feel "an overwhelming need to respond with action designed to deal with the specific events of [an] accident." Modern search and rescue, with its crews, radios, phones, beacons, and helicopters, is such an action.

Gimme Shelter

In 1963, as fifteen-year-olds, my friend Brad and I set out from the Appalachia parking lot for a first Presidential traverse. We had twenty-five-pound packs with food and sleeping bags and extra clothing, and we were expecting a summer walk across the August peaks. I'd recently completed my 4,000-footers, many climbed with my father (whom I'd beaten to completion, a contest that seemed necessary then) and others with a Maine camp group where I'd been a counselor's aide. So I had some foot miles on my boots and in my mind. Still, as my parents dropped us off and pulled out of the lot, I felt the string system of my nerves tighten a bit.

Brad, too, was strong and fit, and we went quickly up the Valley Way, stopping briefly at Madison Hut for a snack and a look at my father's photo on the hutmen's wall of photos. Then we climbed on across the Gulfside, passing the point of Joe Caggiano's death from exposure in 1938, a tale from family lore since my dad had been the searcher who found him. This was not to be a one-day traverse. We'd begun around noon, and our aim was to overnight at Edmands Col, where the inverted, metal U of an emergency Quonset hut would offer shelter. We got there around 4:00 p.m. to find a number of others with the same idea—clearly, whatever "emergencies" were in the air were planned ones. Edmands Col had become an aim point for campers.

That air, however, also brought a hint of what true emergency might look like as night came on. The clouds dropped onto us, and the temperature fell to just above freezing; even in the fading light, the droplets of water that gathered on every surface shone. The drainpipe shelter had room for six, and by now there were ten of us shuffling around outside, trying to shelter stoves from a thirty-five-mile-an-hour wind and mumbling about the cold. Some stoves went out; we shared flames that kept on; everyone had something to eat eventually. Then, in the intimacy of even small emergency, we packed ourselves into the lightless, dripping metal shelter and pretended to sleep. I was near the back and experiencing waves of claustrophobia until distraction finally arrived in the form of negotiations with my bladder. How, I hissed, am I supposed to get over all these bodies? Don't care, said bladder. The only other option is pissing on them.

At fifteen, we're sure everyone's watching and judging us but, of course, everyone was really wrapped in his or her dark misery, so I got no resistance or complaint as I groped and stumbled to the shelter's narrow outlet. There, I slipped on my boots (good boy, you remembered them) and stepped out to pee. And almost fell. The ground was glazed with ice; I wobbled a few steps and added to it. I was aware dimly in that moment that this night was a near thing. Even in the shelter rich with body heat (and scent), I was cold in my summer sleeping bag, and now colder still from being dampened by going outside. Two bodies away, someone moaned and babbled in a bad dream; the night never ended, until finally it did.

Brad and I owned no tent that would have repelled that mix of water and cold; without the Edmands Col emergency shelter, we would have encountered real emergency. But some thirteen years later, in the mid-1970s, the shelter was removed. Our evening tensome and countless others had made a beaten, trashed, poop-littered landscape of the col, a little version of what Everest expeditions have done to that giant's South Col.

Built for emergencies, such shelters could be seen as a passive rescue presence. Where rescuers might not be able to go in a storm, these structures would serve the purpose. Dark, damp, and uncomfortable, the shelters were meant to be the opposite of an attraction; they were conceived of as places only the desperate would seek out. In the Whites emergency shelters were stand-ins for the Appalachians, then the dominant force in White Mountain climbing, who could not always be there. The implementation of emergency shelters also helped transform the White Mountains from tourist destinations to adventure sites. The drive to test oneself in slanting terrain, a drive that keeps marching toward extremes today, was partially rooted in these stolid shelters, which adventurers then took to factoring into their plans.

The shelters that remain in today's mountains are sited and maintained for regular visitors. In all mountains it seems that untended shelters get trashed. We, the public, often don't confine ourselves well to the visions of experts.

6

THE WOODS ARE WHACKED,
AND THE FEDS ARRIVE

Bushwhacking—climbing or meandering off established trails—is the art of threading what often seems impassable and discovering what's hidden from everyone else. Early explorers are, of course, bushwhackers. But as others arrive in an area, they follow the tracks of those explorers, and the tracks become trails. Most woods walkers and mountain climbers like their adventures without the shin barking and puzzle solving of making their own way; they like Arnold Guyot's or Charles Fay's discoveries, but they want Rayner Edmands' paths. In short, they like meeting their mountains with guidance from and in the shelters of the "improvers."

The early twentieth century saw the arrival of society's largest improver, the federal government. It reached the Whites in response to the rampage of a heretofore-unmentioned group of White Mountain shapers: the era's timber barons and their cutters. While much of southern New England was shorn of old forests well before the mid-nineteenth century, reservoirs of pine and hardwoods still covered parts of the north as that century waned. The heartland of the Whites can be seen as the broad valley of the Pemigewasset River, which rises within a fine horseshoe of mountains—the Franconias, Twins, and Bonds—that describes its bounds. To the west, Cannon Mountain, the Kinsmans, and Moosilauke form the Whites final tier, while to the east the Presidentials rise as exclamation points before the Carters and the Mahoosucs bring news of Maine. But "the Pemi" offers the White Mountains' most expansive wild expression, even today. In the late 1800s it offered old trees, lumber for the growing country, and, along its river corridors, a way of getting that timber out to market. The land was cheap, and a cutting frenzy ensued.

The full-scale logging in this heartland went forward in a series of stages,

The reforested heart of the Pemigewasset Wilderness, with Mount Carrigain and the Hancocks prominent in the center. Photo by author.

and it lasted there far longer than in much of the rest of the Whites, ending finally in the 1940s. At its height, logging in this area was served by railroads that ran for more than seventy miles. Today, nearly seventy years after the last locomotives ran, their trunk lines are easy to follow, and the loggers' relic encampments still rust away in the woods. But though logging provided jobs and contributed to the economy in several ways, its effects on rivers and streams and on the tourist industry led to an active resistance to what some considered its depredations. In 1902, a savvy forester named Philip Ayres helped found the Society for the Protection of New Hampshire Forests (SPNHF). Its advocacy, joined with that of other groups such as the AMC, set the stage for the Whites' grandest, enduring creation: the White Mountain National Forest.

From what did Congress create this forest? When the first purchase was made in 1914, much of the White Mountains looked like the set in a disaster movie. Logging in that era favored clear-cutting, and residue from that cutting was simply that: leftover slash. That slash lay in great tangles and heaps. Invariably, fire found it, burning through the accumulated fuel and residual trees, and the mix of fire and erosion then choked the streams and rivers. What only a few decades earlier was untracked wilderness through which early mountain explorers had forged became a scarred, smoking wasteland in many places. The era's nature lovers were appalled, and they were a growing breed, as more and more city dwellers sought to color their urban worlds with the green of city parks and country sojourns. So, too, were businessmen whose downstream factories and other enterprises needed river power. The newly naked watersheds were now being washed into the rivers, choking them with silt and debris, hobbling their dependent industries. The bush of the backcountry had been whacked in a way that begged remedy.

Modeled after the newly formed national lands of the West, the WMNF now covers more than 780,000 acres, creating public ownership of and access to virtually all of the White Mountains. For an area that had been divvied up into private holdings long before the idea of public land ownership took hold, this forest is a stunning achievement, almost, one could argue, a pure good. Yet it emerged from meetings and methods that aren't often tagged as pure: the conversations and compromises of two politicians, Massachusetts congressman John Weeks and Speaker of the House Joe Cannon.

Weeks joined Congress in 1905. He arrived as a man with banker's credentials and a business mind-set, not the background we commonly associate with a wildlands savior. Yet Weeks also carried with him an affection for forests and wildlands, and the cutting chaos in the Whites bothered him. Early on, when Speaker Cannon proposed that Weeks be assigned to the Agriculture Committee, Weeks balked. What qualifies me for this sort of work, he asked? I'm a banker; I know little of agriculture. Cannon's answer was revealing: he wanted Weeks there, he said, to bring a business eye to various projects favored by "specialist" congressmen, who were inclined toward the natural and cultivated worlds. So Weeks took his assignment.

A few years later, when Weeks turned his attention to the timber trouble in the White Mountains, he went for help to Cannon, who was not known for favoring conservation issues ("Not one cent for scenery," he had been quoted as saying). Cannon's response was typically pragmatic: bring me a proposal that you, as a banker, think sound, and I'll see if I can support it. Weeks went to work and brought back such a bill, and I'm sure he wondered what Cannon's next move would be. The day the so-called Weeks Act came up for a vote, Cannon took the unusual step of voting last, and the momentum of the early voting carried the bill without Cannon's having to reveal his hand.

Conservationists, including those at Ayres's SPNHF, continued to revile Cannon for his resistance to conservation, until Weeks felt compelled to speak. In an address to SPNHF (likely given in 1915), Weeks told the backstory of his legislation and Cannon's role in getting it passed:

> I am saying this of the Speaker because I know that his activities in opposition to this legislation have been very severely condemned by every friend of the forestry service, and I want to say further that after two years having prepared a bill which I believed was sound and which I was willing to support, Mr. Cannon kept his agreement, recognized me when the bill came from the committee, and in that way I was enabled to get it passed through the House by a majority of seven, he doing the unusual thing of directing the Clerk to call his name at the end of the roll call and voting on the bill. We could not have passed the White Mountain forestry bill in that Congress or any other Congress. It was a practical proposition legislatively. (whitemountainhistory.org)

Thus on January 2, 1914, a new landholder arrived in the White Mountains: "The E. Bertram Pike Tract, US #59, is historically significant as the first tract of land acquired for the future White Mountain National Forest. The tract consists of 7,072 acres in Benton, New Hampshire. The tract was acquired on January 2, 1914, at a price of $13.25 per acre. This tract includes Oliverian Pond, portions of the South Peak of Mount Moosilauke, a ridge known as the Hogback, portions of Black Mountain, and the west slope of Hurricane Mountain" (whitemountainhistory.org). Nearly 800,000 acres later, that acquisition has made all the difference.

Those results, the spawn of compromise and collaboration by unlikely allies, prefigures what's best about the White Mountain National Forest and White Mountain culture today. It also prefigures the arrangement of the search and rescue forces that work within that forest. The SAR work of today, with its mix of state, federal, and volunteer rescuers, is an efficient cooperative. It is also hopeful counterpoint to the antagonistic relations in government and in public where credit and control are seen as necessities, and where compromise is seen as weakness. Yes, this paragraph tends toward rosy, and away from tensions that arise among a disparate group of rescuers, but we'll note some of those as this story deepens. For now, it's good to keep in mind the partnerships that created this forest and set up those groups that find us when we go missing in it.

7

GETTING INTO DODGE

Incidents from the Joe Dodge Era
in the Whites

If there is a father to the modern Whites, he is Joseph Brooks Dodge. Dodge arrived at the rude AMC camp in Pinkham Notch in 1922. Over the ensuing thirty-seven years, he built much of the AMC's hut system, made the Mount Washington Observatory a central year-round weather site, and formed a net of relationships that made him the "Mayor of Porky Gulch," "Hizzoner," and, arguably, the best known character in the state. Dodge was a colorful figure and, as generations of young men found out, a demanding, gruffly affectionate boss. But his chief effect was to teach us, the public, how to be in the mountains—how to climb them; how to revere them; how to survive them. Search and rescue in the midsection of the twentieth century was, like much in the Whites, all about Joe.

My father, who worked for Joe Dodge in the AMC huts in the late 1930s and maintained a friendship with him throughout Joe's life, liked to tell this story: Once, at a major New York city dinner in honor of skiing, Joe was to be the main speaker. The ceremonies stretched out, and one speaker went on at a length Joe found excessive. As the time arrived for Joe to speak, he folded the speech he'd prepared and strode to the podium. "Skiers," he said in a voice that would have carried without being amplified, "are the damnedest people." And then he sat down.

In 1955, Joe was offered an honorary degree from Dartmouth College. He attended their commencement and received that degree, which he deemed a high point in his life. There was Joe, a master of mountain language, up on the stage with another master of language, Robert Frost. The citation on Joe's degree was proffered from "one New Hampshire institution to another," and praised Joe for "rescu[ing] so many of us from both the harshness of the mountains and the soft ways leading down to boredom that you, yourself, are now beyond rescue as a legend of all that is unafraid, friendly, rigorously good and ruggedly expressed in the out-of-doors." Dartmouth got it right: Joe Dodge did save generations of White Mountain wanderers, often from themselves and, at times, from the mountains and weathers he loved. Dodge often did this personally, and he did it also through extensions of himself, the AMC hutmen, and others who worked for him. The White Mountains of the mid-twentieth century had a lot of Joes in them.

One day, when I was ten and our family of four was on vacation and staying at the Old Hutman's Cabin a few miles south of Pinkham Notch, my father announced that we—he and I—were going to "go visit Joe." What my younger brother and mother were up to that day has slipped from memory, but what remains is my early instinct that my father was a little amped up as he said this, and that excitement tinted the day throughout. Like many ten-year-olds, I was used to my father's being in charge, and that feeling redoubled whenever we were in "his mountains," the Whites. There, in his early twenties, he had made a name—actually, a few names—for himself as an AMC hutman. Variously as Mac, Fireball, and Mad Mac, he had worked for Dodge, and the stories of his capers and Dodge's idiosyncrasies and responses were family legend, a legend amplified by chance meetings along various trails. Everyone seems to know Dad, I thought to myself. It also occurred to me as he drove toward North Conway that my father was a little nervous—he muttered a bit to himself and leaned forward toward the steering wheel.

"Um, Dad, what are we going to do at Mr. Dodge's?" I asked. "We're going to *visit*," he said, and the car jumped a bit as he goosed the pedal.

We got to the front of a small white house, and my father rapped on the door. A few seconds later I heard footsteps and what sounded like grumbling. Then, the door swung open. "For Chrissakes, it's Mac," said a solid figure with a gruff look going to smile. "Come in, come in. And what's this?" he said looking at me. "Sandy," my dad said, "say hello to Mr. Dodge." "O Christ, Mac," said Joe, "he can call me Hizzoner."

My father relaxed visibly and, these years later, I can see that he also slipped into another self. My years of being a high school teacher and the memory of nosing about the Dodge house while my dad talked with Joe and his wife, Teen, make me realize that I was meeting my father's other or third parent. Each of us, if he or she is lucky, finds some adult who, at a pivotal point in life, shows and helps us discover who we are—and what we can be. Joe Dodge had been that person for my dad in the late thirties and early forties, just before he went to the Pacific war as a combat marine. I gathered a glimmer of this when I looked at a wall of photos in one of the Dodges' rooms that day. There, in the center of the wall, amid photos of his own two children and various other young men, was a large photo of my dad in his dress uniform. "Oh . . .," I recall thinking, without being able to finish the thought.

Later, as I sorted out my third-parent thinking, I realized that this visit also contained some of the reversal of care that happens as a parent ages. Dodge was a powerful presence and a vital man when I met him, but he had also just retired from the AMC and his thirty-seven-year position as master of the huts and almost everything else that went on in the Whites. That retirement had been a nudged one; hard feelings and the questions that follow us as we leave long work were near the surface. My father was checking in with his third parent to see how he was doing. Years later, in his professional role as advocate and fundraiser for good ideas (the AMC among them), my father would be instrumental in getting AMC to honor this central figure in White Mountain history, by having them name the AMC's new Dodge Center at Pinkham Notch for Joe. We do, in our various phases, search for ways to honor our fathers.

The White Mountains, we shall see, held a number of these sons of Joe, and many of them had learned his knack for saving others.

Fathering These Mountains

Among the gifts that the young Joe Dodge brought with him to the Whites was a fascination with and a facility for radio communication. Dodge had begun to tinker with radio as a boy, and he'd later gotten training as a radioman in the Navy; he knew how to make waves work, and he saw their potential in linking the various outposts in the Whites. Dodge also saw that radio could be the next layer of human knowledge to drape over the landscape. Maps and trails had already brought the fame of name and some ease of access to the mountains; now radio would add voice and instant report. Some of the time.

Dodge was, in Malcolm Gladwell's phrasing in his book *The Tipping Point*, an "early adopter," an embracer of new technology who, through force of personality, expands the vision and scope of an invention. In 1922, there were a number of outposts in the Whites, including the constellation of summer buildings atop Mount Washington, but each place was and felt remote. It could take hours, for example, for a message to get by foot from the summit to the AMC camp at Pinkham Notch. Yes, there was, even on Curtis and Ormsbee's fateful day, a phone wire that connected the summit to the base on the west side, but even the most optimistic lineman wouldn't envision a web of wires strung across the Whites, with phones tacked to trees at intervals. Radio waves, if they could be mastered and bent around landforms, would offer extended connection for those going into the mountains and those who sometimes faltered there. Dodge knew and helped to implement that. As he did, he also extended the creation of the AMC huts, outposts that would allow average hikers the experience of taking multiday walks, of seeing the mountains up close over time. These huts, staffed by young, fit men, brought rescuers already in place to the upper slopes of the Whites.

By the time Dodge retired in 1959, the string of modern AMC huts was in place along a walking line of fifty miles from Lonesome Lake in the west to Carter Notch in the east. The Mount Washington Observatory, which he also helped found, was a famous, vital site in meteorology. So the man who dominated life and development in the early and mid-twentieth century Whites was both a builder and an explorer, a deeply practical man with a wild, colorful spirit. As a rescuer, Dodge brought both gifts with him when he went looking for you.

Saving Us (from Ourselves)

Each of the three incidents that follow is well known. Each offers insight into mid-twentieth century search and rescue, and into Joe Dodge's ways of conducting them. Told in excellent detail in Nicholas Howe's *Not without Peril*, covered extensively in the day's papers, and often chronicled in *Appalachia*, these stories get at the spirit of Dodge's saving work. What they add up to is the way one man's presence joined, in the end, with another's to become the shape of search and rescue in the White Mountains.

The first story, which I will shorten, took place early in Joe's tenure at Pinkham. The story displays Joe's physical strength and resilience and the way those attributes defined his day's search and rescue. Word arrived that Max Engelhart, a friend, who worked as a cook at the Glen House and had been sent to the top of Washington days earlier to serve snacks to hikers, was missing.

Engelhart's story began as such tales do with a turn of the weather: 1926 had featured a chilly early fall, with snows from the prior winter lingering and new snows arriving. Still, there were hikers abroad in the October mountains, and the Glen House had sent Engelhart up to man the old Stage House at the summit for their convenience. Engelhart arrived not long before an epic storm, which began on the evening of the eighth and dropped thick snow even into the valleys, while it howled white for four days across the upper ridges. As the storm persisted and Engelhart didn't return, anxiety about him grew. Finally, when the storm eased some, two guests at the Glen House ascended through the drifts, with instructions that Engelhart come down with them. They found an empty, snow-clogged Stage House and a note: "Laf at 12 for Tocmans Arien—no wood."

The note occasioned head scratching and more anxiety, and both were conveyed to Joe Dodge when he stopped at the Glen House on his way back from Gorham on the afternoon of the twelfth. Apprised of what details were available, Dodge said he'd be back with his assistant, Arthur Whitehead, to conduct a search in the morning. On the thirteenth, Dodge and Whitehead were back at the Glen House with full kit, and they led a rescue party of five others up the auto road, traveling the first three miles in a car before it became mired in the snow. From there, they climbed on foot. As they did, they reached tree line and entered the cloud deck and a wintry zone hard to imagine in October. Waist-deep drifts alternated with wind-scoured ice, and their vision dropped to thirty feet in the snow-and-ice choked air. The storm had eased in the valleys but not high on the mountains.

These ninety years later, despite the tellings and retellings of Engelhart's and others' stories, people still climb into trouble especially during the "shoulder seasons" of fall and spring. Just as suburban skiers from southern New England won't believe there's good snow at northern mountain areas unless they can see snow in their own backyards, so too are tourists winding north along color-washed valley roads in the Whites unaware that monochrome winter can have bled all life from the cloud-cloaked ridges above them.

Dodge and Whitehead and a third searcher forged ahead of the other four, checking the tiny refuges placed at half-mile intervals along the road above tree line. No Max, nowhere. When they reached the summit, they found a scene in the Stage House that signaled a quick and desperate departure. There, Dodge uncovered another message that spoke of life-threatening weather and trouble. That was two days ago.

After a search of other summit buildings (the two hotels and a refuge called Camden Cottage) and no further sign of Engelhart, Dodge set to puzzling out their next moves. It was clear Englehart had fled, but not to the logical other summit buildings. Where to then? Down the auto road they'd just ascended, perhaps, but the implicit panic of Englehart's departure argued for another direction. The auto road faced northwest, directly into the tempest, and when people beset by wind flee, Dodge reasoned, they almost always go downwind, helped along by the wind's strong hands. Dodge, Whitehead, and the third volunteer set out to search the downwind side of the summit cone, while the four other volunteers, already beyond their experience, decided to descend to the Glen House via the road. They were certain Engelhart was long frozen.

For four hours, the three men wallowed through drifts, fell into them, and searched for the missing man, as the wind whirled snow above and around them. Possible footprints dissolved into illusion and possible bodies resolved into rocks as they drew near. From their descent of the summit's backside, they worked along the Alpine Gardens, skirting the ravines and eventually coming around the cone to where they were again fighting the wind. No Max; no sign. Back on the summit, they reconsidered again, aiming next down to Lake of the Clouds hut, a mile down the west side. Again, no Max, and, as the day faded and cold intensified, the three searchers headed back down the auto road to the Glen House. They had traveled and searched over an estimated twenty-five miles. In the valley, everyone was sure that Max Engelhart had perished.

Dodge and Whitehead, however, returned to Pinkham Notch intent on searching again the next day. Dodge knew Engelhart to be smart and woods wise, and he wondered if the missing man might have made it down into Tuckerman or Huntington Ravine. These two great stone bowls dig into the east side of the mountain, and they are in the downwind direction that Dodge had reasoned Engelhart would go. Dodge asked for snowshoes from the Glen House, and around 11:30 a.m. on the fourteenth the shoes arrived. A little late, thought Dodge. Elliot Libby, who brought the shoes down, said he had been delayed by several hours of conversation with Boston newspapers about the search. Clearly, no one else thought Engelhart had a chance, so what was the hurry?

> Dodge and Whitehead took the snowshoes and their packs and soon returned to wallowing. Bindings kept breaking and the snow was thick and wet on the way up to Tuckerman Ravine. Still, the two men climbed quickly, reaching Hermit Lake in a time that signaled they still believed Engelhart could be alive. They paused at a register the Forest Service used to keep track of foot traffic in the ravine. As they rested, they heard an odd sound, a call perhaps. Wind, animal, strange settling of snow? They heard it again, and this time they began the auditory tracing of sound that leads us, we hope, to a mouth (sound origins in the echoings of a ravine and amid the mutings of snow can be tricky to find). But the call kept sounding, and Dodge and Whitehead kept following until they came to a spot on the rushing Cutler River. There, down by the water, was Max Engelhart, calling up into what must have seemed an endless void. "Help," he called. "Help!"

That is the saga of finding Max Engelhart. But once found? Modern recovery calls up all sorts of conveyance, from sleds, to snowmobiles and ATVs, to helicopters. Often the rescued are prepackaged in litters that make hauling or hoisting them easier. But there, in 1926, were Dodge and Whitehead and their find, who had been without shelter for three days and was stiffened beyond walking. What next?

Carrying someone out is the less glorified part of search and rescue. Unless the person found is in life-or-death crisis (which is very rare, even as it is amply reported), the energy and adrenaline that have fueled the search drain away. What remains is very often simply hard work and, for Dodge and Whitehead, that hard work needed to be done after the demanding twenty-five miles of snow bashing the day before and this day's struggle on balky snowshoes into the ravine. Once they had hauled Englehart up from the creek and given him some warm liquid and tried via body heat to warm him a little more, they began with Dodge carrying Engelhart and Whitehead lugging their gear. Dodge was young and built like a bruin, but his burden weighed some fifty pounds more than he, and their combined weight drove Dodge's feet deep into the snow and tipped him over more than once. He and Whitehead tried to make a litter of their snowshoes, but that offered little improvement. Finally, as their charmed third attempt in these seemingly charmless, snow-clogged woods, they cut some pines to make a drag. Engelhart, a French Canadian woodsman, even offered advice for rigging the travois, and his return to lucidity must have encouraged the two rescuers.

The trio set out, and on both the levels and ups, the going was a slow, heavy labor; even when the downward slope helped, it was simply hard work. Covering the three-plus miles took all afternoon, and as darkness came on, Dodge and Whitehead flicked on their flashlights and kept on. Finally, in the last third of a mile, they were able to draw some help by flashing those lights. When they arrived at Pinkham Camp, they found a clutch of attention gathered. Newspapers had been reporting on the missing man, and now here he was; locals and reporters peppered them with questions.

Imagine the scene: after all the isolate hours of looking for and then hauling out Englehart, during which the three of them had heard only their own stories and cursings, suddenly, they were surrounded by the babble of people who were decidedly not of their tribe. Dodge and Whitehead turned away to prepare a space inside for Englehart while he waited for medical attention. Then, when he was on his way to the hospital, they turned away again, went inside, and shut the door on all the others.

Media attention hasn't diminished in the ensuing ninety years.

At Madison Spring Hut, 1938

Whether the AMC's hut system or the Mount Washington Observatory is Joe Dodge's signal achievement is open for debate. Both institutions have had,

Rescuers Joe Dodge (*left*) and Arthur Whitehead a few days after they found Max Englehart. Photo courtesy of the AMC archives.

and continue to have, a profound influence on White Mountain culture, and both will be vital players in its future. But it's beyond argument that, as Joe Dodge built and maintained the huts, they also became an extension of his personality and way of being in the mountains. For generations of visitors, it was true that you couldn't go anywhere in the Whites without meeting Joe, or a Joe. Like many managers charged with hiring, Joe often hired himself. I need to clarify, however: Joe was, as may already be clear, a one-off; his blend of talent and charisma was unique. But as the earlier story about my father, Fred Stott, suggested, Joe was also a mentor to a group of young, physically inclined and able young men, who were often at the age of deciding who and how to be in the world. Who better to be than Joe? So a mountain walker in the 1930s, '40s, and '50s was likely to meet Joes at any of the seven huts scattered from west (Lonesome Lake) to east (Carter Notch) across the high spine of the Whites. These were the hut crews, or "croos" in their own parlance.

The "croo" at Madison Spring Hut in 1938 numbered four: Bob Ohler (hutmaster), Ernie Files, Sumner Hamburger, and Fred Stott. By late August, when oncoming school and weather begin to shut a White Mountain summer down, they were experienced. The night of August 23 saw between thirty and forty guests at the hut, including a group of hiking ministers, who called themselves the Red Shirts. The twenty-fourth dawned gray and damp, with temps in the low forties, clouds down to the ground, and a forty-mile-per-hour wind from the north. Not unusual for the date at 4,800 feet, but not promising either. Most of the guests opted not to press on for what would be a cold, soggy day of hiking with no views. It was what we now call classic hypothermia weather.

The day dragged and the hutmen went about their practiced routine. A torpor took over the hut. As my father later pointed out, waiting out a day in an unheated hut stuck inside a cloud has little appeal or energy. That changed at midday, when a twenty-something burst through the door with news that his two companions were back up the trail and having trouble moving. Files and my father began to gather supplies for a trip out to investigate and, perhaps, help, but they were unhurried. They knew the twenty-something, Philip Turner, as a nuisance, who recently had been hanging about the hut trying to cadge food without buying either lodging or a meal. When Turner and his two friends had departed unseen from their nearby campsite earlier that day, they had not been missed.

Slow prep turned to haste when the second young man stumbled through the door. Frank Carnese was slurring his words and barely able to walk; he said that he'd left their third friend, seventeen-year-old Joe Caggiano, back up on the trail, unable to move. The two hutmen got what information they could on Caggiano and set out on the run with a volunteer from the Red Shirts. A mile above the hut they reached Thunderstorm Junction, a confluence of four trails and realized that, from Turner and Carnese's descriptions, they must have passed Caggiano. From there the trio fanned out, Files going twenty yards above the trail, Stott, twenty below, and the Red Shirt staying on the track. They then began picking their slow way back among the glacier-split rocks. Travel like this, away from the leveled stones of a trail amid the huge angled rocks, is very tough and often occasion for trouble. Add in rain, wind, and sleet, and you have a very tough day.

Madison Spring Hut in the late 1930s. Photo by Harold Orne, courtesy of AMC archives.

Twenty minutes later, Stott found Caggiano, fallen amid the rocks, covered with lacerations and downed by what appeared to be a broken knee. Even cursory examination said Caggiano was dead. It seemed that, in a final effort to save himself, Caggiano had gotten back up but been unable to follow the trail. He had, instead, done what most will do when impaired by cold: he had turned in the direction of least resistance, downhill, and stumbled and fallen in that direction until he couldn't go on. In 1938 the huts were sparely equipped with rescue gear, and the croo had to unbolt a bed from the bunkroom to use as a litter. They bore Caggiano back to the hut and brought his body in the back door. Hutmaster Ohler, a premed student, worried about rigor mortis, and so they attached a box to a packboard and folded Caggiano into sitting position for his trip down the mountain.

Sixty-five years later, during his final climb and visit to Madison Springs, my father, asked to speak to the fifty assembled guests by Hutmaster Liz Mygatt, recalled the moment. "There was utter silence as I carried Caggiano out through this dining room," he said to an equally silent room. "It is so different now," he continued after a pause. "Liz and her crew all have wilderness first-aid certifications, and there's a litter and a full first-aid kit at the hut. Crews expect to rescue. They're prepared for it. We were prepared to go find people, but not always for what we found."

Stott and his fellow croo members traded carries on the way down the Valley Way until they reached Thousand Yard Spring, where they met a rescue group headed by Joe Dodge. The hut Joes handed Caggiano over to Joe, as happened repeatedly over the years, and he went to the valley to notify the survivors.

Though it may be a trifle out of context, that incident brings up Joe Dodge's famous "bedside manner." The story goes that during one of these difficult phone calls in the aftermath of a rescue attempt in 1952, Joe was having trouble making the widow understand what had happened. Finally, Joe said, "Jesus Christ, no, lady. It's worse than that; the sonofabitch is dead." As noted earlier, Joe was a one-off, even as his progeny were everywhere in the Whites.

< 8 >

THE GATHERING

— — — —

Steep Enough to Slide, 1954

Perhaps by the time Joe Dodge had the phone conversation just excerpted he had become inured to death in his mountains. Over the twenty-six years he'd been there, he surely had carried many, both living and dead, from their slopes. Partnering with the two other authorities in the Whites (the U.S. Forest Service and New Hampshire Fish and Game), he had developed the outlines of a template for search and rescue that endures to this day. But this man—by then a legend—with his big brain and big heart had a final contribution to offer his public and its searchers and rescuers, one he had been developing all along. Dodge would provide an example of how new technology could be infused into the hills he loved to serve the people he hoped would love them, too. That he would seek to blend new technology with old spirit marked him as an optimistic precursor to an age he could not have imagined, when technology would threaten the very definition and spirit of the wild hills.

Travel to the Whites was much easier by the 1950s, and many from the growing cities only a day's drive away headed north for short trips, often on a moment's notice. Such proximity and ease of approach brought new waves of novice wanderers into the Whites, and it brought them in all seasons. Many of these new wanderers went out onto the trails without much preparation or inkling of what lay ahead, which marked them as trouble waiting to happen. Joe had long called such novices "goofers," a name that persists in some spots today. Going out to look for or rescue goofers was an increasingly common pursuit by that time. Goofers didn't yet have cell phones, but the influx of newcomers ensured plenty of calls, albeit slow ones, for help.

As Nick Howe points out in his illuminating and enduringly popular book, *Not without Peril*, the post–World War II years brought a boom in winter mountain recreation, in no small measure because of the war's surplus clothing and equipment. All the research and development that had gone into equipping troops to fight in cold-weather regions in European mountains and the north countries had produced a bonanza of gear—parkas, footwear, sleeping bags—that was now cheaply available. Many mountain lovers bought in, and the winter hills began to fill with them. A mountain season that had formerly been mostly about skiing on known slopes with many others had suddenly issued a license to wander.

On a January night in 1954, Dodge was hosting the Saturday evening meal at Pinkham. At the table's far end, NHFG officer George Hamilton was enjoying his roast beef. Three young women sat near Hamilton, and he overheard one of them talking about her brother and a friend, who were camping in Tuckerman Ravine for the weekend. Given the weather (very cold, deep and ongoing snow), Hamilton hoped he'd not heard right and asked the young woman to explain. Polly Longnecker said she'd been with her brother Philip and his friend, Jacques Parysko, the day and night before in the ravine, but that she'd found it too extreme, so he'd brought her down to Pinkham before returning to the mountain. He was up there right now, she said. Where "there" was wasn't fully clear to Hamilton, but the scenario made him nervous, especially with the week's new snow having been blown toward the east-facing ravine by a strong west wind. He sidled over to Dodge to confer. Dodge too didn't like the sound of the young men's plan, but he figured he'd have to wait until morning to check on it.

Sinking temperatures and more snow arrived Sunday morning, but the afternoon brought an odd tale. A skier who'd been on the Sherburne Trail arrived, saying he'd come across a partially buried mannequin a few miles from Pinkham. He'd poked the figure and found it a hard sort of plastic. Who would dump a mannequin up there? he'd wondered. A few people from Pinkham went up to have a look, and they uncovered the body of Jacques Parysko, partially clothed and fully frozen. Tracks led uphill from where he lay toward the ravine.

When Parysko's body arrived back at Pinkham, Polly Longnecker gasped; this was her brother's friend. And so up along Parysko's tracks went Dodge's rescuers. What they found presages many modern rescue and retrieval scenes. Earlier, Philip Longnecker and his friend had reached the ravine's headwall and burrowed into the deep snow to form a shelter. That they were sited directly beneath avalanche slopes loaded with a week's fresh snow hadn't occurred to them, even as signs posted on the trails leading there had warned of the danger, as had, apparently, one or two people they'd met as they climbed.

The storm continued that Sunday, and in the intense cold (−10F°) and wind-whirled snow, the searchers couldn't see much or find Philip Long-necker's camp. They retreated, and at Pinkham Dodge summoned the best team he could find for another attempt on Monday. Part of that team was NHFG officer Paul Doherty, or in Dodge's parlance, "a goddam fish cop," making him fishing-Joe's natural enemy on the streams and rivers, but in all other seasons a search and rescue ally. Later that year, New Hampshire governor Hugh Gregg would formalize that relationship by putting NHFG in charge of search and rescue throughout the state, a development many attributed to Doherty's mix of ability and zeal for the work. A similar pro-fessional-volunteer composition of search and rescue endures to this day.

An added note about the modern patchwork of SAR in the Whites: be-cause the national forest, first envisioned by the Weeks Act of 1911 and ex-panded over time to more than 800,000 acres, is a federal government en-terprise, the U.S. Forest Service and its rangers figure into this patchwork too. Today, USFS rangers, called, delightfully, snow rangers, are the first-line authority in the Cutler River drainage—the eastern-facing ravines on Mount Washington—from December 1 to May 31, the mountain's snow season. The rangers' daily bulletins on the Mount Washington Avalanche Center web-site (www.mountwashingtonavalanchecenter.org/) are winter must-reads for anyone who plays or works on angled snow. The snow rangers typically lead all winter-season search and rescue efforts in this drainage. Figure 3.1, though from a different season, let's you look right into the two ravines that serve as the snow rangers' living rooms. Beyond those boundaries, the legal responsibility for SAR work passes to NHFG.

But on this January Monday in 1954, the arrangements for searching were still informal, which meant they ran through Dodge, who had gathered a mix of Forest Service, NHFG, AMC, and U.S. Army personnel to look for Philip Longnecker. Up again to the ravine they went, and the way they went up merits mention. Though the going was made tedious by deep unconsolidated snow, the search party rode up to the USFS campsite in Tuckerman Ravine on Weasels. Perhaps that sentence wrinkles imagination's brow, but Weasels were another leftover from World War II: an early version of snowcats. They made this search the first mechanized one in the Whites.

What the searchers found in Tuckerman Ravine could be called a comedy of winter errors except that Parysko's body had already classed it as a tragedy. The two young men had crossed the floor of the ravine and dug into the steep slope of the left-central headwall. In the now-clear air, Dodge and his crew could see that the whole headwall had avalanched, and that, above the fracture line two-thirds of the way up, more snow "hung fire." The mix of windblown snow carried by prevailing westerlies and sliding snow from the steep ravine walls can pile snow to depths of over one hundred feet in Tuckerman, and this January storm had been a major contributor. At great risk to themselves, Dodge's crew set to searching, an action that, with all the snow still above them, might not get rangers' sanction today.

Polly Longnecker had accompanied searchers to the ravine to see if she could recall the approximate location of her brother's camp. Once she'd pointed it out, the searchers dug a series of trenches across the slide rubble to see if they could uncover any sign of encampment. Failing that, they began to use avalanche probes, long aluminum poles that, if used by a sensitive, knowing hand, can feel the resistance a buried body makes to their passage. In the early afternoon, searchers hit some of the debris from Philip's camp, and, as they dug, they uncovered more evidence strewn downslope by the snow. Finally, they found Philip's body under four dense feet of snow. They also found Jacques Parysko's sleeping bag, boots, and clothes, left behind when he made his long, partially clothed run from the site to where he was found.

Such discoveries always shift rescuers toward forensics, a puzzling out of what happened to satisfy curiosity and provide lessons for those who will go next into the hills. The Appalachians' detailed 1901 parsing of Curtis and Ormsbee's deaths, written up in *Appalachia*, is an excellent early example of this sort of analysis, and the USFS snow rangers' recent look at Quest's 2014 story on Mount Washington provides a modern bookend. How did this incident occur, and what might we learn from it? These are the sober, rational questions behind such reports. But this intent raises another, less comfortable, question: Is there any relationship between sober analysis and increased knowledge and the impulses that drive us outward into experience? In short, do we learn from others' incidents and follies? Our continuing tendency to step into the same snow piles again and again suggests that we do so only sporadically.

As best Dodge and company could work out from looking at the layered snow they dug, two slides had reached the young men's campsite. The first had been minor, but enough perhaps to spook Parysko from his sleep and set him running half-clothed for help. His panic and lack of familiarity with his surroundings had taken him by three telephones, two first-aid caches, the then-new Tuckerman Ravine Shelter and finally along the Sherburne Trail near to the Harvard Cabin, where ten people slept. Longnecker hadn't run; instead it seemed he'd simply inhaled, and the snow-dust blown into his shelter by sliding snow had filled his lungs. There, it quickly melted and he'd drowned. A later slide had then buried the campsite.

9

IT'S THE LAW

— — — —

New Hampshire Fish and
Game Assumes the Lead

As the Weasels bore their burdens down to Pinkham, the future of search and rescue in the Whites was largely there. In Joe Dodge and Paul Doherty, we find its relationship between volunteers and professional authorities personified. Doherty's stories come down to us from his memoir, *Smoke of a Thousand Campfires*, which draws liberally from a newspaper column, "The North Woodsman," that he wrote for more than forty years. Doherty's legend is still fresh in many mountain walkers' and North Country residents' minds.

The Law

Some say that the mid-twentieth-century White Mountains had two sets of rules: one set described Joe Dodge's way of being in the woods and the world; the other adhered to New Hampshire Fish and Game officer Paul Doherty's provisions for staying on the right side of the law. You might say that in those White Mountains, Joe Dodge was the word and Paul Doherty was the law.

After an apprenticeship throughout the districts of southern New Hampshire, Doherty arrived as a New Hampshire Fish and Game conservation officer for the Berlin area in 1949. When first hired in 1948, Doherty had requested this posting "north of the notches," and the NHFG director, Ralph Carpenter had granted that request. But in doing so, he added a wry, careful-what-you-wish-for caveat for his young CO: "I might as well tell you," said Carpenter, "we consider [your new area] the toughest in the state." The paper mills of Doherty's new headquarters, the "city of light" of Berlin, New Hampshire, were full of workers who found their freedom in the woods. Those mills were also fed by legions of loggers who knew those woods and resisted any attempts to rein in their ways of living there. The fish and game Doherty was sent north to serve and preserve were under pressure from the northern natives in season and out. COs preceding Doherty had worked hard to catch out-of-season poachers, but they were still very active. As Carpenter added, "There's something else you should know. The North Country is different from the rest of the state; they do things different up there. . . . You're going to be the first new man assigned a territory up there since prewar days. Lots of eyes will be on your every move. Good luck" (*Smoke from a Thousand Campfires*, 96–97).

Even a retrospective glance at Doherty's long career in the North Country shows he did well with "lots of eyes on [his] every move." Like Dodge, who had arrived a quarter century before him, Doherty brought an unusual ability to blend the old and the new. In doing so, he gathered attention, sometimes effortlessly, sometimes forcefully.

Here was his secret: Doherty, an indifferent student in usual schools, was an avid scholar of the backcountry. He first went out into the woods not to impose but to learn, even as his blunt, muscular personality (backed by an impressive physical presence) made enforcing the law natural for him. He cultivated relationships with veteran COs and woodsmen alike, and as he did so, he gathered a trove of knowledge about his district and its characters. Like Joe Dodge, Doherty had an energy and endurance that made him seem, at least to some, omnipresent. Being the law in Doherty's era was no less an extension of personality than being the word was in Dodge's. Poachers, deer-jackers, and over-fishers learned quickly that Doherty was, at times uncannily, everywhere at every hour.

Doherty also had an eye for opportunity, and postwar America and these uplands seemed to him a place where he might forge a notable self and a meaningful life. In his memoir, he looked back at this time:

> For those of us hired during the early years of this period of expansion and change, a golden opportunity was ours to take advantage of. The era of the old-time game warden was coming to an end. A new breed was moving into place; two-way radio communication, faster cars, better and more efficient equip-

ment, special training, courses at the University of New Hampshire. Things a world apart from what the old-timers knew were on the horizon. The changing of the guard was under way

Still on the payroll, however, were at least a dozen men, who, like Harry Hurlbert [an early Doherty mentor], represented the passing of an era. And there were others, not yet considered to be old-timers, that had much knowledge under their belts that they were ready to pass on.

Here then, was an opportunity for those of us so inclined to mold the best of the old with the new and hammer out, upon the anvil of our own character and individuality, the direction and accomplishments we hoped lay ahead for each of us. (*Smoke from a Thousand Campfires*, 82)

Though not often given to metaphor, Doherty hammered hard on that anvil, and the self he forged was to have a large influence on all things out back, including search and rescue, in the North Country.

The Goddam Fish Cop

Paul Doherty became an iconic conservation officer, and Joe Dodge was a consummate fisherman. In those two identities lay an overlapping tension that suited each man. For Dodge, fishing was escape from the burdens of administration and from the duty of explaining the mountains to "goofers," and looking for them when they strayed. If a stretch of free time arrived and didn't happen to coincide with a state-approved season or body of water, Dodge sometimes fished anyway. Doherty knew of this, or suspected as much, and being his own hard nut, he wouldn't have minded snaring Joe. That surely would have spread his reputation. Dodge, for his part, knew this also, and, over time, managed to avoid being caught. "When you're smart enough to catch me, I'll shake your hand," he said to Doherty more than once.

But their ongoing game and Doherty's emergence as his own North Country character helped to cement a relationship between the Mayor of Porky Gulch and the Goddam Fish Cop, which bolstered both men in their legends and work and led to a cooperation that helped form White Mountain search and rescue for the modern era. In Dodge's claim that he "taught the goddam fish cop everything he knows" [about search and rescue] there is even the whiff of parental approval, though neither man would likely have called theirs such a bond. Doherty, who estimated he had taken part in and mostly led over five hundred searches and rescues during his time as a conservation officer, did indeed begin his tutelage in these arts with Dodge:

> I cut my teeth, as it were, in this field with Joe as tutor. I remember well the day I was having coffee with Joe when a report of an accident on the mountain came in. In those days the state didn't have any policy relative to search and rescue. This would come later when Fish and Game would be assigned the responsibility.
>
> "Got some poor bastard with a busted leg up on Lion's Head, you might as well get off your ass and come along," was how he put it to me.
>
> From that day on, I went on every search and rescue that Joe was called upon to handle. He got to telling people I went along "to make things legal like." He knew the mountains and directed a well organized search. He used to tell me about lost hikers and his advice went like this: "Find out where the stupid bastards were going, then look for them in the opposite direction."
>
> Joe, after he retired from AMC, often said, "I turned everything over to that God-dam Fish Cop from Gorham, he took over where I left off. Taught the bastard everything he knows." (*Smoke from a Thousand Campfires*, 277–78)

November 1954 brought a high-profile incident that pointed out just how much Doherty had absorbed from the senior North Country figures he cultivated as a young conservation officer. On the thirtieth, a Northeast Airlines DC-3 crashed while approaching the Berlin airport. While a location had been pinpointed by an air search, rescuers were debating where exactly that location was and how to get there. Doherty was at this meeting, and he had in tow a woodsman friend from the Brown Company, the dominant paper outfit in the area. Doherty's friend identified both the location and an approach; others thought differently. But Doherty had already gathered a search group, and they went to the spot predicted by his friend and found the plane. Governor Hugh Gregg was in attendance, and he was impressed with Doherty's knowledge and response. When Gregg returned to Concord, he drafted an executive order putting Fish and Game in charge of search and rescue; Gregg followed up by promoting legislation that made this responsibility permanent.

Gregg's action ended the uncertainty of an informal era wherein nominal responsibility rested with the USFS, which oversaw the now-vast White Mountain National Forest. But USFS resources and funding couldn't marshal responses to the growing number of searches and rescues during the postwar outdoor boom. Dodge and his AMC cadre of hutmen had long been the first responders, with other groups summoned as available, and throughout the 1950s and beyond, their volunteer manpower would continue to dominate. But the legal, lead agency had now been tabbed, and "fish cop" Doherty personified that authority.

Nick Howe points to an additional factor in NHFG's ascendance as designated leaders in search and rescue, and that factor appears prominently in Doherty's memoir, too. Almost all of the conservation officers appointed across the North Country district had wartime, military service backgrounds, and that experience suited them well to the demands of organizing and supervising search parties. In *Not without Peril*, Howe writes:

> This combat experience meant that they were accustomed to taking orders
> and giving orders, and when those orders wouldn't suffice they knew how to
> improvise. That was a major factor in World War II; the organization of both
> German and Japanese forces was rigidly vertical and the lower ranks could not
> make a move without the proper orders. American forces were accustomed to
> fighting by the book, but when the book ran out, they did whatever worked.
> These habits paid large postwar dividends in the mountains. (199)

Doherty, a Marine with underwater demolition experience from the Pacific theater, fit the description precisely.

That military cast of leadership shows clearly in New Hampshire Fish and Game's enforcement division today: led by a colonel and staffed by majors, captains, lieutenants, sergeants, and officers, Fish and Game's enforcement division establishes command posts wherever and whenever a search and rescue is called throughout the state. At the head of whatever body of people goes looking for us when we're missing in the White Mountains is an officer. But much of the searching, finding, and carrying—much of the body work of rescue—still gets done by the many-handed, many-legged composite called the volunteers.

10

WHEN THE ANGLES AND THE ODDS RISE

————

The Need for a Technical Team

A 1959 tragedy on Cannon Cliff in Franconia Notch entranced the public, in part because it played out over two days on its airy stage above what was then Route 3. It would be thirteen more years until the founding of North Conway's Mountain Rescue Service, with its elite climbers and high-angle capabilities, but the absence of such a group in the Whites was already glaringly apparent. Rick Wilcox, one of MRS's founders and its long-serving president, points to the Cannon incident as one catalyst for creating MRS.

Cannon Cliff, 1959: "There's Nothing We Can Do, but We Have to Try"

August is a fickle month in the Whites. Dog-days' heat often bakes the valleys and softens the tar, but the summer season has grown measurably shorter, and along the ridges, fall can appear with an icy suddenness. Mount Washington, the center pole of the White Mountain tent, usually feels a first touch of snow during the month, with a record fall of 2.5 inches. Snow's precursor, cold rain, is a possibility verging on certainty. Even as summer's cicadas buzz on, hypothermia season arrives. In August 1959 such change took the form of a cold front that brought a chill rain to the Whites for the first time since mid-June.

Before the rain fell, on the pleasant morning of August 23, two young men, Alfred Whipple, twenty, and Sidney Crouch, twenty-one, both from the Ledyard, Connecticut, area, set out with homemade tools and not much else to climb Cannon Cliff, a 1,000-foot sheet of rock atop which the Old Man of the Mountains then perched. The pair ascended an obscure route just to the south of the Old Man, but halfway up the cliff, they got stuck. By then the weather had shifted; cool rain was on the way, hurried on by rising winds. Unable to go up or down, the men began signaling their distress by flapping their shirts, and, after some time, their flailing caught eyes in the valley below. Clearly they needed rescue, and, as the day's light faded, a call went to George Hamilton, Appalachian Mountain Club manager at Pinkham Notch. Hamilton had recently taken over for Joe Dodge. With this new command came the calls for help that Dodge had fielded for more than thirty years. Arriving home late that night, Hamilton got the message and turned to a series of calls, including one to the noted climber Miriam Underhill, which asked her to help gather a rescue. Underhill, thought Hamilton, would have the contacts of the region's best climbers, and Cannon Cliff would call for the best.

All of this seems a scenario that could play out in today's White Mountains. But what unfolded over the next forty-eight hours was unique to its era. Though rock climbers were often spotted on cliffs such as Cannon at the time, they were a much rarer breed than exists today. Also, the route the young men had taken was largely unclimbed, and so, little known. Those two factors would turn what today would be a routine, albeit dramatic, rescue into a drawn-out tragedy. As hundreds watched from the road below the

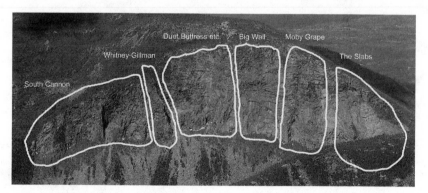

Cannon Cliff with its six climbing areas outlined. The 1959 tragedy took place in the middle of the wall; the 2016 rescue in chapter 17 happened near the top of Moby Grape. Photo by Lee Hansche.

cliff, the two men finally succumbed to the rain-occasioned cold just as their rescuers reached them.

When Hamilton and Underhill started pulling together rescuers during the wee hours of the twenty-fourth, they had to reach a long way, drawing rescue climbers from Massachusetts, New Hampshire, and Vermont. In an interview for a 1959 article in *Appalachia*, John Taylor, who would climb first that morning, recalled answering his phone: "My first sleepy thought was that surely there must be someone else, nearer Cannon Mountain than Princeton [Mass.], who could help. . . ." A second rescuer, the noted climber David Sanderson, had to drive north from Portsmouth, New Hampshire, and a third, Robert Collins, hailed from Brookline, Massachusetts. Driving the open night roads at speed, sometimes with police escort, the climbers converged on Cannon. During his drive, Taylor thought ahead to the rescue, and assumed he would be trying to help accomplished climbers, who could be counted on to assist. Probably, he thought, we'll be able to lower men or gear from the cliff top and they can self-rescue. But when the rescue climbers had arrived, they'd found that the trapped men were neophytes, and the low clouds and rain-spawned rockfall meant that any rescue from above would be too risky. Climbers would need to ascend. As they began their attempt to reach the men amid the torrents of cold rain on August 24, they had to invent their way up, hammering in pitons and fixing their ropes at a rate of just feet per hour.

Trapped and strapped into their two-foot-wide ledge and clothed only in summer cotton (their pack with more protective gear had been blown ten feet away by a gust), Whipple and Crouch could only wait. Once they'd started climbing a little after 7:00 a.m., the eight rescuers took more than seven hours to reach the pair, even as one's urgent cries for help goaded them on. The difficult mix of distance, response time, hard terrain, and cold doomed Whipple and Crouch, while putting their rescuers through an ex-tended ordeal. At day's end, rescuers were so tapped by effort and weather that, once they were assured both men had died, they had to leave the two bodies roped to the cliff and descend. One rescuer, when he finally reached ground and untied from his rope, needed support to walk.

The December 1959 issue of *Appalachia* led with a twenty-page analysis called "The Cannon Mountain Tragedy" (vol. 32, 441–61). It is especially notable for the rescuers' accounts of the event. A reader is taken inside this rescue, seeing it from both the command post at the cliff's base and from the often harrowing slabs of the cliff itself.

Hamilton set up his base on the scree below the cliff, and he was careful to stay far enough from the sheer face to be out of range of the rain-loosened rocks that careened with regularity down from above. He was joined by John Perry, chairman of AMC's Rock Climbing Committee, an experienced climber who looked up in some awe:

> It was noon before the last man on the 2nd rope disappeared over the overhang about 300 feet above my head. During this time I coordinated the climbing party with the ground party. . . . During the course of the morning the storm increased in intensity. At 10 a.m. the temperature was reported to be 38 at the summit, while a 50 mph wind was whipping rain onto the rocks. The whole face was awash. A stream of water jumped out over the overhang above, fell about 50 feet and was blown off into the clouds.

On the face itself, Taylor recalled a tricky moment:

> The next few minutes were very exciting. I moved left out from under the overhang along a sloping ledge, right into the fury of the wind and rain. The wind was so strong that I gasped for breath. The problem in front of me would not have been a difficult one in dry weather: it was a short vertical face with fine handholds at shoulder level. But the needed foothold was covered with lichen and so slippery that my foot kept coming off whenever I tried to put my weight on it. I began to lose my nerve. I moved farther to the left, to see if there might be some alternative easier route. What a sight! There was no possible route in that direction—rivers of water poured down the slabs and the wind whipped it at right angles to the cliff.

By the time Taylor neared the trapped boys, he had finger cramps that had "never happened to me before," and he realized he didn't "have the muscle" to make it up the last bit of the route. He retreated, grabbed a little food and then tried again on another approach.

At the same time, he recalled:

One boy kept calling weakly, unaware that we were only a hundred feet to the left of him. I climbed up the gully, perhaps 20 feet, and then began traversing to the right across slabs of rock at a slightly higher level than the ledge on which the boys were located. Finding an old piton, I pendulumed farther to the right over a more difficult section of slab. I ended up in another gully only 25 feet from the boys, but this maneuver left me utterly exhausted. After resting a few minutes, I looked for a piton crack, found one, and with considerable effort drove in a piton. I had to rest again. I realized that though I was only a few minutes away, my strength was spent. I felt certain that, once on the same ledge with the boys, I would be a definite handicap to the rescue.

David Sanderson, who took over the final approach to the boys, remembered some moments from that effort:

We inched gingerly over the place where we had seen a block of granite, the size of a football strike just in front of Bob Collins and bounce over him as he dived for cover. . . . On the 3rd pitch I had a bad time, as the wind seemed determined to blow me off the cliff, and I climbed by a piton which Jack had placed in the roof of the overhang without seeing it. I remember being very angry at being in such a predicament. Once in the wind, I felt myself moving very much more slowly and I completely lost track of time. . . . We worked up another hundred feet and I had my worst moment of the day when Jack pointed out the two boys. They were much closer than I had expected, scarcely 50 feet away, but they seemed to take no notice of us. Behind the veil of mist they were gray silhouettes, almost at home among the gray rocks. Their heads bobbed up and down, but I heard no voices.

A little later Sanderson was on the ledge with the boys. "At about this point one of the boys gasped a few times and died," he reported. At 500 feet above the cliff's base, Sanderson tried to lower the boy who was still breathing, though he too seemed almost gone. And soon he was.

After lowering the dead pair to a next ledge, Sanderson estimated that it would take four hours to descend. In assessing what it would have meant to retrieve one or both of the bodies, he figured it would have taken six climbers, "rested and in good condition" and probably been an "all-night proposition."

Spencer Wright, climbing with Dave Sanderson, added some final words to the *Appalachia* analysis. Embedded in those words, a reader can also find more hints of the toll such work takes on rescuers:

> None of the questions asked of the rescue party were as penetrating as our own soul searching, I am sure. Could anything more have been done? As an active First-Aider and First-Aid Instructor, I should perhaps add some observations.
>
> My most vivid recollection is one of sitting at a point opposite the boys, after leading the sixth pitch, and watching in complete frustration as they made occasional feeble movement, not more that 75 feet out of reach. More than once they looked directly at me, without seeing. As Dave came up, I said, "There's nothing we can do, but we have to try."

A bit later, Sanderson and Wright reached the boys: "They were insensible, and their condition—equivalent to deep shock—was caused by the serious lowering of body temperature, and certainly aggravated by fatigue, hunger and terror. They could not survive where they were, yet they surely would have succumbed under the added strain of evacuation by whatever awkward means we might devise. I could detect no pulse or respiration in the Crouch boy before I tied him in to a bush. Nor was there evidence of life in Whipple as we prepared to leave."

The next day, another team of climbers, this one led by a noted climber, William Putnam of Springfield, Massachusetts, retrieved Whipple's and Crouch's bodies in another extensive effort, as an estimated one thousand people, including New Hampshire's governor, Wesley Powell, looked on. Summer had returned as had the sun. How, many wondered, do two twenty-somethings die of exposure in this season? And why couldn't rescuers get them off the cliff? Few could fathom what had taken place only a day ago in a maelstrom of cold rain inside a cloak of cloud.

Mountain Rescue Service Forms

Fast-forward a dozen or so years from the Cannon tragedy. Drop down into North Conway, New Hampshire, and survey the local scene. As ever, tourism is the major economic mover, and the Eastern Slope Inn caters to those who want to be in the mountains' presence. Some want merely to gaze, to drive to points from which they can wonder up at the peaks; others want onto those slopes, as amblers, as skiers. Increasingly, another mountain group seems to be gathering. North Conway, with Cathedral and Whitehorse Ledges nearby, is becoming a hub for rock climbers. These athletes, when you look at them, seem the perfect spawn of the 1960s, a time when order is being tested. Often hirsute, shaggy, living in cars and cold-water flats, many of these climbers are not exactly economic engines. Yet their specialized equipment needs have given rise to Eastern Mountain Sports, a new shop in the inn. Managing and dispensing all those ropes and carabiners and nuts is a young and compelling figure. Someone meeting Rick Wilcox for the first time might think him diminutive, until he took in the large hands and ropey forearms and then listened as Wilcox filled the space between them with words and stories. He might think, "This Wilcox fellow certainly has a lot to say." And, "He seems to know what he's talking about."

By the early 1970s, AMC people concerned with search and rescue knew they needed a local solution for the growing number of incidents happening in technical terrain. Calling on those who happened to be climbing in the area or summoning rescuers from afar took crucial time, and AMC's many seasonal employees couldn't add specialized rescue training to a lengthy list of demands. So AMC's eyes turned to the area's burgeoning climbing community. Here were technically skilled, physically able climbers, who also were beginning to find work as guides; here were people who sought out high angles and extreme conditions and knew how to negotiate them. Famously idiosyncratic and independent, rock climbers posed only one question as AMC leaders looked their way for an answer: Could they be organized into a dependable group?

It took a few years to arrive at a short answer, but yes, it turned out, they could. In 1972, a core group of local technical climbers would become the Mountain Rescue Service. For MRS's first decade or so, other groups concerned with safety in the mountains peopled the new nonprofit's board of directors: AMC, NHFG, USFS all assigned representatives. Then, in 1976, they located Mountain Rescue Service's final organizing piece; in that year, they appointed the twenty-eight-year-old climber and Eastern Mountain Sports store manager Rick Wilcox as its president, a post from which he retired in

Mountain Rescue Service group photo. Photo by Joe Lentini.

2017. Until current president Steve Dupuis took over, Wilcox had been MRS's only president, and, if the Whites have a high-angle spirit, he is it.

In the summer of 2016, sitting at a broad-boarded pine table in the upstairs section of his current store, International Mountain Equipment, Wilcox looked back at MRS's formation. Hands moving, eyes alive, he ranged across the years, dipping down here and there for emblematic stories.

Before MRS organized, what happened if you went climbing—with or without experience—and got stuck on a cliff? One answer was the heroic effort gathered from afar that fell just short of having a happy ending on the Cannon Cliff in 1959. The other could be found in local fire and police departments, which often had the word "rescue" tagged to their primary responsibility. Wilcox recalled the scene at Whitehorse Ledge in the early 1970s:

> They [local officials] weren't so much worried about climbers doing crazy stuff, because they began to see us in action, and we did a good job. We're good

climbers. But we'd stand around and watch North Conway Rescue spend five hours trying to get someone off Whitehorse. There'd be some guy in a bathing suit up 300 or 400 feet, and they'd all be standing around figuring out how to get up there, and I'd come over and say, "Can we help you?" "Oh, no, Oh no," they'd say. "Stand back, stand back." The police would be there too and have it all roped off. "Give us fifteen minutes," I'd say.

So finally the chief came over one day and said, "Okay, go get 'em," and I went shoo shoo, up with my guys. It's like a hike for us. And he goes, "Oh, wow, you guys are pretty good." And I said, "This is what we do. We don't run into burning houses, we don't go to crash-cars, we don't go down into wells, we go on cliffs. So if you need us, call us."

They call us all the time. . . . They want to be involved, but they can be at the bottom; they can get the guy when we bring him down; they can put him in the ambulance. We work great together.

Wilcox, a self-described "cautious climber," who, nonetheless, has been up the world's biggest mountain, Everest, and a number of its notable companion peaks, is an instructive figure when thinking about risk and rescue in the mountains. A favorite joke revolves around his primary worry: "My greatest fear is being rescued by Mountain Rescue Service. What I tell them is don't rush, because I carry a cyanide pill and they're not going to take me alive."

But when you set aside the self-deprecating humor, you find Wilcox has a clear-eyed, experience-based take on how to make decisions when climbing, and his ethos has had a powerful effect on MRS and its remarkable record of safety and rescue in the Whites.

In an interview for the book *Mountain Voices*, Wilcox thought aloud about a climber's primary tool, his mind:

> I think you process Mount Everest the same way you process a hike on Mount Washington in the winter. You go to Lion Head, you stop and look around, and if there's no wind and it's clear and it's noon, then you keep going. If it's three in the afternoon, you can't see a hundred yards, and the wind's blowing, well, you process that information [and go down]. A lot of times, you try to second-guess yourself. *Should I have kept going? Could I have done it?* That's a bad thing, I think. You have to accept your decisions and live with them. I did the right thing on Makalu [5th highest peak in the world, where Wilcox and partner

turned back a few hundred yards from the summit] by turning back in high winds. I thought I would be just another dead guy up there if I kept going.

I'll give you an interesting example of something that happened to me. I started to cross the knife-edge ridge on Everest [Wilcox summited Everest in 1991; the knife-edge ridge is near the top]. It was scarier than I thought it would be. I was all set for the Hillary Step, which has 40 feet of rock climbing, no net, and 10,000 feet on both sides. I was ready for that. I'd been studying that for years. Nobody told me that the knife-edge would be really pointed and really scary with huge drops on either side. It was about 100 yards long. I got into it and I went, "Holy—" you know. I'm thinking to myself, *Boy, I didn't plan on this*. I thought I knew every footstep of the summit day. Well, I didn't.

Accidents are never one event. They're usually a combination of things that happened beforehand. So here's the scenario. I'm going across and I'm scared, so what do I do? Turn up the oxygen [Wilcox is breathing bottled oxygen for better function at this altitude]. You've got a little valve, and you think, *This'll give me a little go power. I'll get across the knife edge sooner and I'll turn it down*. So I turned it up. I started moving and my goggles immediately fogged up. The reason they fogged up was there was this teeny crack in the goggles and there was just enough extra heat coming off my body with the oxygen turned up, so they fogged right up. Now I can't see. So what do I do? Take my goggles off. If you take your goggles off at 28,000 feet, you're going to be blind in twenty minutes. Then we're into this scenario: Are we [his climbing companions] going to help Rick, who's blind, or leave him behind? I put the goggles up and sure, I could see, but I knew that my eyes would be damaged very quickly and I couldn't keep going like that. So what do you do? Turn down the oxygen. Less oxygen, less body heat, and then the goggles returned to normal.

The accident report would have read, "Rick tripped and fell off the ridge. But he didn't trip and fall off. He turned up his oxygen, he couldn't see, he took off his goggles, he went snow-blind, then he fell off the ridge." That's how it happens. (*Mountain Voices*, 47–48)

"It" hasn't happened to Wilcox during more than sixty Himalayan trips and countless forays into the Whites, and he attributes much of that good fortune to a lifelong education in the mountains, a gradual accruing of experience that began as a teenager and continues today. Trouble intrudes, he says, when we seek shortcuts, when we skip the step-by-step learning and go straight to the test:

> I always felt that if you wanted to be a climber—not a client but a climber—you had to pay your dues. Imagine climbing a ladder with rungs in the ladder. You go from rung to rung to rung. First, you learn to backpack in the White Mountains, then you learn to rock-climb, then you learn to ice-climb, then you learn to winter camp. You learn all these skills, go take some avalanche courses, then go to Mount Rainier. You find out about crevasses. Then you go to South America, and you find out about bigger mountains, maybe get up to 23,000 feet on Aconcagua. Then you go up to McKinley and freeze your ass off.
>
> And then, when you've done all that—then you're ready. It was my twenty-fifth expedition that I was on when I led Everest. . . . But my attitude was this: You took it a rung at a time. What is happening with guiding is that you're eliminating a huge number of the rungs. . . . People who have never worn double plastic boots are going on big arctic mountains on their first trip. (*Mountain Voices*, 49–50)

That brings us to the idea of apprenticeship. "Apprentice" is an old-fashioned word for "trainee," but the idea of being an apprentice contains a sense of relationship between the learner and a master. It is a word of long contact, of living relations. An apprentice lives in and through the master's work until he or she can know everything that shapes that work; then, and only then, does the apprentice go out on his or her own.

Trainees, on the other hand, receive their lessons, their training, much as other animals do, responding over a short stretch of time to commands and stimuli, feeling the lick of criticism's whip when they bumble, learning the various yeas and nays. But their training is short-lived, just long enough to foster the illusion of knowing, but shallow-rooted, and so prone to the first winds of trouble. Both "trainees" and "training" are modern words that denote a narrow efficiency in learning, born of the assembly line and its predictable demands. Trainees seem ill-suited to the dynamic mountain and backcountry worlds, where change is the rule and adaptability and wisdom the handrails of safety.

Rick Wilcox knows he was lucky to get an apprenticeship, beginning as a teen in the Whites and ranging finally throughout the world's mountains. He would argue that the learning goes on still, even as he has become a master in mountains to whom others turn to learn.

MRS and NHFG

One of the key relationships in White Mountain search and rescue is that between Mountain Rescue Service and New Hampshire Fish and Game's law enforcement division. While many of the state's rescuers are highly skilled, when the terrain tilts toward vertical or the weather goes arctic, NHFG calls MRS. Steve Larson, a longtime MRS member and accomplished climber, explains a central reason for this:

> We're unusual, because we have some of the best climbers in the region. In most areas, the climbers and the rescuers are two separate groups—the other exception I can think of is in Yosemite. The best climbers just climb; they don't go on rescues. Here, it's different, and I give Rick a lot of credit. When MRS began and throughout its history, he worked to create a culture where the best climbers wanted to be part of this group. So on rescues, you have climbers who have been up the world's biggest mountains and in the worst conditions. And most of us have been doing it for so long that, even when it's terrible conditions, we are comfortable.

Larson points to another plus from the gathering of so much mountain talent, of so many climbers with lead capabilities:

> Virtually all progress in the MRS during my involvement has percolated from the bottom up rather than the top down. When I first got involved with the MRS, we did not have any medical training and basically no protocols for how to rescue a victim. Albert Dow's death [a tragedy in 1982; see chapter 11] motivated most of the team to get EMT certification, and rescue specific techniques were to follow. None of this progress began as a vision from top leadership, but rather from motivated lower-level members, who had the perception to recognize the need, and the initiative to develop the methods and trainings necessary to conduct high-angle rescues.

"When we began, it was the hippies and the guys with guns," said Wilcox about MRS and NHFG. Wilcox's characterizations of these two central groups in White Mountain search and rescue are stereotypes, and he knows it. Still, the bald relief of the statement points to the sort of partnership that is in short supply in our era. It is the synthesis of so many seeming opposites that gives this region a SAR organization that has room for many and serves well those hobbled by accident or ignorance. "In New Hampshire, we're blessed," says Wilcox. Though some argue for a fully professionalized, more robust, insurer-funded rescue presence akin to that in Europe's Alps, they are a minority.

11

ANSWERING THE CALL

— — — —

One for Many—Albert Dow

Choosing a volunteer to stand for the hundreds who work or have worked in White Mountain search and rescue could be a fool's errand had not those workers, their work, and their sacrifices been illustrated so clearly by an accident within an incident in 1982. That incident, a protracted search for two missing climbers, turned on and is remembered for the accidental death of the rescuer, Albert Dow, a generous and gifted climber, who died in an avalanche while searching for Hugh Herr and Jeff Batzer. Dow is, to date, the only volunteer to die doing SAR work, and his death has shaped professionals' and volunteers' approach to their work and the very law that offers workman's compensation to any volunteer injured or killed while engaged in SAR under the authority of NHFG or the USFS. Before 1982, the informal aggregates of rescuers common to the Dodge era still did much of the leg- and lift-work for SAR in the Whites. After 1982 that began to change, and SAR has become, when seen from some distance, an orderly (and colorful) mosaic of volunteer groups all working under the shelter of government.

Dow's story, which I'll recount briefly, is ably folded in to Alison Osius's lucid book *Second Ascent*, the story of Hugh Herr. Herr was one of the two climbers Dow was searching for when he and a fellow rescuer, Michael Hartrich, were avalanched in Raymond's Cataract on the eastern side of Mount Washington on the first day of the search. *Second Ascent* is, by agreement between Osius and Herr, dedicated to Albert Dow, and in an epilogue, Osius cites some of her correspondence with Marjorie Dow, Albert's mother, as a way of remembering who he was:

> [Marjorie Dow] wrote that Albert's sisters, Susan and Caryl, wished that this account of their brother would stress that he had always been willing to assist at rescues and searches. He had felt it his duty to other climbers and out-doors-people, his community.

Marjorie Dow closed one letter by describing a rescue. Only a few days before his death, Albert had joined a difficult search for a man, who, although a veteran Thiokol snowcat driver, had become separated from his vehicle. Sweeping the mountain in a wild storm, all the rescuers were tied to one another for safety. Even so, the weather prevented communication between people who were only an arm's length apart.

Albert told his mother afterward that he thought the search was hopeless, that only by falling over the man would the searchers have found him. (In fact, the man managed to make his way to safety alone.)

Anxious for her son's safety, she asked why he had even gone. "No hesitation on Al's part as he responded, 'Mom, if I was in trouble, I would want to know someone was looking for me.'" And he went out again, a few days later.

That "few days later" was Sunday, January 25, 1982. Albert Dow and other members of the Mountain Rescue Service headed up into Huntington Ravine to look for two ice-climbers who had not returned to the Harvard Cabin on Saturday evening. A storm had begun on Friday night, and intense cold, high winds, new snow, and low visibility combined to make the Sunday searching hard going.

Some thirty-six hours earlier, after a long drive from Lancaster, Pennsylvania, two young men had stepped from their car into late afternoon light and looked up at the still-visible white bulk of Mount Washington above. It crowded the sky and quickened their pulses. Already fit and accomplished on rock walls, seventeen-year-old Hugh Herr and twenty-year-old Jeff Batzer grabbed their gear and headed up the trail to Huntington Ravine, where they intended to spend the night at the Harvard Mountain Club's small cabin and climb the ravine's ice the next day. Herr, in particular, was a phenom. Known throughout the East for his climbing on rock, he might already have been the best climber in the whole region; surely he was on his way to being among the world's best.

But as can often be true, when the search began, rescuers knew little of those they sought and where they might be, and their mission began amid weather that limited vision and upped the ante of danger.

What happened over the ensuing four days was the amply chronicled story of Herr and Batzer's losing their way, and the search that gathered for them. In that gathering were two young climbers, Michael Hartrich and

Albert Dow. On Sunday afternoon, the first day of the search, they were descending from the Alpine Garden along the summer trail from Lion Head. Their radio squawked a warning relayed from fellow rescuer Misha Kirk via the AMC Pinkham Notch base radio: be wary of a cornice of fresh snow, deposited by the current storm on an old crust on Washington's eastern slopes. Okay, they thought, and they cut over to the winter trail that runs in a diagonal toward Huntington Ravine, the trail favored when there is possibility of avalanche. As added prudence, the pair made their way along into the thickest woods, which, they knew, might help anchor the new snow.

Still, the snow on the thirty-degree slope didn't stay put, and Hartrich, in the lead, suddenly found himself caught and carried by a wave of white. Hartrich worked to "swim" in this wave, fighting to stay up near its surface and not be dragged into its lower flow, and he managed just enough. When the wave slowed, he could punch an air pocket around his face and thrust his hand above the snow's surface. At that point, the snow behaved as it will after an avalanche: it set rapidly like concrete, holding Hartrich immobile; he couldn't dig himself out, though through luck and determination he did reach his radio with his free arm. "This is unit four," he radioed. "We've been avalanched." Then he lay there, hoping.

Already mobilized for the Herr and Batzer search, rescuers hurried toward Hartrich and Dow. Kirk and Tuckerman's caretaker, Joe Gill, were there in twenty-five minutes, climbing into the slid snow even as the rest of the slope issued warning *whoompfs* that could presage more avalanches. Amid the debris, they saw a single mitten waving.

Hartrich could breathe, but Kirk and Gill couldn't get him out without shovels. Kirk dug out more of Hartrich's airway and they began looking for Dow. Twenty minutes later, six more searchers arrived with avalanche probes. The eight men did a hasty, rough probe with the twelve-foot poles, feeling for the resistance a body makes when poked. One pass, during which the snow shifted again, brought nothing, and they began again, this time using a finer probe, where searchers stood nearly shoulder to shoulder. The searchers found Albert Dow ninety minutes after he'd been swept down. An examination revealed only the coldest of comforts—Dow had died quickly from collision with a tree. A cut on his chin had not bled, and they did not find the grim ice mask that sets up when an avalanche victim suffocates.

The search for Herr and Batzer ground on over more days, and it was resolved only by a chance discovery of their footprints in the Great Gulf, a ravine no one had thought likely because of the pair's intended ice route in Huntington's. Their story, and Herr's in particular, is wonderfully told by Osius, also a noted climber. Herr and Batzer survived their frigid ordeal, but the cost in body parts and battered psyches was frightful. Herr lost both lower legs and also had to absorb Dow's death. He lost, too, the climbing for which he was noted and through which he seemed set to chart his way to an adult self. Herr's recovery from those losses, and his discovery of a new self, one who would return to climbing at the highest levels and then use his experience and formidable drive to build remarkable prosthetics for other amputees, became the focus of Osius's story.

But it is Albert Dow's presence and spirit that direct us here and that has helped shape search and rescue in the Whites from 1982 until today. Not far from the Harvard Cabin in Huntington Ravine, there's a memorial to Dow, a plaque and, fittingly, a rescue cache. The plaque reads: ALBERT DOW CLIMBER RESCUER FRIEND KILLED IN AN AVALANCHE WHILE ON A SEARCH FOR A FELLOW CLIMBER JANUARY 25, 1982. Not long ago, a handful of mountain SAR people walked up to it to mark the anniversary of Dow's sacrifice and rekindle memory.

Though commemorated in this place he loved, Dow lives particularly in the heightened imperative to look first to your own and fellow rescuers' safety, a tenet that permeates White Mountain search and rescue, even as his selflessness in service of his "outdoor community" also inspires. If you look back to this book's opening incident, as NHFG officers and MRS volunteers climb into the coldest weather and complete night to look for Kate Matrosova, you may recall incident commander Mark Ober's injunction to rescuers to look after themselves first. You may recall the unquestioning support a conservation officer gets when he feels subpar and retreats that night. Or you may recall the complete absence of second-guessing of MRS team 1, when they decide to come down after finding no sign of Matrosova at the coordinates of a second beacon hit. As I've talked with searchers and rescuers across the state, even when they don't mention his name, it's clear they work under the guardian spirit of Albert Dow.

12

COLORFUL CHIPS

‒ ‒ ‒ ‒

White Mountain SAR's Modern Mosaic

Bill and Barbara Arnold's screened-in porch and living room on the south side of New Hampshire's Randolph Hill look directly up into King Ravine, a deep glacial pocket on the north flank of Mount Adams, at 5,800 feet the second tallest White Mountain. It's late afternoon on an amber-lit May day in 2016, and a few just-hatched black flies wing dazedly through the air. Seemingly uncertain of their life's mission to torment and draw blood, they are simply aloft in the miracle of being here. Outside, a hummingbird feeder draws an airport's worth of traffic; unlike the flies, the birds are clear about mission and aggression. They whirr in with purpose.

A Pair and a Volunteer Group: The Arnolds and AVSAR

Here, looking up at the northern flank of the Presidential Range, Bill, co-ordinator for one of the White Mountains' prominent volunteer search and rescue groups, Androscoggin Valley Search and Rescue (AVSAR), and Barbara, AVSAR's secretary, reflect on years of missions in that range and others nearby.

"Everyone manages a rescue differently," says Bill. "Every rescue is different." In that individualized description, in that evocation of a rescue's fingerprint, you get the essence of White Mountain search and rescue: each search and each rescue is personal; each is carried out by a hybrid of professionals and volunteers who set aside their usual lives to go out. Yet though "every rescue is different," each is carried out with a mix of mountain professionalism and altruism common to them all.

Bill Arnold first went to work in the Whites in 1963 as a sixteen-year-old, when he climbed to the Randolph Mountain Club's Crag Camp shelter and settled in as its summer caretaker. Sixteen is a bit young to be in charge of a mountain hut—at that age, most of us have trouble assuming command of self—but that season's caretaker had decided against his job just a few days before he was slated to begin, and RMC knew that Arnold and a friend had been unofficial helpers up there the summer before. Yes, they were young, but they knew the territory. They also had summer lives in Randolph that made them available, so they got to split the job.

That same summer, I was a fourteen-year-old counselor's aide at a Maine summer camp not far away, and we were led on our mountain forays by a gung-ho, twenty-year-old, who drove us hard so that we could tell hero tales when we returned to camp. On one such trip, I spent a night at Crag. After supper, the wind came up, and I recall a hurried, late-night negotiation with a fellow aide: "Look," I said, "the caretaker warned us. He said the outhouse isn't stable in a high wind. We need to go out there together so our combined weight keeps it from blowing off the cliff."

These years later, it's clear to me that at a young age Arnold was already having fun at the expense of "goofers," Joe Dodge's term for flatlanders who wander the Whites' trails. To my knowledge, the outhouse at Crag, though, at that time, perched on a cliff near tree line, never was blown from its spot, even as northwest gales far in excess of what we found routinely raked it.

In a 2011 interview for the book, *Mountain Voices*, Arnold reflected on accomplishments from his years in the Whites. Two rose to prominence: his years of going out to help those who had foundered or were lost; and his having fashioned a meaningful life on the side of Randolph Hill and in those mountains. That life has seen Arnold work for the AMC, the RMC, the USFS, the timber industry, and the Randolph Fire Department. He has also served the local medical community as an EMT, all the while fitting volunteer work into seams of time between these assignments. The sixteen-year-old who manned Crag Camp has become a sixty-five-year-old who sees and knows the surrounding terrain like few others. When Arnold presses the keys to send out an AVSAR phone message seeking volunteers, he knows deeply what he asks and where it may lead.

Arnold's first summer as a caretaker also marked the start of his searching and rescuing. From his outpost high on the side of Mount Adams, he was often the first to hear when something or someone went askew up there. "Mostly," he remembered, "our rescues were the sort where some members of a party show up late in the day, saying that another or others are coming along behind them. Then, as it gets dark, people start to worry. It could be rainy and cold; the wind could be blowing pretty good. We'd get our Coleman lanterns and go out to look for them. Even then, we knew the area so well that we almost always found them. I learned that that felt pretty good."

Again and again, rescuers I've spoken with have cited the good feeling of helping another as a powerful motivation for their work. Volunteers are drawn by it, but, of course, there's more to joining a search and rescue group than good feeling. Barbara Arnold, who also works as a nurse, manages the applications of those who would join AVSAR. Here are some of her thoughts on what such joining entails and who becomes part of SAR's fabric:

> We have a regular application form that was developed ten or fifteen years ago, and it asks a lot of the usual questions. But what's most important is your experience: What equipment do you have? What are you comfortable doing? So that's a good starting point. Once we have the application, the board of directors looks at it, and they say yea or nay. They know so many people in the mountains that there's a good chance one of them will know the individual. As a rule of thumb, nobody comes on as "winter qualified" [capable of searching in winter's extremes] until that person has gone on what we call "a shakedown cruise." The people who run the shakedown cruise are very qualified; they've climbed all over these mountains and many have climbed all over the world. They'll come back to the board and say, "This person didn't have the gear to be above tree line in winter extremes, but they're okay in winter below tree line." Or "sign 'em up; they're great." And then I get back to the person and say, "Welcome to AVSAR. We've put you on the three-season list," or whatever list they've qualified for. We then encourage them to meet with all our people, come to all our trainings; everybody gets invited to the trainings [AVSAR offers two or three trainings per year, one of which is winter focused]. And with our winter people, we encourage them to take an avalanche course.

Talk of winter brings on talk of gear. Winter asks for a lot of gear, and a lot of gear can be expensive. Not having it can disqualify someone from the team. "Sometimes we'll get pro deals for someone who is qualified but without some of the equipment," says Barbara. Bill adds, "AVSAR has done fifty-fifty purchases with volunteers, where we help get GPSs or [avalanche] beacons, depending on how our budget looks." But that budget hovers in the $1,500 range, so lavish expenditures aren't possible.

Even as our talk ranges toward gear for heights and extremes, Bill is quick to point out that when rescues get technical, Mountain Rescue Service most often gets the primary call. "We're grunts," he says, referring to the litter bearing that is a staple of backcountry rescue, "even as many of our members are highly capable in technical terrain and some are members of both AVSAR and MRS."

Both Arnolds return to "experience" as a rescuer's primary asset: "Medical training is good, but if you're going up there in the middle of the night, experience counts for way, way, way more. There will always be someone who has medical knowledge. . . . Being on a mountain rescue is a lot like being a firefighter. You can't just go charging into a fire. You might get hurt, and then there are two people who need help. The first thing is not to become a liability. That takes experience."

Experienced mountain people tend to know each other, crossing paths during long days in the hills, or in their aftermath. It's no surprise, then that most volunteers arrive at AVSAR and other groups via word of mouth. "We've had eight or ten inquiries or referrals from social media, but none has panned out," says Barbara.

A Rescuer's Mind

Later that afternoon, as I prepare to leave, Bill Arnold offers me a final story that helps me see with a volunteer rescuer's eyes.

> This spring we took a trip to the Southwest. It was spectacular. But we're in Canyon de Chelly, and there's one trail you can take down to the ruins. We decided to go down for a hike. It was a weekend, a beautiful spring day, and it was jammed; it was like Tuckerman's. The trail's about this wide [not very], and people are in flip-flops, kids running around, one person pushing a stroller, and if you go over the edge you're done. And part way down, I said, "I can't

take this. Somebody's gonna fall, and I'm gonna feel responsible and think, why didn't I warn these people. We gotta get out of here." So we turned around and went up.

All this time I thought Mount Washington was unique, because you go up there on a good day in the summer, and there's flip-flops and heels and bloody blisters. People don't realize how many thousands of people go up there and get away with it. Then, one will get hurt, and somebody will say, "It's amazing he got hurt," and I'll say, "No, it's amazing how many made it." But it's the same thing out there. They have all these big warning signs. You can't miss them. We had hiking boots and extra clothes and water, and these people are in flip-flops. That was an eye-opener for me that day.

I get up to go. Bill looks over and says,

It's still impressive, the way people show and go out. Some are funny, some are not funny at all. But until you've been on a rescue. . . . I'm thinking about the Timothy Hallock recovery [Hallock died of cold after a medical emergency, while hiking alone in February of 2016] near Edmands Col. We had a caretaker who went on this one and later wrote a piece about it for the RMC newsletter through the eyes of a rookie. In it he spoke so much about the camaraderie, everybody there for a common cause, everybody working together. Everything clicks on those; you get mistakes, of course, but by in large things click. There's so much experience, and the few rookies are going along doing their part, watching. He was very impressed with that.

And I also remember from that one at two o'clock in the morning I was at the trailhead in my truck. By then Fish and Game was there too. And we're looking where the trail comes out over the last couple of hundred feet, and seeing this army of maybe thirty headlights all bobbing in the dark. Incredible stars up above, and knowing what they had done, what they'd been through, and there they are saying "nice night" and just matter-of-fact. And I said to Wayne Saunders [veteran NHFG lieutenant in charge], "Take a look at that. It's too bad we can't get a picture. Seeing just one after another pop out of the woods, all those lights." And he just looked out of his truck and said, "Whoa!"

Here's Who's on the Way: The Structure
of Search and Rescue in the Whites

The Authorities: New Hampshire Fish and Game's law enforcement division oversees search and rescue throughout the state, except from December 1 to May 31 in the Cutler River drainage on the eastern flank of Mount Washington. Then and there, the U.S. Forest Service is in charge. Also, atop the popular, train-, trail- and road-approached point of the mountain, the Mount Washington State Park has legal authority.

Embedded within this arrangement is a common question: How is it that the federal government controls nearly 800,000 acres of White Mountain National Forest, but oversees search and rescue in only one river drainage, for only six months of each year? That question will recur with added force when we consider how White Mountain SAR gets funded. The longer answer stretches back into the history we've looked at; a shorter answer is a practical one that stems from staffing: the U.S. Forest Service has a limited number of rangers and support personnel to manage those acres, and, though their rangers are often very skilled in the hills and woods, they are too few to conduct the many SAR missions within the forest. An exception is made for the precipitous and peopled ravines on the east side of Mount Washington where, during seasonal winter, snow rangers run rescues. This is an area where sliding snow requires avalanche experts, and the USFS snow rangers are those experts.

These two government agencies cooperate to promote safe recreation in the mountains and supervise efforts to rescue those who run into trouble. Both see education of backcountry users as a key part of their missions and a way to limit the number of accidents. In 2003, NHFG and the USFS launched the hikeSafe Program, a primary educational effort aimed at preparing hikers for their travels in the state's forests and mountains. This well-publicized effort promotes a code of hiker responsibility and recommends carrying a minimum of ten essentials with you when you head out.

The Volunteers: Like much of White Mountain culture, the volunteer spirit of search and rescue began on the slopes of Mount Washington. The Appalachian Mountain Club's twentieth-century role, developed under the guidance and within the gruff, generous spirit of Joe Dodge, set both expectations and tone. In 1939, in the midst of the Dodge era, the Mount Washington Volunteer Ski Patrol formed, and it continues to provide ski-season help for the USFS snow rangers in Tuckerman Ravine today. As MRS spokesperson and USFS ranger Justin Preisendorfer says, "Volunteers are the big story in White Mountain rescue. If you tallied up the effort of all those involved, the vast majority come from volunteers. The media always wants to talk about funding, about who pays, and then the role of volunteers gets lost. To me, that's the big story of what makes it work in the White Mountains. We know there are people who are gonna show up because they want to, not because they're getting paid to."

Though the volunteer rescuers from the groups described below receive no pay, they are, as noted in the chapter on Albert Dow, covered by workman's compensation when they are searching and rescuing on behalf of NHFG or the USFS. That coverage (and simple safety) occasions a sign-in-sign-out ritual at the base of every SAR incident. Volunteers arriving to help sign in with the incident's supervising officer, so every incident has a roster of those searching and rescuing, and they are covered. A proposal is now being brought to the legislature to extend that coverage to SAR groups' training sessions as well.

Androscoggin Valley Search and Rescue (AVSAR): Founded in 1993, AVSAR's mission is "to save lives and lessen suffering." We've just met AVSAR's coordinator and secretary, and its volunteers are prominent in these pages. As is true in many realms, location helps shape participation, and AVSAR's home base on the north and east sides of the Presidential Range ensures plenty of calls. Its approximately fifty members live in various corners of the White Mountains, with a core residing in the Gorham-Randolph area. AVSAR also boasts a Winter Above Tree Line Team that often works in concert with MRS's alpine experts.

Pemigewasset Valley Search and Rescue Team (PVSART): The western flank of the White Mountains includes the oft-visited and incident-rich Franconia Ridge, an airy 1.7-mile walk above tree line that matches the Presidential Range's reputation for hard weather in all seasons. But until PVSART's formation in 2005, this crowd magnet and surrounding terrain had no immediate team of responders. Now, with more than sixty members who, by bylaw, must live within fifty miles of Exit 32 on Interstate 93, PVSART is the Whites' largest and among its busiest volunteer groups. Like AVSAR, its rescues and rescuers appear frequently in these pages.

Mountain Rescue Service (MRS): MRS's formation and presence in White Mountain SAR is fully represented in this book's chapters and stories—see in particular chapter 10. It is the region's oldest volunteer group formed specifically for search and rescue.

The Appalachian Mountain Club (AMC): Most White Mountain visitors know the AMC as the region's biggest conservation and recreation outfit, with a backcountry hut system and two large centers, one in Pinkham Notch, the other in Crawford Notch. With hundreds of employees, especially in the summer high season, AMC has a lot of feet on the ground, even as they are scattered across the Whites. So they appear frequently on rescue rosters, even as their purposes are many. Of particular note are the number of searches and rescues that never happen because hikers sought advice from or crossed paths with a mountain-placed AMC employee. As NHFG's sgt. Mark Ober said to me at one point, "It's impossible to know how many rescues don't happen because of AMC, but it's a lot." In addition, when called by NHFG, AMC contributes rescuers from its SAR group, and it also hosts the monthly SAR working group meeting that helps organize and work through issues among the prominent SAR groups in the Whites. Beyond those immediate mountains, AMC's facilities and influence stretch throughout New England and down the Atlantic seaboard, with its 100,000-plus members and lobbying capabilities giving the club a large regional impact on conservation and recreation.

Upper Valley Wilderness Rescue Team (UVWRT): The year 2016 proved to be the "busiest yet" for this group, which formed in 1995. Based in the Hanover, New Hampshire area, UVWRT works on searches and rescues in Vermont as well. Of the year's forty-one missions, thirteen were in Vermont. The following mix of brief incident summaries points to the scope of search and rescue work for UVWRT and other volunteer groups. It involves not only classic mountain retrievals, but other searches as well.

From UVWRT's 2016 incident log:

> On February 26, we were called out to assist with a carryout of a subject with
> a broken ankle on Mount Cardigan in Orange, NH. The trail was very icy, and

we had just completed our own shakedown hike on the same trail the Saturday before, with one slip and fall resulting in an injury. The next day (2/27) we were called to help with a carryout of a subject on Mount Kearsarge in Warner, NH, with another broken ankle, again as a result of the icy conditions.

On May 15, we were called to help search for a subject who had gotten separated from his companions while looking for shed antlers in Stark, NH. He had been out overnight, and we were called the next day and fielded several search teams. The subject ended up walking out on his own quite a distance from where he was last seen. This was the second callout of the weekend, which was also our new member-training weekend, so we really got stretched to the max.

On September 26, we were called to Brownington, Vermont, to help search for a missing subject who was found deceased before any UVWRT teams arrived. But at the same time, we were called to help the Hanover Fire Department with a carryout of a subject with an ankle injury on Moose Mountain in Lyme, NH. So we had members headed in two directions at the same time.

The Randolph Mountain Club (RMC): "Little club, big presence." I heard this from a number of people during my research travels, and its origins are easy to understand. Named for and centered in this small town on the northern flank of the Presidential Range, the roughly thousand-member-strong RMC has had a large effect on the use and culture of these mountains for the past 107 years. Founded by hoteliers and summer residents in 1910 "to put the paths in order," RMC members, like many in the early twentieth-century White Mountains, worked first to repair the disorder brought by extensive lumbering. Paths devised during explorations of the late nineteenth century had been rendered impassable, and a new progressive ethic sought a solution.

A century later, the RMC maintains more than one hundred miles of trails in the northern Whites and offers the public inexpensive, overnight shelter at four facilities on the slopes of Mount Adams. One enclosed cabin, Gray Knob, has a caretaker year-round, while its neighbor, Crag Camp, is staffed by a summer caretaker. The other two sites are three-sided shelters that get regular visits from these caretakers. This RMC presence "on the mountain" tabs its caretakers as rescuers in residence. They often go out on "hasty searches," when incident calls arrive and before a full rescue is mounted.

Like their AMC counterparts in the huts, RMC caretakers offer advice and orientation that prevents trouble, or nips it before it blossoms fully.

Mahoosuc Mountain Search and Rescue Team: Named for a rugged, cross-over range, this team, located and responding primarily just over the border in Maine, has recently assisted with a number of nearby incidents in the eastern White Mountains. Their presence in both states' rescue scenes points out that only "authorities" recognize borders. Wherever they rise, mountains are simply mountains.

Stonehearth Outdoor Learning Opportunities (SOLO): Begun in 1976 by Dr. Frank Hubbell, SOLO describes itself as "the oldest continuously operating school of wilderness medicine in the world." Its first and central location is a campus in Conway, New Hampshire, and that location on the edge of the White Mountains makes SOLO a player in the region's search and rescue scene. When courses are in session, SOLO contributes people-power to rescues (see their presence in the Gulfside rescue in chapter 3). But their greatest influence has been in the proliferation of hikers, climbers, and skiers with wilderness medicine skills. With courses ranging from two-day Wilderness First Aid training to their flagship, 170-hour Wilderness Emergency Medical Technician course, SOLO aims to serve a broad spectrum of the backcountry community. Their success in doing so is evidenced by their growth—SOLO now offers courses in locations throughout the United States and abroad.

Closer to home, SOLO's website offers a story that underscores the value of such training. A local hiking club, the Denmark Mountain Hikers, takes a refresher course each year. On May 27, 2016, they had a chance to use their training. That day members of the club set out on their weekly climb. This one would take them over Mount Jackson and on for a night at AMC's Mizpah Spring Hut. At around 4:30 p.m., around a mile from the hut, Christine L. slipped and fell from a rock ledge. A snapping sound augured bad news. Recalling their training, the hikers gathered to help, assessing the injury and stabilizing it. Then, they began the work of self-rescue and, realizing they needed further help, summoned rescue. They sent word ahead to the hut, and Allen Crabtree, one of the leaders, called MRS's Rick Wilcox, who called NHFG, who organized the rescue—a carryout.

From there, it became a question of waiting and persevering, which Christine L. and the others did with spirit, all the while making slow progress toward the hut. Crabtree offered this description of what he saw at about 9:00 p.m.: "I went to the trail junction with the Mizpah Spring Cutoff and waited. Then I spotted the first headlamps coming up the mountain—first one, then another, then a whole line bobbing along toward me. What a welcome sight!"

Once gathered, rescuers made quick work of Christine's carryout, traveling down the 2.6 miles in two and a half hours. Later, she would recall their work: "They never slipped or tipped me, always kept me level, and kept up my spirits by singing and telling bad jokes. I could look up and see all of the stars and the trees on the sides of the trail going by."

*White Mountain Swiftwater Rescue Team (*wmsrt*)*: Water, the most volatile of backcountry elements, asks for its own specialists when it comes to searches and rescues. An easy route to appreciation for White Mountain Swiftwater's work and the element they have to master is a photo scroll of the more than fifty images offered on their website. The water pictured is indeed swift, but it is the varied light—rescues and trainings at all times of day or night—and the rigging for safety and rescue that draw the eye. Always suited for immersion, Swiftwater's volunteers set up ropes to catch "swimmers," leap into currents (while tethered themselves), ferry people with their boats, and often search or probe waters, looking for someone who has gone missing. One arresting photo shows a rescuer preparing a victim to be hoisted into an Army National Guard helicopter, all the while being blasted by a rotor-wash estimated at between sixty and a hundred miles per hour. The water, already running fast, is misted by the helicopter's air blast.

White Mountain Swiftwater practices for "live recoveries," really an extension of "saving ourselves regularly," said its director, Crispin Battles. But "there's an added element of difficulty in our work, because we are often working on recoveries."

Battles said that a search in the late fall of 2015 illustrated that aspect of Swiftwater's contributions to regional search and rescue:

In November 2015, the White Mountain Swiftwater Rescue Team was called in by New Hampshire Fish & Game to aid in the search for a missing Plymouth State College student, Jake Nawn. Many search and rescue organizations were involved in land-based searches, but the Swiftwater team was the primary group responsible for the water-based search of the Pemigewasset and Baker Rivers. These rivers flow south from the mountains to their confluence in the town of Plymouth, nearby the college campus. Searchers using polarized glasses scanned both rivers, and, in the low water conditions, they could see most of the bottom.

Two areas with deep pools were mostly opaque to team members searching from their kayaks, however. One was at the base of the hydro dam upstream from Plymouth, where the search area began. The other was at the confluence in Plymouth where the Baker and Pemigewasset rivers joined. In a debrief after the search, the Swiftwater team noted that they were fairly sure that the victim's body was not in the shallower ten miles of river they had searched. Searchers did think it could be stuck on bottom in either of the deeper pools and suggested that Fish & Game dive teams search these locations. Several days later, the body surfaced in the confluence pool and grounded in a shallow section downstream.

*New England K9 Search and Rescue (*NEK9*):* Founded in 1981, New England K9 Search and Rescue is a volunteer group that uses air scent dogs. NEK9 provides life-saving assistance, at no cost, to New Hampshire Fish and Game and Vermont State Police, the lead SAR agencies in each state. Averaging about forty searches per year, NEK9 has now responded to more than eight hundred searches, primarily in those two states.

When the average citizen thinks of canine help finding someone, a picture of a bloodhound snuffling along a scent track comes to mind. That long-eared, baying hound has first been given a good sniff of an article of clothing and then sent off to find its owner. Searchers follow that mournful baying as the hound, nose to the ground, tracks its quarry. That's a tracking dog. NEK9 uses a different dog, an air-scenting one.

Tracking dogs follow a specific person's path of travel (track). Over time, that track fades; weather obscures or washes it away, and contamination from other sources—passersby, for example—can muddle the scent. Air-scent dogs don't work nose to the ground. Instead, as their name suggests, they sniff and sort the air for telltale signs of what they seek. Humans, whether alive or dead, constantly emit microscopic particles bearing scent. These particles become airborne and are carried by the wind, sometimes for considerable distances. Such a scent is concentrated near its source and more diluted farther away. Air-scent dogs are trained to locate these airborne particles and follow them to the source.

When an air-scent dog arrives at such a concentration of scent, the dog will seek out a person who is "out of place." This could be a person who is frightened or stressed, or someone who has been in the same location for a long time—a lost person, or a body, for example. During training, the dogs learn to rule out as their target odors hikers, other searchers, or folks doing normal tasks. So to use a backyard example given to me, if an air-scent dog were to be deployed in my neighborhood to search for a man in hiding, that dog would ignore me if I were mowing the lawn and go, instead, right to the man skulking behind the pine out back.

Air-scent dogs work off-leash and range out in front of the handler, who walks a grid pattern at right angles to the wind. Once the dog picks up a scent and locates the subject, the dog comes back to the handler and leads the handler to the subject. (The dog communicates such a find by jumping, barking, or grabbing a toy from the handler.) NEK9 dogs are also trained to find articles that fit that same category of being "out of place." Each handler-and-dog team covers about eighty to a hundred acres per assignment in two to four hours, depending on the variables of terrain, weather, and vegetation. Most handler-dog relationships are monogamous, developing a trust and understanding during one or two years of training (with six certification tests) and then throughout a search career that can, given health, last until the dog is ten years old. "Trustworthy teams," wrote NEK9 spokesperson, Donna Larson, "are a result of the partnership between the dog and handler, not simply an accumulation of skills."

So who gets to be such a dog? NEK9 gets its dogs from all sorts of breeds. They are, as I was told, "elite athletes with a body type and coat that is adaptable to work in both heat and cold." The other characteristics they need are "excellent scenting capability, strong prey, play, and pack drives, physical stamina, and a high degree of intelligence."

Though its typical searches involve looking for lost kids, elderly folks, mentally challenged people, and the dead, NEK9 has worked on Mount Washington many times over its thirty-six-year history. These searches have usually been focused on the lower half of the mountain, below tree line. On May 11, 2016, NEK9 was contacted by NHFG's lt. Wayne Saunders to assist in the search for François Carrier, a missing Canadian. With support from Upper Valley Wilderness Response Team (UVWRT), who are field assistants for the dog teams, NEK9 searched for a total of four days. As information and sightings of Carrier filtered in, search assignments were shifted accordingly. A video surveillance shot placed Carrier on the Mount Washington Auto Road on May 8. Two NEK9 dog teams along with UVWRT members were then assigned to search the woods on both sides of the auto road from the tree line to the parking lot. At the elevation of 2,800 feet, the team on the east side located an abandoned backpack that was later identified as belonging to Carrier. Additional dog teams were immediately assigned to all the trails leading from the west side of the auto road to the Pinkham Lodge. Though no new clues were discovered, teams covered approximately two thousand acres of land, including area searches and corridor searches of trails and roads in an effort that concluded on May 22. In the end, Carrier's body was discovered by passing hikers a little off the Tuckerman Ravine Trail, high above tree line, on May 28.

> But let's leave our brief sojourn with NEK9's dogs and handlers with the happiness of a short story of a "find." An overnight search for a sixteen-year old in Rindge, New Hampshire, on November 5, 2015, ended happily at 1:00 p.m. the following day, when NEK9 dog Jackson followed the boy's scent to the shores of Island Pond, then plunged in and swam over a hundred yards to an island. There, Jackson found the boy, swam back to alert Jeremy Corson, his handler, and then swam back to the island to be with the boy. NHFG officers followed in a canoe and brought the boy back across the water and then to his nearby school.

New Hampshire Army National Guard (NHANG): As part of their training, pilots from NHANG fly search and rescue missions in Blackhawk helicopters from bases in Concord and Lebanon. Their work and contributions are covered in chapter 21, which discusses air power in SAR.

Dartmouth-Hitchcock Advanced Rescue Team (DHART): As a service to the communities of New Hampshire and Vermont, DHART pilots, medics, and flight nurses provide help with rescues where time is a critical factor or where a quick look from above can clarify a search. Like NHANG, DHART's contributions to the region's SAR are covered in chapter 21.

Local Police, Fire, and Rescue Squads: The advent of NHFG's role as legal lead in SAR and the founding of the volunteer SAR groups listed above has freed these local agencies of responsibility for leading backcountry rescues. Still, members of these departments appear frequently on SAR rosters at various rescues.

Behind These Groups: New Hampshire Outdoor Council (NHOC): Founded in 1986 as a vehicle for promoting education and awareness in backcountry travel, and raising and channeling funds for volunteer search and rescue groups, NHOC is an all-volunteer partner for NHFG. It joins the organizations it serves as an advocate for "appropriate public access to and vital services in the backcountry of the Granite State." That also makes NHOC a grant-making group, with typical awards to SAR groups ranging from $200 to $2,000.

On December 1, 2016, I listened to the details of an AVSAR grant request for a Sked, a lightweight, sled-litter that can be "snaked" through rough terrain—a boulder field in Huntington Ravine, for example—that would make for a very difficult traditional litter carry. Given AVSAR's work in the northern Presidentials and their willingness to have the Sked borrowed by others, and given the modest $850 price tag, the White Mountain Working Group (for SAR) approved making this request of the NHOC. Also in that conversation, I heard a reminder of the training that makes SAR volunteers effective. USFS snow ranger Frank Carus noted that the Sked, while remarkable and lightweight, also requires a lot of practice. Rescuers need to have had their hands on a loaded Sked to understand its strap system and how the Sked moves. MRS's new president, Steve Dupuis, agreed, having seen its use during practice sessions he helps lead for elite military ParaJumpers.

NHOC provides search and rescue teams in the Whites with a representative organization that brings perspective and balance to the tricky question of funding. Who gets the gratitude-laced donations that rescued hikers and skiers sometimes make? That's a common and vital question, especially for volunteer groups that need to replace equipment and provide regular training. Rick Wilcox recalled that, during the early years of MRS's work, its often-dramatic presence on cliffs caught attention and a lot of donations, sometimes at the exclusion of other SAR groups that also put in heavy time and labor. NHOC's board, composed of representatives from the state's major SAR groups, helps to redress some of the imbalances in support through its grant making. That advocacy helps SAR groups keep their focus on the work of rescues rather than on promoting themselves to attract funding.

13

WOMEN AND MEN IN SAR

I wasn't very deep into my research for this book—a few scans of rosters from rescues sufficed—when I noticed the large male majority in SAR's ranks. A number of women peopled those rosters too, but there were many more men. As I worked forward, I kept my eye on this discrepancy, asking questions and noting down answers.

The source of this disparity in numbers is easy to explain from an historical point of view. Volunteers for search and rescue, whether the specialist climbers of Mountain Rescue Service or the generalists of the Pemigewasset Valley Search and Rescue Team, tend to come from the group of people who have chosen to make their lives (and often their livelihoods) in the outdoors. Traditionally, more men than women have made this choice. The guides and climbers of the Mount Washington Valley area, who make up the MRS roster, for example, are heavily male. Yes, climbing rock, ice, and snow is attracting more and more women, so some are also showing up on rescuer lists, but these numbers shift slowly.

Generalists' rosters, drawn from many professions, do include more women. PVSART's current sixty-six-person roster lists seventeen women, AVSAR has ten women in a complement of fifty members, and a scan of rescuer photos on various volunteer group websites reveals rescue scenes and carryouts that almost always show women among the rescue crews.

As I was wondering about this, I drove to Concord for a meeting with NHFG's colonel Kevin Jordan, leader of the law enforcement division. High among Jordan's hopes for his division is the hiring of more women as COs. That goal led him to say, "You need to meet Lt. Murphy," which, a little later, I did.

Lt. Heidi Murphy currently serves as the division's administrative officer, but not long ago she was a CO in District 3, a rescue-heavy district that includes the western Whites. Murphy patrolled the district's lower southern tier. But as is true with all COs who work the mountains, she got called often into searches and rescues, "especially in summer. Then, you couldn't really bank on being at home on a lot of nights, because that's when the callouts happen," she said. Murphy is also New Hampshire Fish and Game's only female CO.

A self-described "physical and athletic person," Murphy found that she liked SAR work: "For me, it was easy to enjoy because, first, you're getting paid to exercise, and second, for the most part you get the instant gratification of helping someone." That pleasure in the work led Murphy to apply to be part of NHFG's sixteen-person Specialized Search and Rescue Team. "I liked the challenge," she said. "It takes a lot of mental and physical stamina to go on a rescue and know that, as long as you follow the right steps, you'll be okay." To join that team you must complete an application that explains why you want to be part of it, pass an agility and fitness test, and attend trainings. Murphy joined the team on her first attempt.

Allan Clark, head of the Pemigewasset Valley Search and Rescue Team, worked often on rescues with Murphy. He said, "Rescues just seemed to go better when Heidi worked with us. She was very good." While she retains her place on the Specialized SAR Team, Murphy's administrative role, located in Concord, means she gets "out into the field" for rescues far less often than when she worked as a CO. "I miss it," she said. "It was such a great antidote to solo patrolling. It was fun to catch up with search and rescue people, to build relations with them. There's great respect within that community. I think we do a good job trying to make it all work."

Near the end of our conversation, I wanted her thoughts on how the division could meet Colonel Jordan's goal of bringing on more women. "It will take a shift in thinking," Murphy said. "Typically, we get COs from the hunting and fishing community, which, by the way, is shrinking, and the percentage of women in that community is small. So we need a paradigm shift where it's okay to look for someone who has a background like mine." Murphy arrived at NHFG along a circuitous route: a biology major in college, she worked outdoor jobs out West and, when she returned to New Hampshire, she decided to take NHFG's law enforcement entrance test on a whim. She didn't pass and went on to teach middle school biology in New Hampshire for three years. Then, she decided to look into taking the test again. "I was curious," she said. "And this time I studied." Murphy passed, and went on to succeed at the rest of the lengthy requirements. "The classic game warden has known he wanted to be a warden since age five," she said. "I found out much later."

Then, there is the law enforcement part of the job: "Some people apply, and then say, 'Wait, you guys carry guns?' And we say, 'Yes, we're certified police officers.'" Murphy's childhood as the daughter of a state police officer who worked for a long time as an investigator for the major crimes unit made that requirement familiar. Both Jordan and Murphy are hopeful that NHFG's appearances on the popular television show *Northwoods Law*—the first show aired in March of 2017—will encourage more women to consider becoming COs.

At one point in 2017, as I mulled all this over, I exchanged notes with James Wrigley, AMC's huts supervisor and also coordinator of their search and rescue response. AMC had caught my eye because not so long ago its hut crews were male preserves, but now their staffing is more than 50 percent women, who carry loads, go on the long hikes or runs that often mark young mountain people as exceptional, and work the Whites as equals with their male counterparts.

Throughout my work on this project, I identified the hut crews and caretakers of the White Mountains as rescuers in place, but they share another characteristic too: they tend to be young. They are the next generation of backcountry exploration, living, and ethics, which might make them also the future of search and rescue there. That would be one of Sally Manikian's hopes. Manikian, currently a thirty-something dogsled racer and shaper of a life in the mountains and woods, got an early taste for the life as a caretaker at the Randolph Mountain Club's Gray Knob shelter on the side of Mount Adams. She followed that work at 4,300 feet with ten years at the AMC, where her responsibilities included hiring caretakers and trail crews. As we kept trading e-mails, she had this to say:

> Women are appearing in roles they have not appeared in before. During the ten
> years I worked at AMC, and during the eight years I was responsible for hiring
> seasonal staff, I charted a very real rising up in women in seasonal positions,
> and in the backcountry caretaker program that places them in remote locations

with canvas tents and no running water. When I was a caretaker, I was one of three out of twelve. When I left the caretaker program, I had hired seven women, more than 50 percent of the crew. There is a wave at work.

It takes a long time for these things to percolate. It takes women who were raised in situations where they are truly able to do what they want to do, and are allowed to even think they have the ability to make those decisions. It takes families and communities that are supportive of dynamic gender roles.

As our exchange continued, we explored the composition of search and rescue teams. Manikian's thoughts on that sort of women's presence in the backcountry are pointed and incisive. During this time, *Outside* magazine's online site had published a piece on Mount Washington's deadly nature, and it featured Kate Matrosova. Manikian wrote back to me expressing her frustration that, despite any number of men dying there too, Matrosova is being "forever punished. 'Mount Washington Kills Women Who Dare Try to Climb It,' is the continuing message." Then she made a powerful link between that ongoing attention and search and rescue:

> There remains a confusion about professional women in the outdoors. Over a decade ago, I once had a man ask me what I thought of myself, as a caretaker, and I responded, "It's my job. I steward natural resources." But he was not satisfied with that, and instead said, "No, but don't you see yourself as a maiden in the woods, waiting?"
>
> That Kate Matrosova is still the most prominent example of why Mount Washington Kills, is an example of why there are not a lot of women in SAR. There is a deeper and limiting framework at play here, and for more women to be on those rosters in SAR, to be on the very team that is doing the saving, they can't all be viewed as isolated "trailblazers."

Manikian thinks we need to emerge from the "trailblazer phase" of women in the woods and consider women's presence to be an everyday matter. In short, we need to see a female caretaker or rescuer and say, "That's usual," or better yet, think nothing of it.

> I wrote back to Manikian, and part of my thinking reverted to the young people I see working in the mountains:

Your point about "trailblazers" resonates, which is why I looked at huts-people and caretakers as counterexamples. A former student of mine was Galehead's hut leader last summer, and I stopped through there one evening and hung out with the crew—mostly, given the disparity between my age and theirs, I was observing. I saw three women, two men, and, leaving aside all the dynamics of living in close quarters for the season, an absence of usual gender roles. Part of what fascinated me was watching the guests watch the crew and take in the way they were living. It lodged in my mind as a sliver of optimism in a world that threatens regression to a less inclusive time.

Manikian's response arrived just before she departed to race with her dogs in the Can-Am dogsled race. It occasioned a shift in my thinking . . . and raised further questions: "After I wrote this [earlier] response, I thought more about the crew piece. It is very different to be hired into a hut crew, in a building where water runs for a daily shower, electronic devices can be charged with regularity, and the primary responsibility is to host and cook food and dress in costumes every morning, than to be welcomed into the elite ranks of protectors and saviors, which is what those elite SAR crews represent. It is the difference between the dispatcher at our local police department and a Navy SEAL."

Yes, I get the elite saviors characterization, and the way that would draw men. I've certainly witnessed a lifetime of actions that support Manikian's thinking. Still, to me the perceived distance between the SEAL and the dispatcher seems too great. Perhaps it is the word "elite" that creates the wedge of separation and distance. I see the heroism in the everyday saviors, those rescuers in place who have taken up residence, even temporarily, in the backcountry as not very different from heroism writ larger. As noted earlier, this generation just emerging from school is much more gender balanced than those aging out in front of it. Perhaps they aren't so much blazing trails in the backcountry as populating it in a natural sort of way.

Still, this migration toward a new usual is slow. As Manikian and others have pointed out, women in positions of power or rescue in the backcountry are still often seen as exceptions. To be the "only one in the room" is its own burden. It can make any room, even the backcountry, feel like an isolation booth. But between the wave of women Manikian helped hire and those my trail time and readings in the Whites keep introducing me to, I look out with hope.

If I need reminder of this, thinking back to a night at Galehead Hut in August of 2016, offers it. The Galehead croo, three women and two men, were at ease in their late-season familiarity, slotting into the various parts of their work without fuss. Dinner went off without a hitch; they gathered into cleanup. At first the soundtrack was the usual boxed sort, but soon human voice took over, erupted really, in the kitchen. "El camino," they all sang, "el el camino / el camino, el el camino / el, camino, el el camino / The front is like a car, / the back is like a truck / the front is where you drive, / the back is where you. . . ." They chanted on, their repeated verses rising in volume. In and outside the hut, it was audible; the thirty-some guests all paused. Louder still, the implied four-letter punch line ever clearer; their voices were indistinguishable from each other. Rowdy exclamation point of relationship. Okay, they like each other, I thought; they like and respect and play as equals.

Morning brought a quiet second sample: gray light, ridges rising outside the small kitchen windows. It is 5:30, and the whole crew is up, half remembering to whisper. The three women are taking on fuel—oatmeal, bagels, coffee or hot chocolate—they are eating with purpose. What's afoot? I wonder. Ah, just a Pemi-loop, a fifty-kilometer circling of the Franconias, Bonds, and Twins. "How long will that take?" I whisper. "We're good as long as we're back for dinner prep at 5:30 p.m.," says Anna. The little math tumblers in my mind click over. With a few stops for fuel and photos, that's around ten hours for the loop. Those are quick mountain feet. When I checked later on that week, those six quick feet had brought them home in time for the work of setting and serving the dinner the two men had prepared during the day. Yes, the example is a trifle ham-handed, a bit obvious, but it is also real. Looping long distances in the mountains can be seen as a personal heroic. As can making dinner.

< 1 4 >

GO-GO OR NO-GO

Up against Extremes

Northern Presidential denizen, writer, and longtime RMC and AVSAR volunteer Doug Mayer tells a story of a rescue he helped with on Mount Adams one day. It was, as is often the case when a call for help comes in, an uncomfortable day in the mountains—some rain, cold enough to make hypothermia a concern, and cloud-bank fog from 2,000 feet up. Near the top of Adams, a man had injured his leg and called to say he couldn't walk anymore. Okay, Doug and other AVSAR folks thought as they gathered in the Appalachia parking lot, a slog up and a litter carry down over roughly four miles. In short, a long, albeit routine, rescue day.

Litter carries, a staple of rescues, sound simple. You get a litter, walk to the injured person, strap him or her in, and then walk the litter out. That might be true along the wide, gravel paths of a local park, but along mountain trails, a number of variables flesh out this easy-to-carry skeleton story, and it can easily become weighty with exhaustion and exasperation. In short, a body of trouble.

A litter carry asks for at least six people, each lending a weight-bearing arm to the task. As you imagine this task and flex your stronger arm, think of your favorite mountain trail, one you know even down to some of its individual rocks and roots. Now describe the terrain a few feet either side of that trail. What's the walking like there? Why worry about what's off that trail? you may ask. Because often we must, answer litter bearers. The litter takes up the center of the trail; typically, the carriers walk beside it. Next time, you're out on your trail, try one hundred yards of walking a few feet to either side. If you're lucky, you may only have to avoid a tree or two, but it could also land you in thick scrub, among angled rocks, or tottering on a bank. Imagine bearing weight at the same time.

"How much does he weigh?" My friend Steve Smith, a veteran with PVSART, smiled as he echoed a rescuer's first question. "One day we'd been called up on to Jefferson," he recalled, "where a guy had broken his leg, and we were looking at a carry down the Caps Ridge. There are sections of rock on the Caps where you want to use your hands but, of course, a litter makes that impossible. Plus, this guy weighed around 225 pounds, and, already, when we'd carried him a couple of hundred yards to a trail junction, my arm was toast. I was praying we'd be able to find the DHART helicopter a landing zone, because I didn't know how we were going to get down the Caps. When the copter landed, we all cheered."

So weight matters too, over the short or long haul. SAR crews aim to have eighteen or more carriers so they can rotate teams as needed, though, as you may imagine, getting eighteen or more rescuers to a remote spot in a hurry can also be a problem. Add in steep terrain, where litters must sometimes be secured by ropes and lowered; add in stream crossings; add in seasonal ice underfoot; add in the difficulty of balancing when you are being tugged one way or another by the landings of ten other feet. That's real work. Now, back to Adams.

There, high on the mountain, they were, Doug and his AVSAR cohort. They succeeded in packaging the guy in the litter and set out down the Airline Trail, then over to the Valley Way, going down over 4,000 vertical feet on terrain that's rough in the trail's center and worse to the side. The carryout was exhausting, and the parking lot never looked so level or welcome. Then—what's this? As they unstrapped the injured hiker, who had complained of being jostled all the way down, he rose, stood on both feet, tested the "injured" foot a little, took a step, and announced, "I'm okay now. I think I'll drive back to my motel. Thanks for the lift."

"We had to restrain a couple of the guys, who really did want to injure him," recalled Doug. "That was, to be fair, unusual, but some sort of disregard for the difficulty of rescue in the mountains isn't all that unusual."

≻ The writer Nick Howe and many others point to 1994 as annus horribilis in White Mountain search and rescue. In *Not without Peril*, he chronicles four winter-spawned incidents of the kind that take lives and drain rescuers. Two of them were born of a disregard that put rescuers at extreme risk, and one also served notice that lawyers would be watching the action on the heights to see if those in charge of these state and federal lands were "ensuring" everyone's safety. Even the phrase "ensuring safety" is enough to make any backcountry advocate quail.

Safety must have been far from Jeremy Haas's mind when he led his friend and fellow University of New Hampshire student Derek Tinkham up the side of Mount Madison and then over Adams on a very cold January day. The pair's goal was the iconic Presidential Traverse, with a stopover planned in Clay Col for the night. As Howe tells it, Haas's system coursed with the juice of heroic journey.

Much of the action in Western culture's ur-tale for such a journey, the *Odyssey*, turns on the ancient Greek ideal of *kleos*, which translates as "what others say about you." Life in the worlds of the *Odyssey* and *Iliad* was often short and violent, and death offered only the noncorporeal yearnings of being a "shade," a sort of ghost who could only recall life or be reminded of it by fellow shades. So no paradise or afterlife would be there for either. How then to live, and, perhaps, live on? *Kleos* suggested doing so in others' eyes and stories; your afterlife lay in the narratives and songs people sung about you. That, of course, meant you had to do something worthy of song. Like go and conquer Troy and then survive a ten-year passage home full of monsters and sirens. Jeremy Haas had a hankering, as do many young men, to be sung about. And the mountains were the place where he wanted those songs to be realized. He'd begin in the Whites, but he had higher peaks in mind.

Derek Tinkham was a quieter sort, given to following and in some thrall to his friend's self-singing. The traverse seemed like a good thing to do for the weekend. The weather that day on aimed-for Washington surely provided heroic backdrop for the pair's climb. The temperature was −27°F, and the winds were in the—for this mountain—humdrum forties; worse was slated to blow in. On the south side of Adams, Tinkham began to falter. He was growing cold and slowing, signs that hypothermia was infiltrating his body. Haas, impatient to move along in his narrative, would go out front and then wait for Tinkham; they made their halting way to Edmands Col.

As Howe and others have pointed out, here the pair had an irrevocable decision to make. To their north lay three nearby Randolph Mountain Club shelters, the Perch, Gray Knob, and Crag Camp. The latter two have weatherproofed walls, complete shelter from wind, and Gray Knob also has a caretaker and a stove. Haas and Tinkham carried only bivy sacks for their sleeping bags, and Haas was aiming for an ice cave in Clay Col that he'd noticed two years earlier. Tinkham's fatigue and the deepening cold and now-thick wind—it was nearing −40°F with winds still near forty—argued for a shelter, Gray Knob especially. Getting there over two exposed miles into the wind would be hard work, but it was probably doable. Haas argued for going on. Later, he would say that Tinkham agreed, but that persuaded few who looked closely at the incident. Rescuers pointed to Haas as the decision maker. Tinkham couldn't confirm or deny. He was dead.

Jefferson rises nearly 1,000 feet above Edmands Col, and the pair climbed into the dusk. Near the top, Tinkham couldn't continue and, after trying to get his friend into the shelter of sleeping bag and bivy sack, Haas left, staggering along the ridge toward Washington in winds now reaching eighty miles an hour. Shorn of use of his hands by the cold (he was wearing gloves and had left his heavy mittens at home), Haas stuffed his hands in his armpits and, miraculously, covered nearly three miles, pounding finally on the Mount Washington Observatory's windows and being finally heard and let in to the rest of his life. Asked later by the press if he had any regrets, Haas said he was sorry he had left his mittens behind.

All of that is bad enough, but what this incident put rescuers through gets told and retold by those who were called to it. Their stories underline the risks they endure, even under the protective memory of Albert Dow, and the ways in which rescue work can tug at a person's psyche.

Jeremy Haas's 8:00 p.m. arrival at the observatory and the ragged outline of his story triggered the gathering of a rescue attempt for Derek Tinkham, even as those who made this attempt considered it the longest of shots. Two volunteer groups got the call, the technical crew from Mountain Rescue Service and the nearby Androscoggin Valley Search and Rescue (AVSAR). Quickly, rescuers agreed that going up in such desperate weather at night

The Randolph Mountain Club's Gray Knob shelter. Staffed by a caretaker, this shelter features prominently in SAR work and safety in the northern Presidentials, especially in winter. Photo by Carl Herz.

was out of the question. They knew only that Tinkham was somewhere above tree line on Jefferson, and finding him in the howling darkness would be nigh impossible. What was certain was that rescuers would be at extreme risk in such conditions; they would wait for morning's first light.

> That decision, while a difficult one, was straightforward for those in the valley. As Bill Arnold of AVSAR recalled, "We just weren't going up into those conditions at night." But for one potential rescuer the crawl of those night hours was excruciating. Paul Neubauer was in his first of two winters working as winter caretaker at Gray Knob shelter, and that placed him a mere—albeit dark, wind-and-cold-blasted—two-plus miles away from where Tinkham lay. While the weather's reality made that distance as good as transcontinental, in the windless interior of the cabin, Neubauer ago-

nized. Yes, he could hear the storm outside and, even after a few months as a caretaker, he had the mountain savvy to know what he was hearing. But he also had recurring visions of how quickly he had reached Jefferson any number of times. He was so close. How could he not try?

Neubauer was in radio contact with Arnold at the Arnolds' home on Randolph Hill. As the night deepened, Arnold recalled that a pattern of calls set up. Every so often, Arnold's radio would squawk to life, and Arnold recalled a sequence that went roughly like this: Gray Knob to Base. Base to Gray Knob; come in. Bill, this is Paul. I think I can get to this guy. I want to try. Paul, there's no way; it's too tough out. I won't let you go; you can't go. Please, Bill. I'm his only hope. No, Paul. You're not to go out. You can't go.

Arnold said, "This went on through the night. I had to keep talking Paul down from going out, which would have put him at extreme risk. But I also sympathized. He *was* so close."

> Neubauer remembers a hard night, too, though the repeated call sequence is missing from that memory.

Morning brought a galaxy of A-team rescuers to the Caps Ridge trailhead at 5:00 a.m. MRS has some of New England's finest mountaineers, climbers who have tried and succeeded on the world's most challenging peaks, including Alaska's Denali, considered by many the coldest major mountain in the world. Still, what ensued as they worked to find and then retrieve Derek Tinkham matched or exceeded what they'd encountered elsewhere.

Rick Wilcox, Everest summiteer, worldwide mountain presence, and a local climber who helped found MRS and has led it since 1976, recalled what he heard during this rescue turned recovery:

When we went on the Tinkham and Haas mission, it was the first time I've ever seen frozen eyeballs. One of our members crossed the line of safety, and that's a very serious thing. You've got your goggles—we all carry two or three pairs of goggles, especially clear ones for night for high winds. . . . Your goggles fog up and you can't see anything. You've also got ground blizzards. And so you take your goggles off and put on another pair and that one fogs. Pretty soon you have a choice—you either take them off, or you won't see. But you take them off, and then you go blind because your eyes freeze. . . ."

Not quite a whiteout, but close. A hiker steps up into snow blown
by seventy-mile-per-hour winds. Photo by Carl Herz.

The nearby Mount Washington Observatory reported winds of eighty
miles per hour, with gusts to one hundred and a temperature of −32°F.

> Barbara Arnold related a radio conversation with rescuer Mike Pelchat, a
mountain presence so experienced and ubiquitous that, as I researched this
book, I began to think of him as Mr. Everywhere—there seemed no slope or
storm that could keep Pelchat from helping a marooned or injured climber.
That morning, Pelchat and other rescuers had reached Tinkham's body on
Jefferson's cone. "So I'm on the radio with Mike, and I hear something I've
never heard before," said Barbara. "Mike's saying, 'We're in trouble. We got
a guy with his eyes frozen shut, and I don't know if we can deal with this.'
What really got me," she said, "was that I'm talking with Mike Pelchat . . .
Mike Pelchat . . . and he sounds terrified."

Such moments are indelible. Both Arnolds grew more animated as they
remembered back into that night. It has stayed with Paul Neubauer too.
During a 2016 interview, he read me an entry from his journal, kept that
winter and written during and right after the incident:

What I've always dreaded has finally happened. Bill called me on the radio. A party of two got split up near Jefferson summit; one made it to Washington Observatory very frostbitten; the other lies in a bivy. In bad shape when his partner left, his only hope now is to make it 'til morning. I'll be leaving at 6:00 a.m. Who knows what I'll find. It's −35 degrees and 70 mile-an-hour winds on Washington; I'm scared.

This morning I and two of the most prepared guests, Paul and George, got up at 5:00 a.m. via Bill Arnold's radio call, preparing for a go-ahead from New Hampshire Fish and Game to go look for the victim. Temperature at Gray Knob, −36 degrees, winds blowing hard. Fish and Game tells us via radio to stay put, because people are going up Caps Ridge on Jefferson and will be much less exposed. The Obs [Mount Washington Observatory] recorded record temps for that date, −41.9, peak gust from west 103 miles per hour. Forecast for today, high −20s, winds 70 to 90.

The search party finds the victim near Monticello Lawn. Although I know nothing about the trip logistics, rescuers seem to think he didn't live very late into the night. He was perhaps two hours away from here, maybe two and a half with the weather. With the wind chill of −100 or more, his odds of rescue were minimal. Nobody knew of trouble until at least two and a half hours after the victim stopped hiking. That was the time it took his pal to make it, miraculously, to the observatory. Add three hours to that, and that would be a minimum of six hours 'til our arrival. Then four more, probably six hours, to get him out. All those are optimistic time estimates. I guess it boils down to the question of how much risk rescuers should take. I will wonder about their logistics, their parting words, their thoughts for a long time. Is that morbid? One of last night's guests used the word "humility" to describe his feelings. I didn't swing by Perch last night [The Randolph Mountain Club has three shelters in this area, Gray Knob, Crag Camp, and The Perch, and the Gray Knob caretaker is responsible for all three, paying daily visits to Crag Camp and The Perch]. Would I have crossed paths with them? I'll find out. I don't know why, because I know how risky it would have been, but I can't help it—Could I have saved him had I left? Bill told me not to; I'm sure he was right. But I know what Bill's itinerary was—had the wind been calm I would have been dispatched; it would have been me who found him.

Last night, they sounded rightly pessimistic, and I went to bed and awoke thinking of what could have been. A break in the wind, and I would have been the first person on the scene. Already I will see and feel the dark, the snow, the wind and Jefferson in different ways; "remorse" is a fair word, "humility," however, fits much better.

"And that's what I have," Paul said, and we let a little silence fill the phone space between us. Even these years later, his quiet, hard words offered sympathetic warmth in contrast to the winds howling outside. It was also clear that the night's effect had dimmed little over time.

THE OTHER SIDE

————

The Case for Doing Nothing

Guy Waterman, that winter's other caretaker at Gray Knob, was on his week off when Haas and Tinkham reached Tinkham's endpoint on Jefferson. But even from his home in Vermont, Waterman's spirit and close considerations of who we are in the mountains colored the aftermath of the incident.

Though he was a White Mountain legend, whose familiarity with their terrain exceeded others' and sometimes even imagination's scope, Guy Waterman was not much of a searcher for or rescuer of people. A deep believer in self-sufficiency, of both getting into and out of life's territories on one's own, Waterman had arrived at his winter caretaking duties along a singular route. Well, not singular in life—Guy's partner and frequent companion on all manner of trails was his wife, Laura, with whom he had composed a life off all sorts of grids in Corinth, Vermont. There, on acreage a mile from the nearest road, they had fashioned a home and an independent life on roughly thirty acres of land, where they tilled soil, tapped trees, and wrote prolifically on New England's mountains and the ethics of living in and visiting them.

One of Waterman's prominent characteristics was an insistence on control. Whether it was a line of words or a line of march, he liked to take each step with assurance that he was ready to do so. But that did not mean he hung back from challenge or risk. As both a climber and a wanderer, Guy Waterman went where and when few others dared venture. Rather, it meant that whatever he set his mind and body to, Waterman did fully, and, whatever he got himself into, he expected to get himself out of. So as you may suppose, he tended away from sympathy for people who got themselves in over their heads, or without much use of those heads, in the wild lands he threaded so often.

Jeremy Haas and Derek Tinkham would not, then, meet with much sympathy in Waterman's world. Yet as AVSAR veteran Bill Arnold recalled that incident, he remembered that it had moved Waterman. "Guy wasn't a great believer in rescues," Arnold recalled. "But after Tinkham died and Paul's week at Gray Knob was up, Guy climbed up to Jefferson to retrieve the gear rescuers had had to leave behind as they fought to bring Tinkham's body down in that gale. And that led to contact with the family and their grief, when he took the gear to them in the valley. All of that shifted Guy a little farther along the spectrum toward a rescuer's point of view." The deep personal toll and grip of a story of mountain loss can unsettle even the most closely held principles.

Still, Waterman and others of his ilk tend to hang out on the rescue-lite end of that spectrum, and their case was made persuasively (and, perhaps, extremely) by the veteran mountaineer Robert Kruszyna in a provocatively titled essay from the mid-1990s called "Let 'Em Die." (Full disclosure: I edited and titled this essay, drawing the title from the author's opinion as expressed in the piece, while serving as editor of *Appalachia*, though the beliefs contained in the piece were, most assuredly, Mr. Kruszyna's.)

Kruszyna was no novice wanderer offering opinion from a newspaper office or the heated interior of some diner. Winner of the Canadian Alpine Club's top honor, the Silver Rope, he offered an essay that reads like a libertarian tract that supports individualism, choice, and self-sufficiency. But it looks most intently at wilderness search and rescue, and there it makes an essential point: "In our society we have decided somewhat arrogantly and self-righteously, it seems to me, that we should be our brother's keeper. And we have assigned government to the task. But the moral obligation of watching out for our brother ends at that point when he knowingly and willingly places himself in the way of danger."

From Kruszyna's point of view, stepping into "the way of danger" happens whenever and wherever we step between two trees and head off into the woods and the mountains. In his essay, Kruszyna cited the search for Hugh Herr and Jeff Batzer that led to rescuer Albert Dow's death and argued that the search shouldn't have happened. He viewed altruism as a need for attention (personal or organizational), rather than in the commonly voiced brother- or sisterhood of "it could be me out there." In perhaps his most persuasive point, he argued that knowing there are rescuers ready to come get you leads to greater risk-taking. In the background of every decision a climber or wanderer makes "out there," he said, lies the promise of someone else's help. It's only a small leap of imagination and logic to envision all the cell phones and "spot" devices lodged now in packs as people head up in to the mountains and wonder how much their courting of risk will be affected by those devices.

Near essay's end, Kruszyna wrote this summary:

Unlike many of the issues we confront, search and rescue poses no real philosophic or ethical dilemmas. It is a simple matter of free choice and responsibility. The prospect of a guaranteed search and rescue robs climbing of its sense of adventure, which is probably the only meaningful justification for an otherwise useless activity. Risk is an intrinsic part of that sense of adventure. Those who seek out the wild country must accept it and its consequences. If one's desideratum is complete security, then one should get one's thrills by watching them climb El Capitan on TV from the safety of an armchair. When I go into the mountains, I avoid notifying anyone of my intended whereabouts or my timetable so that by the time anyone should discover I am missing, it would already be too late to launch a search. No "thrills without chills." Nix on the fix. . . .

Therefore I offer the least expensive, the least complicated, the least regimented, and the most moral solution to the problem of what to do about people in trouble in the mountains: DO NOTHING! Abandon all contingency plans. Disband all mountain rescue groups. At every trailhead, erect a sign bearing the inscription Dante found over the gate of Hell: "Abandon all hope, ye who enter here." For if it is immoral for the climber to exercise his freedom at the expense of placing a burden on others, it is equally immoral for society to seduce him into exactly that position by promising him rescue, no matter what. (*Appalachia* [December 1995]: 53–54)

It's hard to find fault with the logic of Kruszyna's essay. Human behavior provides ample example to support it, and Kruszyna lives his creed. He told an amusing story of being in the Canadian Rockies, where a $25 fine awaited anyone who did not register and leave a sketch of a trip plan before heading out into the wild. Kruszyna buttonholed a warden and asked if he could get it over with and pay the fine in advance; the warden (standing in for society) was not amused.

Such self-sufficiency (twinned with deep competence) at first braces me, firms up resolve to go and do likewise. But upon further reflection, I also feel a hollow space where compassion and relationship live, the place where people overlap, where, in all their messiness, people coexist. Extreme self-sufficiency and individualism seem, finally, lonely. Given the ease with which we bumble in all areas, given the universal truth that we are all strugglers, such standards seem unapproachable. Still, every time I reread Kruszyna's thoughts, especially in the aftermath of considering a moment of breath-taking backcountry folly or careless disregard, I wonder if I should set up camp a little farther along the continuum, a little closer to Robert Kruszyna's neighborhood.

Jeremy Haas, who may have been cold-addled as he made his final bad decision of the day and led Derek Tinkham up Jefferson's cone, may have made his fateful series of errors under the needy prod of ambition. And the rescuers who tried to reach Tinkham came whisper close to multiplying that tragedy with their own. Had Kruszyna been sitting at the other end of the phone, instead of Arnold and Wilcox, perhaps no one would have stirred from safety until the storm had blown away. How might *you* have answered the call?

16

COMMAND

A Meditation on Being in Charge
of Rescue (and of Self)

Brad Ray likes to tell a story from the mid-1960s. In it, Ray, a newly fledged
USFS snow ranger, was attending a winter training of mountain personnel
at the USFS camp in Tuckerman Ravine. The subject was response to emergency, and around fifty other people were there from various groups that
would offer such response—USFS, NHFG, AMC, and MWVSP among them.
Everyone agreed that staying calm was of utmost importance, nodding in
that way that overtakes us when we are being "trained" in something that
seems a no-brainer.

"What we didn't know," said Ray, "was that there was a plant in the training. There we were sitting around agreeing with each other when, suddenly,
a woman came running into the room. 'My boyfriend's been buried in an
avalanche up in the ravine,' she said. And the room went crazy. People were
running everywhere, picking up packs, dropping stuff. No one knew where
he was going, but everyone was running. It was chaos."

Ray sits back, squints a little in the autumn sunlight as he returns from the
memory. Ray, his wife, Rebecca Oreskes (also a longtime USFS employee),
and I are sitting at a table in the early fall sun at their farm in Milan, New
Hampshire, and there's just enough breeze to add a little edge to the air, to
remind us all that cold is coming—and, with it, winter. Which would be
Brad Ray's season. For forty-four years, from 1958 to 2002, Ray worked as a
USFS snow ranger in Tuckerman Ravine, and over that time he developed a
reputation as an authority on snow and human behavior.

"It turned out that no one was buried. When we learned that, we all looked
at each other, a bit embarrassed. No one had stayed calm," Ray said.

A—perhaps *the*—classic shot of Tuckerman Ravine, taken during the 1937 Franklin Edson Memorial ski race. Note the avalanche tracks across the headwall. Photo by Harold Orne, courtesy of AMC archives.

> A conversation a few months earlier with USFS snow ranger Chris Joosen had prompted my question about command for Ray. Joosen, on his way to a new USFS posting in Orgeon after twenty-six years as a snow ranger in Tuckerman, had related a similar story about how he had learned to show authority and be in command in that ravine. During his time there, Joosen became known in SAR circles for his masterful handling of incidents in which he assumed leadership. As the MRS veteran Alain Comeau said, "He knew where everyone was at all times; he knew where to send us so we didn't get in one another's ways. He was *good*." But early in Joosen's tenure, someone had come running down from the ravine saying, "My friend's broken a leg. I need help," and this person had been no plant. Joosen had run off to find

Ray and learn what they should do. "I went running into the room where Brad and his partner Rennie were sitting, and said, 'There's an emergency up in the ravine.' Before I could go on, Brad said, 'Chris, don't run.' And then he made me sit and give him what I knew. I've never forgotten that. It's at the heart of any good response."

When we run, Joosen explained, everyone sees it. It affects them; panic spreads. We don't seem in command of ourselves, so how can we exercise command of anyone or anything else. As Ray knew and Joosen learned, the external show of command must be matched by an internal poise. Just when the juice of adrenaline is loosed in our systems, we must maintain a calm that allows us a clear, rational response. That calm lets us gather full information from any messenger and then fashion a response. Even as the bundled energy of avalanche roars down a slope, whoever is in charge of offering hope to anyone buried in its slough at the bottom, must find the quiet clarity of reason and assert it. Clearly, command must be learned and practiced. Ray knew this; so, too, did Joosen.

The following incidents offer an unusual, extended look at two Mount Washington emergencies and the way they were handled. It is unusual because it allows us to see some of an exchange between one of those rescued and a lead rescuer, Chris Joosen. The exchange, in the aftermath of the incident, is testament to the high level of poise and self-control that safety and rescue in the mountains demand.

During the winter of 2015–16, sparse snow and recurrent rains made for a slippery winter and spring in the high Whites. While most of us were scuffing leaves in the lowlands, climbers and skiers were contending with rock-pocked ice and hard snow. That was especially true in the spring on the people magnet, Mount Washington. Two incidents, both occurring on March 13, showed how difficult it could be to make decisions about getting down such surfaces.

On that day, the expert backcountry skier and filmmaker Jon M. and his friend, Arthur W., arrived at Mount Washington for some end-of-season skiing and filming. They took a couple of pleasurable runs in the Gulf of Slides and then decided to cross over for a day-ending run on Hillman's Highway. That plan entailed climbing the lofty Boott Spur Ridge to reach the top of the "Highway" that drops some 2,000 feet down into Tuckerman

Ravine. Early sunshine had softened the hard snow that day, but by the time Jon M. and five others in a makeshift group gathered atop Hillman's, afternoon shadows had crept onto a portion of the 2,000-foot drop. The six experienced skiers discussed the route at some length, deciding finally that it could be skied, even as they knew parts of its surface would have iced over in the afternoon shade.

While this discussion took place, three climbers emerged from the gully, one on crampons, the other two on snowshoes with claws on the bottom. The climbers' appearance helped the skiers decide in favor of skiing the gully, though later, one of the skiing party recalled that the frightened looks on the climbers' faces should have given them pause. Though the three had made the climb, part way up it two things had become clear: first, that they were in danger if they fell on the ice; second, that they couldn't retreat. They could only go up. So many mountain incidents turn on how much easier it is to go up than it is to come down. Our feet and the equipment we wear on those feet are designed for ascent. In fact, the three climbers would later necessitate the day's second rescue.

The second skier to descend at a little after 3:00 p.m., Jon M., fell near the top of the route. On the slick surface, he couldn't arrest his fall, which took him over a battering of rocks and ice nearly to the bottom of the chute. When his companions reached Jon, it was clear he had serious injuries. They secured him so he wouldn't slide any farther and went for help, which, luckily, was only a quarter-mile away at the U.S. Forest Service's Hermit Lake station.

USFS snow rangers and Mount Washington Volunteer Ski Patrol rescuers reached and assessed Jon thirty minutes later, stabilized him as best they could, supplied oxygen and, deeming his injuries life-threatening, called for a Dartmouth-Hitchcock Advanced Rescue Team (DHART) helicopter. The helicopter arrived just after 5:00 p.m. and airlifted Jon to the Dartmouth-Hitchcock hospital with a speed that likely saved his life.

At 5:16 p.m. the Gorham Police received a distress call from the three hikers, who said they were near the summit of Washington, where one of them had lost control of a glissade and had a broken femur. At 5:45 p.m. a USFS snow ranger and the AMC's Hermit Lake caretaker left to help, climbing quickly up the Lion Head summer trail to near the Alpine Garden junction, where they found the trio. After assessing the hiker's injury and conferring for a bit, they again summoned the DHART helicopter, and, it arrived a little after 7:00 p.m. But the rough terrain and absence of a litter had made it impossible to get the injured hiker to a landing zone, so the helicopter (adhering to flight regulations) had to leave at 7:40 p.m. without him. While DHART helicopters are well placed to respond to White Mountain incidents, their primary work of transporting hospital patients means they do not have winches and lifts that allow them to raise a victim or rescuer by a line. So they must be able to land to take someone on board. Rough mountain terrain can make such landing a challenge.

More rescuers arrived with a litter to carry the injured hiker, and after further consultation, another helicopter was dispatched; it touched down at 9:14 p.m., just after rescuers had reached the landing zone with the injured hiker. At 9:26 p.m. the helicopter flew off to Dartmouth-Hitchcock hospital.

Of particular note during both air rescues was the weather: March 13 was clear and calm. But it takes only passing acquaintance with White Mountain weather to realize that many winter days wouldn't let a helicopter in, in which case both rescues would have needed to be people-intensive hand-carries, with the possibility of very different results.

These two incidents are joined both by date and by their out-of-control slides. That they happened to parties on two ends of the experience spectrum adds to their value as illustrations. Jon M., the skier who fell on Hillman's, was an expert, while the hikers who intersected briefly with the skiers showed themselves as novices.

Spring skiing and climbing can be wildly various on the steep, east-facing slopes of Mount Washington. Both the angle of the slopes and the rising angle of the March sun can heat surfaces to create the happiness of corn snow, sometimes softening the snow so that even a fall in steep terrain doesn't send the skier or climber sliding away. Such snow forgives risk and so encourages it. It can grow so hot in the sun as to make people climb in their scantiest clothing. Then, as the sun shifts west and shadows slide across facets of the ravine, the snow can cool and harden quickly, becoming a surface that only the sharpest edges or spikes can hold on to. At that point, the margin of safety thins to the barest edge.

Jon M. and Arthur W. had found corn snow during their time in the

Gulf of Slides, so they had climbed over to Hillman's hoping for a last run. From the top, with some reconnaissance, they knew the corn was gone and hard surface had taken over. Still, they thought their skill could manage that surface. So their attempt was a calculated one, similar to those many with experience make in the mountains. The hard nature of the route during this thin winter (exposed rocks and ice where normally there would be snow cover) made their decision riskier. In retrospect, that and the example of the three frightened hikers should have tipped them away from skiing and toward walking down on crampons.

Jon M.'s fall was recorded by a GoPro camera, and the video, posted online, offers an inside look at the genesis of a fall (www.tetongravity.com /story/ski/falling-down-mt.-washingtons-hillmans-highway-terrifying).

In addition to this unusual visual record of the slide, the Mount Washington Avalanche Center's website published a written exchange between the fallen and a rescuer that offered a rare glimpse into the mind-changing effects of near tragedy. Jon M. authorized publication of the thoughts he had shared with USFS snow ranger, Chris Joosen, a month after his accident, as he emerged from a long recovery in the hospital.

The exchange began with a note of thanks from Jon M. Within that note were passages that pointed to his reflections in the aftermath of his fall "from the point of view of a survivor": "During my time in the hospital I had a lot of time to think about risk, consequence, and the importance of making sound decisions on the hill—and also how lucky I am to be part of a back-country ski community that looks after its own and is ready and willing to jump in and help when things go wrong." Those reflections encouraged Joosen to write back reflectively. Within a long letter, he offered this summary of what he had seen during his twenty-six years in the ravine: "My attitude toward risk has been developed by many incidents I have seen on the mountain. I have seen the aftermath and outcomes to hundreds of decisions people have made in pursuit of their passions. Each one had its own unique circumstances, and the only commonality is how different they are from one another when you get deep into the details."

Later in his letter Joosen thought about how current behaviors varied from those of the past:

As I'm sure you've seen before, the mountain conditions can change so very fast. As Helon mentioned today in the advisory—as the shadow line creeps along, it flash freezes the snowpack and changes the corn of spring day into instant hell. I witnessed this occur to several groups of people yesterday. As they basked in the sun on the ridge eating, drinking, and laughing, their run fell completely into the shade. Their run went from low-risk, glorious corn snow to high-risk, no-fall skiing. Timing and experience. . . .

I also watched three very good skiers aggressively attack a run through an icefall and deep holes while one filmed from the side. I often think, "would they do that if alone in the Great Gulf with no camera rolling?" I doubt it. What we used to call "Kodak courage" is an increasing problem across the world as technology makes it possible to get some incredibly cool results on film.

Joosen followed his observations with an invitation to Jon M. to write more about his experience. Jon M. responded with a long letter. In its midsection he wrote about a central takeaway:

What has stuck with me the most since the accident are two things: the errors in judgment that my group made that led us to actively decide to ski a run that held so much potential for disaster, and our unwillingness to speak up about nagging doubts we had while preparing to drop in. While mulling over mistakes is normal behavior for anyone who has survived a traumatic event, it has deeply affected me because, prior to March 13, I had prided myself on being an overly cautious and responsible member of the backcountry community, who always went to great lengths to discuss risks throughout the day with my companions.

In Jon M.'s reflections we find a central consideration about individual decision making in risky situations. Commonly, we often repeat the wisdom of tackling tough terrain in groups. Those groups provide us with backup help and, theory goes, with more minds to consider risk. What is less discussed is Jon M.'s insight into the ways that groups can also shut down discussion, can create an atmosphere where hesitancy seems a weakness. Jon M.'s candid reflection is worth reading in full, and, as of March 2017, the whole exchange was still available on the MWAC site. But even if it should be unavailable, this brief summary brings us deeper into both a rescuer's and accident victim's thoughts and the mutual respect that often develops between them. Near the end of his letter, Jon M. wrote what serves as a fine takeaway from this incident: "Simply put, we were experienced enough to know better, and yet we still fell prey to all of the pitfalls that you can read about in other accident reports: group dynamics in making tough decisions; a lack of a complete understanding of the state of the [skiing] line at the time; committing to the run in the face of evidence that was telling us otherwise; and the fact that a number of our group chose to swallow our concerns instead of voicing them before we started."

Such a measured, in-depth exchange and subsequent reflection, unusual in the realm of social media, or elsewhere, may be seen as an ideal. The fullness and lucidity of both men's thoughts also point out how deep reasoning and self-awareness—born of experience—must be if we are to manage risk.

The Day's Other Incident

We return from website to mountain, where in the waning of March 13, 2016, the second DHART helicopter has carried the injured hiker to the hospital. Here is an incident featuring people from the more common end of the rescue spectrum. The hikers atop Washington had made a pupu platter of errors: they were up high too late; they were underequipped; they opted for the shortcut of a speedy type of descent when tired. On the hardening snow of late afternoon, they decided to glissade from the summit, and one of them lost control, precipitating his accident. Perhaps their having made it up Hillman's had inflated their confidence. "If we can do that, we can surely handle the lower angles on the cone," they might have reasoned. But once the climber's slide went out of control, he was subject to the same battering from ice and rock that hurt Jon M. As the snow rangers pointed out in a written analysis on their website, the threesome had already climbed beyond safety when they topped Hillman's. At that point, any way down the mountain (save the auto road) was beyond the equipment they carried. Only one had crampons, and even the clawed, modern snowshoes are unreliable when turned to steep descent; they are not meant for steep ice in either direction. Had they not run into trouble on the mountain's cone, it's likely they'd have found it lower down. We are, in many ways, built to climb into trouble and poorly designed to climb down from it.

Following both incidents, the snow rangers offered a final point for contemplation: rescuers arrived to find that neither group had been able to stabilize the injuries of the fallen because they lacked medical training. Had not emergency medical help been nearby (only a quarter mile away for the seriously injured Jon M.), the results would likely have been different. Whether people who find their adventures in the back- and high-country should get medical training before doing so is an active question for search and rescue professionals and volunteers, who almost always arrive at an accident bearing some sort of wilderness medical training and certification.

Ongoing Command

On December 1, 2016, Snow Ranger Frank Carus drove to Pinkham Notch for a pair of meetings. The first, held in AMC's Woodchuck Lodge, was usual business, the monthly meeting of the Whites' SAR Working Group, a mix of professionals and volunteers, each representing one of the organizations that, stitched together, form those mountains' quilt of rescue. Carus was there as the U.S. Forest Service's rep, and he offered a few calm, clear thoughts about the utility of a Sked, a light and malleable litter that can ease some of the torturous work of carrying/sledding an injured climber or skier through a boulder field at the base of a ravine. His voice was resonant of another snow ranger.

That resonance came clear a few hours later, when I listened to Carus talk with a group of AMC employees about the upcoming season in the Cutler River drainage, which features Tuckerman and Huntington Ravines. "If you take a call asking for help, get as much specific information as you can, make notes, and then, sit down for a minute. Don't rush," Carus said. I paused in my listening and note making. There, in clear echo, were Brad Ray's and Chris Joosen's voices—"Don't run"—and a quick spate of rescue stories that begin, invariably, with the most important command, that of self.

The moment, I thought further, was apt linkage, because December 1, 2016 (which could be called Turnover Day), marked the opening day of Frank

Carus's winter as acting lead snow ranger. He was stepping into the space left when Joosen shifted his USFS work to Oregon in the summer of 2016. If Carus felt some anxiety flapping in his stomach as SAR and much other responsibility in this active slice of the Whites passed to him, he didn't show it. Throughout the ninety-minute meeting, he was clear and unhurried, answering questions fully, and returning in various phrasings to the need for poise and clarity when someone else's emergency calls your name. And yes, Carus was sitting down.

17

THE LAW GOES UP TOO

Columbus Day weekend, any year. For New Hampshire Fish and Game's forty conservation officers in the agency's Law Enforcement Division much of the script for this weekend is clear well before the actual days arrive, especially if the weather looks promising too. Even as summer flees south, a reverse tide of tourists flows north—to see the colored leaves; to catch the late sparkle of brooks; to climb into air that has thinned to transparency. Many are content to cruise the roads and pull over on their margins, but a foot-happy subset wants some holiday trail time before the cold season makes its demands, which many prefer not to meet. On this weekend, the White Mountains, a few perhaps by now white topped, gather their share and more of this influx. Soon, NHFG's conservation officers know, their ringtones will make urgent music. "Help, I need somebody . . . help," they might as well begin singing along like Beatles. Up they go, and the volunteers they summon will go after them.

A casual scan of New Hampshire's North Country news might suggest that conducting search and rescue missions is one of the primary, if not *the* primary, tasks for NHFG's conservation officers. The missing make headlines, and headlines are a type of demand—find them, help them, rescue them, society says. But as COs point out in conversation, being the enforcement wing of a Fish and Game agency aims them primarily at other duties, especially those activities licensed or monitored by the agency: fishing, hunting, and riding backcountry machines. The first two responsibilities are nearly archetypal, stretching back to NHFG's founding in 1865, and they are captured nicely by the admiring and sometimes mock-adversarial relationship between Joe Dodge and Paul Doherty back in the 1950s. The third, which takes place year-round on the outsized wheels of off-highway recreational vehicles (OHRV's) and in winter on the oblong tracks of snowmobiles, keeps COs on the go in the backcountry from dawn to dusk, and beyond. If there is a growth industry in enforcement and getting into predicaments, riding machines in the woods is it, especially as old mill towns like Berlin reinvent themselves as OHRV and snow-machine destinations. Even as I write, Maine's *Portland Press Herald* is running a story about how the former (and now depressed) mill town, Millinocket, has turned its eyes toward Berlin as a model for possible reinvention.

Just north of Berlin, on the edge of the Kilkenny Wilderness, lies Jericho State Park, now a hub for OHRV use that advertises seventy-five miles of trail, connecting to another thousand miles beyond. In early August each year, nearby Gorham and Berlin are mobbed with some 6,000 expected OHRVers in town (and woods) for the Jericho ATV Festival. You can drive into either town, show your license, plunk down your cash, and drive away for the day on your rented OHRV. People do so each day. So search and rescue of upland foot wanderers is an add-on, an extra duty that can stretch a conservation officer's workday into the night.

As noted earlier, in the days of Dodge and Doherty, search and rescue work fell to whoever was around—usually Dodge or Doherty—and those they could muster. But the old makeshift wasn't built to cope with today's crowds of hill-and-thrill-seekers, so a new makeshift, directed by NHFG's conservation officers, has evolved to cope with those crowds.

Imagine, on a recent Columbus Day weekend (all of the incidents described here happened on this weekend in recent years) that you are Lt. Wayne Saunders, or Sgt. Mark Ober, or Glen Lucas, or Chris Egan. They are all COs in NH District 1, which sprawls down over the northern White Mountains and farther north before bumping up against Districts 2 and 3, which include the central and southern Whites and their foothills. Perhaps, as Saturday dawns crystalline, you have an early second cup of coffee to gird for the day. Gorham and Berlin are thick with OHRVs growling alongside leaf-peeper cars and, headed for trailheads, their drivers are also amped up on coffee. You hope that's all the amping they've done. In hundreds of boxy motel rooms, hikers sort through all the gear they remembered, including, you hope, headlamps, before thronging the various trailheads. The whole day has the feel of expansive outrush—"Oh," everyone says, "let's go!"

Your morning proceeds with routine calm. You cruise slowly along OHRV tracks at Jericho Mountain, your machine purring beneath you. As you encounter riders, you check registrations, offer orientation about where they are, recommend a few trails, and hope that the adrenaline of being the pilot of your own starship, or perhaps racing the other Millennium Falcons nearby, seeps out only in manageable doses. You hope, too, that the slower tourists who have set out up the Valley Way to Mount Madison or through Tuckerman Ravine to Mount Washington's summit, have read the weather report and gotten an early start. A storm may not be in the offing, but you know that, up high, a different season has already arrived, and you hope those going there have the layers to be its wandering bears.

The first call comes in a bit before noon. It, too, is routine: not far away (a blessing) an OHRV has hit a lump in the trail at a little too much speed and has rolled. The driver is reported to be "shaken, but okay," but you need to investigate and later report on this crash and its cause, so off you go. No injuries at the scene, and, while the machine is dinged, the rider can still get it back to the trailhead, where he will try to repair his day.

You move on, checking, advising, orienting. An ease takes over, carrying a faint but burgeoning hope—perhaps today will simply go this way. As happens in October, the sun seems to begin to drop before it reaches the high sky. An angled light takes over, even as the day remains windless and warm. High above the valleys, it brings on a flood of good feelings. Such good weather, though, makes you worry, as does, frankly, all weather. Today, no next ridge seems too far for a hiker unschooled in these hills.

The phone startles you. The caller ID says it's the state police. Not good—911 calls go to them, and, when the original call is from the backcountry, the police call you. You take notes: a man has collapsed on the trail to Ripley Falls, a short and popular walk. Those with him had walked along ahead, and then, when he didn't appear, they'd gone back to look. About a half mile in on the trail, they found him lying unresponsive on the ground. One of the group began CPR, and passersby are reported to have joined the effort. Your pulse jumps, and you hurry back to your truck. You call the Bartlett Fire Department and get their EMS team to respond. They're the closest rescuers; they'll get there before you. Ninety minutes later, when you arrive, you find a somber scene: Bartlett Fire's EMTs have determined that the man has died. His wife and friends stand there stunned quiet. The moment doesn't want to move.

In low tones, you confer with the Bartlett EMTs. You'll use their litter to carry the man's body out, and you'll need to recruit volunteers among the knots of hikers who have come upon this moment and stopped to try to help, or simply been stilled by it. You need to explain all this to the man's wife and make sure her two friends stay with her. And then you need to get the whole sad caravan moving. The morning seems another season.

As it probably does for the two twenty-somethings who call 911 from high on the Ammonoosuc Ravine Trail, where one of them has taken sick and can't continue. Even as you begin your drive toward the Cog Railway's Base Station, where that trail empties out, you keep contact with the anxious boyfriend of the stricken hiker. There's always the hope in such a situation that passing time will help and, slowly, it does. The first spasm of whatever has afflicted the young woman passes, and they begin descending again. She feels progressively better as they get lower—still not fully better, but getting down, seemingly returning to usual life. When you and CO Lucas reach the pair a mile from the trail's bottom, they are relieved and grateful, and the four of you walk slowly back down to the base. You note that this pair is well outfitted and prepared for their hike, and further that they had even delayed it a day when yesterday's forecast had looked inclement. They drive off to get medical attention by themselves.

Late afternoon's slanting light seems like a finger that slides under and lifts the lid from Pandora's box. Your phone begins to light up even as darkness comes on. Up north, on the Percy Peaks, a family calls in "overcome by darkness." After a 3:00 p.m. start, the four hikers ran out of light and, some time later, their cell phones, which they had been using as flashlights, ran out of battery-life. So they decide to call 911, and you get this call from the police. A while later, two of your COs, Lucas and Egan, have climbed up with headlamps, distributed them and walked the family out. While debriefing at the bottom, the COs recommend that the family be billed for this rescue, to which the mother replies, "While I was on the phone asking for help, if you had said I was going to be billed, I would have said, 'I'll pay anything.'"

While that all-too-common headlamp rescue takes place, another call comes in from high on Mount Washington, where one of a pair of hikers has twisted an ankle and can't go on. This pair of twenty-somethings differs by many measures from the earlier pair. When they call, they are holed up in the Lakes of the Clouds emergency shelter, a dark room beneath the AMC's summer hut (which is now closed for winter), and they are without warm clothing or overnight gear. The cloudcap makes it darkest night. Their earlier plan, if you can call it that, had been to ascend Washington and come down via the railway, but all the tickets had been sold, and they had set out down the mountain's cone late in the afternoon.

This call means a night mission that will unfold as follows: two COs will drive to the summit; from there, stocked with lights, warm clothing, and food, they'll climb the mile down to Lakes. With medical attention and luck, they'll be able to assist the hikers back to the summit, where they'll drive them down for a return to the usual world. Luck comes slowly, but it comes, and the COs reach the hut at midnight, splint the ankle, reach the summit at 3:30 a.m., and drive down.

It is Monday morning, and in the valleys, weekenders are dreaming of what they'll do with this extra day.

Meanwhile, over in adjacent District 3, Lt. Kneeland and his COs have had their own night adventures on the Franconia Ridge, plucking a sore-footed, lost hiker from the Greenleaf Trail just after midnight. That would seem plenty, but it overlapped with a nighttime helicopter rescue attempt coordinated with the New Hampshire Army National Guard and assisted by volunteers from AVSAR and PVSART, when a young man's heart stopped near Shining Rock on the Falling Waters Trail. There, despite CPR, the lowering of a medic through the forest canopy from a helicopter, and the hoisting up of the young man, he had died. The rescuers' night ends with a feeling of absence in the forest where so many had come together in a saving rush.

A Team within a Team

The roots of backcountry law enforcement in New Hampshire stretch back to 1865, when, on June 30, the legislature authorized the governor "to appoint two Commissioners to consider the subject of the restoration of sea fish to our waters and the introduction of new varieties of fresh water fish." So began the Commission of Fisheries, which, in 1880, added land animals and became the Commission of Fisheries and Game. Implicit in the agency's charge is the need to regulate us when we venture out into the wild; over the ensuing decades that need hasn't changed, though the behaviors covered have morphed and multiplied in ways that would astonish the original commissioners.

By 1890, the state had hired its first Fish and Game detective, who, for the princely sum of $250 per year, stalked the woods of Coos and Carroll Counties looking for those who would take unfair advantage of deer in deep snow. In 1915, the detectives became wardens, whose pay was "limited" to $100 per month, plus expenses, and they numbered seven. Still, a growing conservation movement and cooperation by sportsmen's clubs made this small crew effective where towns' law enforcement had not been. Over time, their numbers grew, as did the equipment they used—boats, cars, even uniforms became the norm.

Today's conservation officers took their title during a reorganization in 1934–35, when they came to work for the New Hampshire Fish and Game Department, and their duties expanded to meet that department's mission of support for the state's wild inhabitants and lands. COs assisted with fisheries, set up feeding stations for birds and animals, and monitored woodlands. I mention this expansion because, while NHFG COs have become the law in the woods and hills, setting and enforcing limits seems secondary to promoting a spirit and practice of responsible use there. Rule breaking and enforcement are high-profile activities that excite media coverage; spirit building has a lower profile, but is at least as important.

Conservation officers now number around forty, and they are spread among six districts that cover all 9,349 square miles of New Hampshire. To say that's a lot of territory per CO is an understatement. Within that total number are two specialized teams that train for work in particularly demanding locations: the Dive Team, dedicated to water searches for those lost there; and the Specialized Search and Rescue Team, made up of the sixteen COs trained to take to the hills and woods when you or I are missing or injured. Lt. Rick Estes spearheaded the formation of the SAR group in 1996, when it became increasingly apparent that this work was expanding and looked poised to keep doing so. Not only were more people venturing into the mountains, but a number were climbing up and sliding (and sometimes falling) down in places where earlier generations hadn't gone. They were doing so in extreme weather, too. In short, the advent of X games and

Lieutenant Jim Kneeland, team leader of NHFG's Specialized Search and Rescue Team and conservation officer in charge of NHFG's District 3. Photo courtesy of NHFG.

the proliferation of extreme backcountry adventure pointed also to extreme rescues. Estes felt that as the state's lead SAR agency, NHFG should respond.

These twenty years later, District 3's lt. Jim Kneeland leads the team. Kneeland is the only remaining CO from the group's founding. He cites as one of the catalysts for the group's existence the belief that NHFG should participate in search and rescue work as equal partners. By going out and up these SAR team members meet the state's expert volunteers where they work and so can better appreciate what they bring to that work. COs also point out that they now know better who to send and how to use them in hard terrain. Veteran MRS volunteer Steve Larson says a good balance has been reached between volunteers and NHFG, even as finding that balance took some time: "For a while eight or ten years ago, NHFG was taking such an active role in search and rescue that we [the volunteers] were getting few calls. It's hard to keep up enthusiasm and training if you're not being called. But now it's different. COs know when to call and who needs to be in on a particular rescue."

What He Can Command

Every day, as he sets out solo on his rounds, NHFG District 3's lt. Jim Kneeland does so behind the wheel of a 2012 Chevrolet Tahoe that's equipped as a mobile command post. Its truck bed can accommodate a snowmobile or ATV, and Kneeland "usually carries enough equipment to equip a couple of rescuers, if they need more stuff." The Tahoe is also supplied with mobile radios for contact with search and rescue units, as well as cell phones and laptops that are loaded with, among other things, a mapping program. "It is a very comfortable rig," says Kneeland. Given that on a rescue-intensive weekend the Tahoe can become a second home for him, that's a good thing.

On November 19, 2016, a 10:39 p.m. call for help from Cannon Mountain summoned Kneeland from a comfortable night at home back to his truck. It had been a moderate, late fall Saturday, with the temperature on nearby Mount Washington averaging 43 degrees with light winds. A colder day was on the way, as was some rain, which up high sounded more like ice. On Cannon's iconic cliff, which rises above Franconia Notch, two Massachusetts climbers, William S. and Michael F., were stuck some few hundred feet below the top. Earlier in the day, the pair, who had climbed quite a bit throughout New England but never on Cannon Cliff, had aimed up a popular route named Moby Grape (see figure 10.1). But after starting late and encountering route-finding difficulties that slowed them, they'd been benighted. Still, they had persisted, until finally they felt unable to go up or down. Later, analysts would wonder if some of their reluctance to descend, as most experienced climbers would have done, was caused by their not wanting to abandon, and so likely lose, some of their climbing gear.

Kneeland used the climbers' call to plot their location, and, after he advised them that they were around 390 feet below the helicopter-landing zone at the cliff's top, the climbers said they'd try to find another route up to that point. Kneeland checked back in with them just before midnight and found them still stuck but game for another attempt. Finally, the climbers called back just after 1:00 a.m., saying they were right back where they'd been when they first called. Noting the wet, going-toward-winter forecast, Kneeland decided a night rescue was necessary, and that meant calling the high-angle experts from Mountain Rescue Service and figuring out how to get them in place to effect a rescue. He made that call at 1:14 a.m. Readers may note some similarity with the 1959 Cannon Cliff tragedy described in chapter 10, even as these trapped climbers were more experienced and the season colder. But the differences between the two rescues point to how much has changed over these years, and to what someone in Kneeland's position can command when called today.

MRS makes, of course, the biggest difference, and in climbers Steve Larson, Kurt Winkler, Paul Cormier, Joe Lentini, Charlie Townsend, and Geoff Wilson, Kneeland had six of the region's finest. Their drive to Franconia was a short one. Still, it was a lightless night, and the climbers in need of rescue were stranded far up the cliff; getting to them would be an iffy proposition. But here, too, Kneeland and MRS had a new resource: during recent years, as Cannon had continued to attract its share of rescues, SAR groups had plotted the GPS coordinates of places where an anchor could be set to lower rescuers from the cliff's top. With the coordinates of the stranded climbers also available, Kneeland and the MRS climbers found that they could choose an anchor directly above the pair, and, if all went well, rappel down to them and bring them back up. That, of course, would be far less work and far quicker than climbing to them, and far safer. Paul Cormier later reflected that the location of the route down to the climbers had been "the perfect marriage of twenty-first-century technology and old-style experience. We had the GPS coordinates, and I had been to this route a number of times. I could say, 'It's just over here a little way,' and the coordinates confirmed that."

Such a plan prompted another concern: It would be great to drop from the top, but getting to that top would take time, too. Must rescuers hike up Cannon before dropping down from its crest for the rescue? Kneeland ran through his list of contacts and pressed a number, rousing one of the Cannon Tramway operators. Here were the fruits of a trade Kneeland had made last year, bartering some work investigating a skier's death for the home numbers of tram operators. He now had a way to get rescuers and as much gear as they wanted to the mountaintop. That carrying capacity counted importantly too: the tram could accommodate both rescuers and however many ropes they needed; lugging as much up on foot would have taken time, and likely led to thinner support for the rescue.

MRS's six climbers arrived around 4:00 a.m. and Kneeland then sent them and fellow CO Josiah Towne up to cliff top on the tram. He then drove the Tahoe to a particular spot on Route 93. "I've got a spot down here for each route on the cliff," he said, reflecting the number of times he has been called there. Each roadside spot gives him clear sight and radio lines for a route up. Also, before CO Towne went up to help the MRS climbers, Kneeland told him that he was to do whatever the MRS climbers wanted, even if that "means sitting in a bush watching." With this directive, Kneeland was setting up a clear chain of authority. He was also calling on experience. The dark cliff top of Cannon can be tricky to read; in a few steps someone can go from nearly level ground to cliffside. Kneeland wanted no added trouble that night. Cormier recalled that Towne was a big help: "He worked like crazy as we hauled the climbers up."

With the anchor set on a preselected spot above the climbers and lined up with Kneeland's truck lights in the valley, Larson went down over the edge a little after 5:30 a.m., dropping right to the two men, while his MRS colleagues tended the anchors. When each stranded climber was ready to come up, the five MRS rescuers and CO hauled hard. One at a time, each was brought back up to safety by 8:30 a.m., and then they all took a much more prosaic walk back down to the base, where they arrived around 10:00 a.m.

With Sunday still stretched before him, Kneeland was back in his Tahoe.

Postscript: the rains washed in, and the temperatures dropped. November 20 averaged only 23 degrees atop Washington. But by then everyone was off the mountain. That offered a happy ending in clear contrast to the draining, two-day saga on the cliff in 1959, when the two Connecticut boys died from hypothermia.

CALL IN THE SUITS

The Courtroom in the Hills

Much of search and rescue's action takes place where expected—out there. But at times, a second field of action beckons rescuers and those who manage them: the courtroom. There, both the garb and attendant behaviors are as rigidly enforced as they are in life-altering storms in the mountains. What gets decided in the courtroom can have as dramatic an effect on our mountains as any storm. Three significant lawsuits—all worthy of consideration here—suggest how a courtroom's horizontal planes may affect the places where we love to go uphill.

A central question attends each of these cases: Who is responsible? How each of us, and how we as a society, answer this question goes a long way toward determining what our lives and lands will look like, in the front country as well as in the backcountry. In every season, political as well as meteorological, it is *the* question.

The Weingarten Case

The spring of 1994, as noted earlier, was slow in coming, in part because the winter had been so intense. That intensity had already bred a hard year for climbers and rescuers in the Whites. Still, warm air and longer days arriving in the lowlands brought on the usual expansive ideas about visiting the highlands, and many who steer clear of icy winter mountains headed uphill. Among them on May 1 were a Tufts University student, Cheryl Weingarten, and three friends, who started up Mount Washington to see what they could see. Weingarten and two of the friends would climb the peak; the other wanted to ski in Tuckerman Ravine.

⟩ In the ravine, the route of the foursome's ascent, USFS snow ranger Brad Ray prepared for another day when visitors' lowland sense of season might collide with Washington's persistent reminders of winter. So too did his assistant, snow ranger Chris Joosen. It was a foggy day on the mountain, with occasional rain showers and considerable melt of the snowpack. Many who climb do so precisely because it gives them footing in two seasons on the same day, but that footing can be perilous, especially when it's time to come down. Weingarten's summit-bound threesome climbed atop Washington's cone and enjoyed the return to snow in the relatively mild, albeit foggy, air. As the day waned, they turned downhill, headed for Tuckerman to meet up with their friend.

Weingarten was new to Washington, as was the second climbing friend, while the third, Nicholas N., had been there before and knew that the slopes in it were steep and demanded caution. As they descended, he was uncertain of the way in the fog. When they neared the feature known as the Lip, where the ravine walls fall away at more than a fifty-degree angle, Weingarten and one friend were making sport of the descent by sliding on their butts; Nicholas N. stepped down more cautiously and, as he did so, he heard one of his friends scream. He followed her voice and found her clinging to brush just before a long drop. Cheryl Weingarten was nowhere to be seen.

The pair heard voices in the fog and linked themselves with two skiers, who were also looking to get down. As Nick Howe notes in his detailed account of this incident in *Not without Peril*, Nicholas N. and his friend made a near-miraculous descent of the Chute, a very steep technical route, to get to the ravine floor. They then made their way as quickly as possible to the ranger station in the ravine to report Weingarten's disappearance. There they found Joosen. After gathering and making sense of the sometimes garbled details the pair provided, Joosen conferred by phone with Ray, who had descended at day's end. Ray sent Joosen and AMC Hermit Lake caretaker Lewis Baldwin up toward the Lip to look for Weingarten. En route, Joosen and Baldwin checked other spring-opened holes and crevasses, finding no sign of the missing woman.

What they found at the Lip was hard news. First, the volume of meltwater from the day's warmth and rain was high, and that made approaching the place where the water plunged beneath the snow risky. While Baldwin belayed him, Joosen worked his way close to the opening, calling down into it and getting no response. He climbed back to Baldwin, and they reset their attempt at an angle that might get Joosen closer. He went back down, and this time he discovered sliding marks such as a person would make going down feet first. The marks led to the crevasse. Now, in the dark and amid the thundering meltwater, Joosen and Baldwin could do no more. As they returned to Hermit Lake, neither man was optimistic about Weingarten's chances. They conferred again with Ray, and he called Weingarten's parents.

Early the next morning, rescuers from USFS, MRS, NHFG, AMC, and AVSAR gathered to look into the crevasse for Weingarten. As Ray had predicted, the cold of night had refrozen some of the meltwater and snowpack, and the volume of water falling into the hole was much reduced. NHFG's lt. Jeff Gray put on scuba gear, MRS rigged their ropes, and Gray went down into the crevasse. Some sixty feet down behind the snow, he found Weingarten and brought her to the surface. All the way down, until the rescuers met a doctor in the valley, they chased the one in a million chance that Weingarten might be saved, providing CPR and oxygen. Dr. Stern met them, examined Cheryl Weingarten, and said she had died of a broken neck.

This sober exclamation point on a sobering winter would have been final punctuation had not Weingarten's parents decided, in 1997, to sue the USFS for negligence resulting in their daughter's death. *Weingarten v. The United States of America* resulted in a trial, whose final judgment was not delivered until 1999, when Judge Paul Barbadoro of Federal District Court ruled that he had no jurisdiction in this case. Barbadoro opens the discussion section of his twenty-page ruling as follows:

> The United States government cannot be sued without its consent. See Murphy, 45 F.3d at 522 (citing United States v. Palm, 494 U.S. 596, 608 (1990)). The Federal Tort Claims Act, however, acts as a broad waiver of the government's sovereign immunity, granting federal courts jurisdiction to hear certain claims against the United States. See Attallah v. U.S., 955 F.2d 776, 782 (1st Cir. 1992).
>
> Under the Act, I have jurisdiction to hear claims brought against the United States for damages caused by the negligent or wrongful act or omission of any employee of the Government while acting within the scope of his office or employment, under circumstances where the United States, if a private person,

would be liable to the claimant in accordance with the law of the place where the act or omission occurred. 28 U.S.C. § 1346(b)(1). The government's waiver of immunity is limited, however, by the Act's exceptions. See 28 U.S.C. § 2 680(a)-(n). Relevant here is the Act's so-called "discretionary function exception," which operates to deprive this court of jurisdiction over claims arising out of "the exercise or performance or the failure to exercise or perform a discretionary function or duty on the part of a federal agency or an employee of the Government, whether or not the discretion involved be abused." 28 U.S.C. § 2680(a). Thus, if the discretionary function exception precludes Plaintiff's claims I must grant Defendant's motion to dismiss for lack of subject matter jurisdiction.

In this case those discretionary decisions had to do with management of Tuckerman Ravine, and those making the decisions were the USFS snow rangers, who work in the ravine during its elongated winter. As lead snow ranger, Brad Ray, by then a veteran of some thirty-eight years in the ravine, was called upon to testify and justify the rangers' decisions and actions. His testimony opens an unusual window into the remarkable complexity of supervising the decisions and actions of citizens who come to visit these mountains and woods. The number of variables at play on any day in Tuckerman Ravine would dizzy the most ardent mathematician.

Here, at valuable length, is some of Ray's testimony; its eloquence and complexity put you right into the roles of risk manager and rescuer in steep lands. If you would judge the action, you must know the terrain and principles on which it takes place:

> As Lead Snow Ranger, I have the responsibility for managing Tuckerman Ravine consistent with the policy goals of the U.S. Forest Service. As Lead Snow Ranger, the Forest Service leaves me with the authority to accomplish that responsibility by using my professional judgment and discretion. Nothing in the statutes, regulations, or Forest Service policies dictates particular actions that I must follow in the handling of hazards, or managing of public safety issues in the Ravine. *The Forest Service Handbook* . . . provides more detailed guidance on things I, or any other Forest Service official, should take into consideration in managing the Forest's trails. It does not set forth specific steps or actions that I am mandated to take. . . . Nothing in the Trail Management Handbook man-

dates specific actions that I, or any other Forest Service official, was required to take in the handling of a safety hazard such as the waterfall crevasse.

In particular, the Forest Plan establishes that the Pinkham Notch Scenic Area is to be managed as a semiprimitive, nonmotorized recreational opportunity spectrum class area—a predominantly natural environment—to be managed with minimum on-site controls. For such an area, although restrictions on the use of the area may exist, they are to be subtle restrictions.

Pause here to recall the story of Cheryl Weingarten's climb up Washington and then her fog-shrouded descent, ending, tragically, with a laughing butt-slide that sent her over the edge. Perhaps you can appreciate the difficult charge of a snow ranger, who is asked to offer "subtle restrictions." Knowing exactly where we are and in what landscape may ask for subtle, deep understanding, but when we are at play, many of us don't "do" subtle.

Ray's testimony continues to provide valuable insight:

> With regard to the Backcountry undeveloped Areas, which would include Tuckerman Ravine, the management emphasis generally will be placed on protecting the natural resources first and the quality of the human experience second. . . .
>
> Thus, in managing Tuckerman Ravine, I and other Forest Service personnel are to balance issues of public safety associated with the use of the Ravine against the policy goals of protecting or maintaining the Ravine in its natural condition, maintaining a recreational opportunity that has minimum on-site controls, and making the Ravine available for multiple public uses.
>
> Over the years, and long before Ms. Weingarten slid into the crevasse, I have been concerned about the dangers presented by the waterfall crevasse when it opens up each Spring. For that reason, even prior to 1994, once the waterfall crevasse opens, the Snow Rangers have listed the presence of crevasses on the Avalanche Bulletin and have specifically noted its existence in other literature. But in addition to providing such warnings, prior to 1994, we considered whether we should take steps regarding the waterfall crevasse. In the end, however, for a variety of reasons, I concluded that the best approach to safeguarding the public in a manner consistent with the Forest Service policy goal for the Pinkham Notch Scenic Area and Tuckerman Ravine has been to continue to provide warnings about the crevasse through the Avalanche Bulletin and other literature, as well as through personal contact with the public. These decisions

were ones that, in accordance with Forest Service policies, were within my discretion and exercise of judgment.

Among the options we considered, and rejected, prior to Ms. Weingarten's death, was to provide some warning at the site of the waterfall by erecting crossed bamboo poles. Crossed bamboo poles are a well-established means of signaling trail closure or danger to skiers. However, I ultimately concluded that taking such a step would not be effective, would be dangerous, and would lead to a situation potentially contrary to the policy goals of the Forest Service. For example, at that time of year, snow often melts in the Ravine at a rate of three or four feet every one or two days. Bamboo poles are eight feet long and usually are planted with at least four feet sticking out above the snow. With snow melting at the rate it does, the bamboo poles usually would fall down at least every other day. To maintain the warning, I would have to direct a team of two individuals, diverting them from other responsibilities, to reset the bamboo poles at least every other day. I determined that, in view of the limited benefit likely to be gained from the poles, I could not afford to divert those of Snow Rangers from their other tasks.

Ray goes on in his testimony to consider the feasibility of erecting a permanent fence above the area, which, given snow depths, would, "to be visible and effective . . . have to be at least 24 feet tall, so that it would stick out of the snow." Then he considers signage above the waterfall, concluding that "to be readable from a safe distance, a sign would have to be quite large, again marring the pristine landscape." In addition, he cautions, "it would be very easy to miss a sign in the large expanse above the Headwall. As a result, to be effective, I considered that we would have to place multiple signs around the perimeter of the Headwall-waterfall area." Finally, he asserts, such signage in one spot would suggest that every "equally dangerous" area in the Ravine would need a sign or signs, which would lead to this direct contradiction of the Forest Service mission there: "Tuckerman Ravine would be a sea of signs and fences."

Having dealt with inadvisability of passive measures, Ray explains the actions available to a snow ranger:

In 1994, and now, there comes a time each Spring when I close the Lip and the Tuckerman Ravine Trail in the Lip area to all use. I use my professional judgment and discretion . . . taking into consideration the historic uses of the Ravine, the feasibility of enforcing the enclosure, the policy goal of promoting self-reliance by users, providing recreational opportunities, and using minimal on-site controls. As a result, I do not close the Lip until, in my professional judgment, I conclude that a good skier or hiker can no longer safely negotiate the Lip, going up or down.

All the while, as I read through Ray's words, I see Cheryl Weingarten, twenty-one years old, nearly a college graduate, smart, alive—but not aware of where she is—sliding on the snow above the Lip. Above my desk, I look up at the classic Harold Orne photo of the 1937 Franklin Edson Memorial Ski Race, a giant slalom descending the mountain, and there, striped by avalanches, is wintry Tuckerman Ravine (see fig. 16.1). There is so much to know before you stand or sit down to slide on any snow. Brad Ray's words from another source come back to me, too: In the book *Mountain Voices*, Ray is quoted as saying, "You start thinking about it when you're still in bed and your eyes are closed. You can hear the wind, and you can hear the pelting of snow or rime crystals that rap upon the window. . . . You're accumulating information all the time."

All that accumulating adds up to deep knowing, and we hope for that in our snow rangers and guides and companions. But even at a young age, when we may be deep on smarts but thin on experience, each of us who heads into the forests and uplands is asked to know where he or she is and make a personal choice. Those who manage our public lands and those who come get us when we fall can't make those choices for us. To ask otherwise is to give up the freedom of the hills.

An afterlife: Even though Barbadoro's decision ended the Weingarten case, it continues to resonate these twenty-plus years later. In December of 2016, as Snow Ranger Frank Carus met with key search and rescue professionals and volunteers at their monthly working group gathering to talk over the upcoming season in Mount Washington's east-facing ravines, he turned to the crucial question of how the thousands who climb into those ravines get information. "When it comes to signage and marking hazards," Carus said, "we go by the standards outlined in the Weingarten case." Those standards, articulated so clearly by Brad Ray, prevail.

The Bacon Case

Careful calculations of risk and probability seem to have been beyond Edward Bacon as he set about a five-day trip in mid-September of 2012. His itinerary, given the trip's intended duration, may have looked short, but Bacon planned on going up along the exposed spine of the Franconia Range bearing a number of limiting factors; among them were preexisting medical conditions, dubious fitness, and a casual approach to weather forecasts. All would slow him. One would, finally, stop him cold. By the time Bacon's story played out its final pages in court on April 30, 2015, where he had sought relief from a $9,186.38 bill for rescue, Edward Bacon was also probably responsible for any number of bruised heads in the mountain community, where, upon learning the fullness of his story, mountain folk slapped their foreheads in disbelief.

On September 18, Bacon, fifty-nine, of Northville, Michigan, was on the third day of a five-day solo hike, when, at around 1:30 p.m., he fell on the Franconia Ridge between Mounts Lincoln and Haystack, dislocating his hip. The weather was wild, featuring cold rain, falling temperatures, and winds building toward near hurricane force. Getting no cellphone signal, Bacon was able to crawl to a point along the ridge where he got brief cellphone reception, and he called 911. Then, fearing his 911 call had been dropped, he phoned the AMC Lodge at Pinkham Notch to ask for help. Equipped with overnight gear, but soon minus his tent, which blew away as he hauled it out, he was able to get into his sleeping bag to try to fight off hypothermia in the rain-soaked wind while he awaited rescuers.

NHFG District 3's lt. Kneeland got notice of Bacon's plight a little after 1:30 and, initially, it seemed that Bacon was between Lincoln and Lafayette. The closest aid would then be at AMC's Greenleaf Hut, so Kneeland called AMC huts supervisor and SAR coordinator James Wrigley, who talked with his crew at the hut. AMC hutman Justin Gay filled his rescue pack with gear and radios and set off up-ridge to try and reach Bacon. As he fought his way higher, Gay encountered winds gusting at hurricane force. Wrigley later reported, "There were extremely high winds, a lot of rain and cooler temperatures, and he was up on Lafayette and getting blown over by eighty-to-ninety mile-per-hour winds. We talked on the phone, and I told him to turn back."

Meanwhile, Kneeland had marshaled a force of fourteen NHFG COs and eighteen PVSART volunteers, who were climbing the Bridle Path to join the rescue. Among them was CO Bob Mancini, who was carrying both his thirty-pound pack and the thirty-plus-pound litter the rescuers would use to carry Bacon. In a follow-up article, a *Manchester Union Leader* correspondent, Kristi Garolfolo, gave Mancini's approach march full voice: "'It felt like small rocks were hitting you in the face the rain was blowing so hard. The visibility was very low, not due to fog or anything like that, but because it was very difficult to lift your head up with the wind blowing in your face and the raindrops were beating so hard."

The litter, borne on Mancini's back, was folded in half, but it still offered the wind a large surface area of contact, and Mancini is quoted as saying, "Carrying that litter is kind of like carrying a kite. It's probably a good fourteen to sixteen inches over your head, and it's large and square, maybe two and a half feet wide. In those conditions, it just really felt like a sail at times. If you got a good wind gust, it would blow you right off your feet."

A second effort by two AMC volunteers from the Greenleaf Hut, Everett Moore and Ben Kine, reached Bacon a little after 6:00 p.m. They were joined not long after that by NHFG conservation officers and then volunteers from the PVSART. At this point, it also became clear that Bacon was a mile south of his supposed location and that the rescue would not rise and descend via Greenleaf Hut and the Bridle Path. Another, more demanding trail lay closer. Thus began a long night of rescue along the ridge and down the steep Falling Waters Trail, which, in the bucketing rain, more than lived up to its name.

Kneeland had to reroute some of his initial group of rescuers, who were ascending the Bridle Path, and send them back down to climb the Falling Waters Trail. That would avoid the risky, wind-fraught crossing of the narrow ridge, but it added hours to the climb and ache to rescuers' legs. Others who had already climbed above the hut kept on across the ridge.

By now it was, of course, dark, and the moment asks us to sit back and imagine the convergence of little lights from headlamps, their beams shaken by wind gusts, all zeroing in on the spot above tree line where Bacon lay in the storm-girt darkness.

Initial rescuers had Bacon strapped into the litter by 7:30 p.m., and they began the hard walk along the ridge to the harder descent of the Falling Waters Trail. Even as they rotated carrying crews of six every few minutes, the rescuers grew tired. Mancini recalled: "It was labor intensive; it was exhausting. We usually can carry the litter for maybe four or five minutes at a time, but toward the end of our stint, just trying to get Mr. Bacon down, it seemed as though we were carrying the litter for a minute and a half and needed to change arms, at a minimum."

> As the night deepened, the steady rain intensified to torrential, and the waters along the trail rose rapidly. Kneeland knew he needed more rescuers, and PVSART sent seven more. With the brook crossings becoming perilous, Mountain Rescue Service volunteers also got the call. By 10:00 p.m., the initial party had covered a little more than a mile bringing them just below Shining Rock, and the new rescuers were climbing toward them.

The rest of the descent was sluiced by the waters falling down the rocks and coursing along the trailside brook. MRS's experts strung ropes as railings for brook crossings in the now thigh-deep water, and they secured the litter to other ropes for lowering down steep sections. In the *Union Leader* article, MRS's Joe Lentini is quoted, saying, "It was extremely slippery; it was a very steep rocky trail and people were cold, wet, and tired. You're looking at the potential of people slipping and getting hurt." Which, aside from the usual knockings and bruisings from an arduous carry, apparently didn't happen. Finally, some fourteen hours after Bacon's call for help reached Lt. Kneeland, the rescue party reached the parking area, where Bacon could be transferred to an ambulance and ferried off for treatment.

Lt. Kneeland commended "the Herculean effort of all the participating search teams working through the night in very difficult conditions to accomplish the nearly four-mile carry that brought Edward to safety." According to Kneeland, "Most likely, they saved his life."

A look into what preceded this heroic carryout, helps explain why rescuers ended up working through most of a tempestuous night, and why NHFG was intent on billing Bacon for that rescue.

A favorite upland for many, including this writer, the Franconia Ridge is remarkably exposed. Its walker is borne up into the sky with only unpromising, unmarked bailouts for retreat between Lafayette's summit and the

The high spine of the Franconia Ridge from the Bridle Path. Photo by author.

drop-off to the Falling Waters Trail 1.7 miles to the south. It is no place to be caught in a storm in any season. September's late-summer days, when heat's oppressing hand and the bugs' incessant whine have gone away, are also best days for this ridge. Still, they can be days with edge. I've seen a crystalline day with temps in the sixties juxtaposed with another that offered a six-inch snowfall and temps in the thirties. That Bacon was in the midst of a five-day walk suggests the likelihood of both types of weather during that stretch.

The forecast for September 18 on similarly exposed Mount Washington promised the following:

> Low pressure moving north over New York State will swing a warm front through today followed by a strong cold front for the overnight hours. A strong southerly flow associated with this low will allow for ample moisture, bringing continued fog as well as 1–4 inches of rain. Heavy rain late this afternoon and

overnight will heighten the risk of flash flooding, especially in narrow ravines and low-lying areas right around the summits. Winds will also be on the increase with gusts possibly reaching upwards of 100 mph this afternoon and evening as the low approaches. As the cold front exits early on Wednesday . . . with temperatures dropping behind the front, mixed showers will be possible by the afternoon. New snow and ice accumulations, if any, will be less than an inch tomorrow. (Mount Washington Observatory)

That's not the sort of forecast that recommends the Franconia Ridge. Given Bacon's starting point at Liberty Springs campsite, with its daily weather posting, he should have been aware of the coming storm. His comments to the *Manchester Union Leader*'s correspondent Garolfolo in the incident's aftermath suggest that he was: "I've been in 60-mph driving sleet before; I saw that up near Madison once," he said. "So I knew what I was getting into."

At this point, readers and surely the forty-nine rescuers who finally got Bacon down from the ridge that night, probably go slack-jawed. It was not only formidable weather Bacon decided to challenge, it was also a series of physical compromises, which District Attorney Philip Bradley summarized in the 2015 court case that decided against Bacon and for NHFG's assessment:

When Mr. Bacon set off on a five-day, solo hike in the White Mountains on September 16, 2012, he was 59 years old, had undergone four hip surgeries since 2005, had an artificial left hip that had dislocated five times—including twice during the previous year, had a bad back, was on over twenty medications for a multitude of ailments, and needed to use two canes (not walking poles) for support while hiking. He had hiked in the area when he was younger and, despite his physical infirmities, apparently believed he could still conquer some of New Hampshire's highest mountains—the respective 5,089-foot and 5,260-foot summits of Mount Lincoln and Mount Lafayette—even in the stormy weather that had been forecast days in advance. Unfortunately for everyone involved, Mr. Bacon negligently exceeded his physical abilities under the circumstances. He made it only about halfway before dislocating his hip, necessitating a challenging rescue in horrible weather conditions that required approximately 50 Fish and Game Department personnel and volunteers during afternoon and evening of September 18 and into the early morning hours of September 19, 2012.

Bacon voiced some contrition in the aftermath of the incident, saying he regretted exposing rescuers to the grim weather. But as the bill came due, he fought the assessment in court and, upon losing there, was characterized as follows in an Associated Press summary published in the *New York Times* on April 30, 2015: "Bacon, an automotive engineer whose father grew up in New Hampshire, said he has hiked the state's mountains hundreds of times and had even considered retiring there. Not anymore, he said Thursday. And while he has hiked the same area of Franconia Notch twice since 2012, he doesn't know if he will return. 'It has soured me at this point,' he said. 'I'm looking at western mountains at the moment.'"

During my research, whenever I mentioned this case, I got sour looks from rescuers who knew it. "He also bitched and complained the whole way down," said one rescuer. Bacon had become that rare victim who was disliked by those who lugged him out and the loser in that rare court case about which there is near-universal unanimity.

Julie Horgan's Dilemma in a Problem Pocket

There are pieces of White Mountain terrain that seem to gather trouble. We've already visited Tuckerman Ravine, where sharp slopes and plenty of people spawn all-season difficulty. Oakes Gulf on Mount Washington's southwestern flank also collects its share of wanderers, blown often from the open ridge above by amped-up northwest winds and storm into a thick-wooded embrace from which they are released only slowly, or not at all. The just-visited Franconia Ridge is another collector. Then there are the more subtle, barely descript little wildernesses of black spruce, such as the one that grows along the ridge between Mounts Pierce and Jackson in the southern Presidentials. It can serve as a stand-in for many other White Mountain pockets that seem, in scale, too small for getting lost, but that can catch us, nonetheless.

During the deep-snow winter of 2014, my friend Paul and I climbed Pierce on snowshoes along the firmly packed-out Crawford Path, reveling in the clear day and the snow-thick treescape. Atop Pierce, it was an average February day—temperature around zero, winds in the twenties—and, after some gorp and gazing, we set out for Jackson and our planned loop back down to Crawford Notch. An evident track led us on through the dense spruce and over some impressive drifts. Then it vanished. We backtracked, found our own and others' prints, and set out again. A little later . . . gone again. "WTF," we said to each other and fanned out to look. I squeezed through a few openings that could have been a trail below the six feet of snow and ended up in a clearing with no evident exit. Sigh. Track back again, this time veering off along another could-be-a-trail route. Um, no. Instead I fell—only partway, blessedly—into a spruce trap, and cursing, fought my way free. Looking down the six or so feet to where I could have ended up, I whispered, "Careful." Probing gingerly with my poles, I retreated.

Paul had had no better luck, and we agreed without much discussion to go back the way we'd come up rather than try to force a crossing that might be a trap, or a series of them. That evening, watching the freshened wind blow snow across the field in front of AMC's Highland Center, and noting a temperature now well below zero, I thought back to a 2011 day, when Julie Horgan had encountered similar route-finding trouble in the spruce a little farther down ridge.

Horgan, an experienced hiker, set off on March 26, 2011, to climb Mount Jackson, a climb she'd done often before, and one she'd chosen in light of the day's forecast. "I'd never have gone up Washington on a day like that," she said looking back. From Jackson, Horgan planned to return to Crawford Notch at day's end. The day was blustery and cold, with deeper cold forecast to move in overnight. Even as spring had begun to announce itself in the southern flatlands, deep winter held on, as it often does, in the heights. All was proceeding to plan until, after reaching Jackson's top, she lost the trail as she sought to return. Horgan remembers that the wind was strong enough to erase her tracks in minutes, so retracing them was impossible. She rooted through the snow and spruce but couldn't get back on track. So as the day waned around 3:00 p.m., she called AMC for help, initially hoping someone might be able to talk her back to the trail, where she could make her own way down. This failed, and AMC called NHFG. As darkness came on and the cold and wind intensified, NHFG launched a rescue. Evening attempts by conservation officers to reach Jackson's upper slopes were beaten back by temperatures dropping to zero and winds that, up high, reached hurricane force. Nearby bellwether Mount Washington recorded winds of eighty miles per hour. At 2:00 a.m., the search was suspended, to be picked up at first light in the morning, when the volunteer specialists of the Mountain Rescue Service would join the effort.

Searchers returned to the mountain early that next morning, and the National Guard sent a helicopter to help, but the conditions had turned everyone pessimistic. The MRS veteran Alain Comeau recalled thinking as he climbed in the wind and cold that they would end up looking for a body. But up high, Horgan, well equipped for a winter hike, though without overnight gear, had fashioned partial shelter in the spruce and weathered the night by hunkering down. When she got cold, she would do "jumping jacks to warm up again." At 9:45 a.m., the helicopter called in from New Hampshire Army National Guard spotted her and, with their guidance, Comeau found her. "I came around a corner, and there she was. I was so surprised," he recalled. Both MRS president and Himalayan climber Rick Wilcox and Comeau were impressed with Horgan's self-possession and survival skills, and the incident had an unanticipated happy ending as the rescuers and the rescued walked down together that morning.

But controversy then unfurled in the winds of public opinion, which gusted with its own fronts. NHFG deemed Horgan negligent and assessed her a fine of nearly $7,000 to cover the department's rescue costs. Horgan's being charged raised some eyebrows: "I still don't get how they charged her," Comeau said during a 2016 interview. "She was equipped, she did everything right when she got lost. She survived when many wouldn't." Unsaid, but clear to anyone who keeps tabs on mountain mishaps, was the sense that so many chuckleheaded moments go uncharged that it seems odd to slap an equipped, resourceful hiker with a big penalty. When asked about the rescue, Colonel Kevin Jordan pushed back, saying he and the agency believed Horgan had been negligent in attempting her climb in that day's conditions.

In a phone interview in November 2016, Horgan reflected on her rescue. For her the rescue came at the end of a chain of events that quickly shifted out of her control. In her initial call to AMC, she said, "I'm fine. Just unable to relocate the trail." She hoped that either through advice from below or help from a pair who might ascend and locate her, she'd get down quickly with minimal fuss. But AMC was short on personnel at that moment, so the call went to NHFG. Once that call went out, the numbers involved multiplied.

Horgan recalled that she'd weathered the night well, and climbed to an open patch to see if she could find her way out, when she heard a helicopter. "Oh no," she said to herself, as visions of simple rescue vanished. Not long after, Comeau and two other rescuers from MRS arrived. After praising Horgan's self-possession on that cold night, they reassured her: "You didn't do anything wrong," they said. After NHFG officers arrived, Horgan had something to eat and drink, and they all walked down. Grateful, Horgan sent in a $500 donation to rescuers, and went on with her hiking life.

Months later, however, a certified letter arrived with the $7,000 fine for her rescue, threatening loss of her driver's license if she didn't pay. NHFG cited two factors that, in their eyes, made Horgan negligent: first, she had set out on the climb with a very cold and windy forecast; second, she had carried no compass for reorienting herself. Horgan obtained legal help from a New Hampshire lawyer, whose bill came to $2,000. The court, however, found for NHFG, and, unwilling to press on further, Horgan set up a payment plan and moved on.

Two final points emerge from Julie Horgan's story. The first has to do with how emergency escalates, even with communication via cellphone. As she waited atop Jackson and worked her way through that cold night, Horgan was also in touch with NHFG. She said she continued to assure them that she was doing okay, that her need was redirection, not being hauled out. Yet as the effort resumed the next morning and teams climbed toward Horgan, a helicopter was summoned too. Here we encounter a common phenomenon: the person needing help hopes that it will be calibrated to her need; those in charge of the rescue want to make sure that they do and have more than enough, and that they are not vulnerable to being seen later as having been unresponsive. So even with Horgan's assurances, NHFG went big with its response.

Clearly, however, weather had a lot to do with that "big response." Cold and wind at those levels are lethal, and once you're in the game of trying to beat them, it makes sense to marshal all your resources. Put yourself in the position of NHFG's incident commander: time is critical in such cold; we need to be as quick as we can in this work; the helicopter may give us the eyes to be fast.

Horgan's rescue has had a small but persistent afterlife. On the 2014

Dreamfilm documentary, *To the Rescue*, about Canadian search and rescue, it is offered as a cautionary tale of what can go wrong when the government bills people for rescue as a way of funding SAR work. On that same film, MRS President Rick Wilcox goes right to the heart of the problem: "We spent $6.8 million last year telling people to come to New Hampshire and have a good time in the White Mountains, and go hiking and climbing and fishing and camping and snowmobiling, and all the things we do up here. And then we turn right around and whack you for a rescue."

The agency caught in the middle is New Hampshire Fish and Game. Colonel Jordan stands by his department's assessment. It's not uncommon for people to downplay their dilemma in the aftermath of a rescue, he says, and the careful parsing of that incident by the lieutenant at the scene suggested billing. The muddled public response grows from uncertainty about whether such billing serves as a penalty or as a way to make budget ends meet. That it sometimes seems one or the other or both confuses people.

Horgan herself carries forward a lesson. "I would never call for rescue again," she told me. No searchers and rescuers want that reluctance to be resolution to this problem.

WHO PAYS?

(AND WHAT THAT SAYS)

A penalty, like the $7,000 assessed to Julie Horgan to help cover NHFG expenses, invites us into the room of budgets, and even writing that word makes this writer wary. While we all have spaces where we calculate income and outflow and search for balance, they are not often rooms of story. We don't recount our latest tussle with the checkbook or online bank balance to appreciative murmur: "And there I was, ten cents off, in a seeming wilderness of decimals, and then I found the dime was my annual interest on the account. It was awesome!" Still, understanding search and rescue in the Whites requires knowing who pays the bills and why. NHFG's head of law enforcement, Colonel Kevin Jordan, put it this way during a November 2016 interview: "On Monday morning, after everyone's gone home [from a rescue], I have to pay the bills."

NHFG's search and rescue bills now come to more than $300,000 annually, and that figure seems bound to swell. "It's a growing part of the job," Jordan said of what used to be a side venture in a conservation officer's work. Here, we bump first against a usual problem: we as citizens tend to assess governmental expenditures on a personal scale. Three hundred thousand dollars seems a lot of money to look for the lost. But on the scale of a state, even a small, tax-phobic one like New Hampshire, $300,000 is a fingernail paring from the body of its total budget. What, then, accounts for the ongoing controversy about funding search and rescue in our mountains? Wherever you go among the professionals and volunteers of White Mountain SAR, funding frustrations come to the fore, sowing confusion and resentment.

> A good place to begin is with a basic understanding of where the money for search and rescue comes from, and then, where it goes. Around $100,000

is realized from a dollar allotment per annual license for boats, snow machines, and off-road vehicles registered in New Hampshire. That source was established by the legislature in 1989, and it remains unchanged these twenty-seven years later, even as costs and deficits have climbed. "Who is still using the same budgeting as in 1989?" asked Colonel Jordan. "We have been to the New Hampshire legislature twenty-one times in twenty years with pieces of legislation to find a better way to fund search and rescue, and it has remained unchanged, which is ludicrous."

This antiquated method of raising money has created what both Jordan and the NHFG website call "a crisis": "Why is there a crisis in funding wilderness search and rescue activities in the Granite State?" It's a good question.

Where does the roughly $200,000 (and rising) additional money come from? The short answer is that it's drawn from the general NHFG budget, which is funded largely by hunting and fishing licenses (the number sold is, by the way, also declining). Perhaps you sense the heat of some of the controversy already: even before we get to the breakdown of who needs finding and rescuing, we see that it's the boaters, snowmobilers, off-road riders, hunters, and fisherfolk who pay for it. Fair enough, if they're the ones being sought and saved. But you suspect there are others, many others, who aren't riding machines, or bearing guns and rods. And you are right. Of 1,023 reported search and rescue missions between 2008 and 2014, 609 looked for hikers or climbers, while only 138 involved hunters, anglers, boaters, or OHRV riders. Fair? The other significant targets of these missions are lost children and the elderly.

To keep cutting checks on Monday after a weekend rescue, as Colonel Jordan must, he has to locate the money to back those checks and try to find fairness as well. "What about the federal government?" a number of people asked me. Given the 800,000-acre White Mountain National Forest at the heart of the Whites and their rescues, it seems a fair question. But as mentioned earlier, USFS staffing and budgeting are too thin to support a robust search and rescue operation, and, if anything, their resources are under threat of further tightening. Jordan also points out that were the federal government to assume responsibility for search and rescue in New Hampshire's federal lands, it would be setting a precedent for similar lands throughout the country.

The most controversial method of finding money for search and rescue, and one still in force, is billing backcountry travelers and adventurers who are deemed "negligent" when they get into trouble and need help. So we arrive back at Julie Horgan and Edward Bacon and a number of related attempts over the years to help balance Fish and Game's search and rescue budget line. In 1999, the New Hampshire legislature passed a law that authorized NHFG to bill hikers or climbers who needed rescue because of their "reckless" behavior; in 2008, the standard for billing got lowered to "negligent," a more common transgression, and easier to prove. The logic, budgetary and ethical, seemed clear to proponents—if you get in trouble through your own hand, you can hand over the cost of rescue when we come get you. Given the consistency of head-scratching incidents in the mountains, it looked like a good way to close the budget gap. The law, however, has proved both controversial and hard to enforce. For one thing, a number of SAR groups around the country have condemned the law, largely because they worry that a possible charge for rescue will delay or prevent people from calling when they need help. That slow trigger could, in turn, put rescuers in more danger when they have to respond late and more hurriedly in a developing crisis. Their argument is also simple and clear: backcountry search and rescue is a public function, just as front-country law enforcement or fire protection is; we should fund it as part of the social contract.

Long Search, Large Dollars

In 2009, the late-April Mount Washington rescue of seventeen-year-old Scott Mason got a lot of people talking, both for its extended, dramatic nature and for its monetary aftermath. Mason, a Massachusetts Eagle Scout with some hiking background and a little exposure to the Whites, set out solo on the twenty-fifth from Pinkham Notch with an ambitious itinerary for a day hike that would take him up Washington, then along the ridge connecting Mounts Jefferson, Adams and Madison, before looping back down the Appalachian Trail to his starting point. Those roughly eighteen miles contain a lot of hard work. Still, with good footing and conditioning, they can just fit into the container of a day. But that day's light needs to be long, and the route is exposed. Should the weather turn—and late April is often a time of extremes and uncertain footing in the high Whites—ice, snow, mud, and rock can appear in all sorts of combinations, and rivers, docile in summer, can be wild with snowmelt. But much of the route travels along open rock, and it was said to be dry and snowless in 2009. So after talking with AMC staff at Pinkham Notch, Mason decided the day was a go, and he left Pinkham at 6:50 a.m.

> All those possible variables suggested a thin margin for error, and when Mason sprained his ankle slightly on his ascent of Lion Head, that margin vanished. The mild weather forecast, while it noted possible thunderstorms and high winds a few days later, favored Mason, even once he was slowed down. He kept on, summiting Washington. Then, inexplicably, rather than returning via Lion Head, he decided to stick to his planned route.

The mild temps also meant softened snow and rising rivers, both of which complicated the search for Mason when he got lost. Real cold would probably have written a different ending to the subsequent four-day (and three-night) search that ended happily with a helicopter spotting Mason as he labored up out of the Great Gulf, aiming for the little settlement that lies atop Washington.

That he was in the Great Gulf at all has a lot to do with why this search broke open such controversy. Mason's actions before, and especially after, his ankle sprain were what led NHFG to deem him negligent, which opened the door for the whopping $25,734.65 charge they assessed him. Most assessments, when they are made at all, are measured in hundreds or a few thousands of dollars, and they typically cover Fish and Game COs' time, which is often overtime, because many rescues unfold after regular hours. The Mason charge ballooned because of the search's unusual length, and because of helicopter expenses, when NHFG had to call in a copter from Maine because those that usually help in New Hampshire were unavailable. Air search and support usually arrives at minimal cost to NHFG, because it often comes from New Hampshire's Army National Guard, where most of the costs are seen and paid for as training. But when the check to be written on Monday includes full charge for air work, then zeros quickly pile up at the end of the total.

When Mason's mother reported him missing on the night of April 25, she was also able to provide searchers with her son's itinerary, and that aimed some of them up along those intended trails. A clear mission if not an easy one. But along the ridge between Washington and Jefferson on day one (and after his inexplicable decision to press on with his twisted ankle), Mason made another poor decision that lengthened his and the rescuers' ordeals: rather than staying on his proposed route or turning back toward Washington, he'd descended the steep headwall to his right on the Sphinx Trail, which he'd lost in some upper snowfields. Then he'd cut across the slope and off trail to the Six Husbands Trail and into the Great Gulf. In doing so, he was aiming to shorten his return to Pinkham Notch to a direct line. But Mason's new route went against the advice given earlier by AMC staff, who said that, should he need to bail out on his loop, he should go down the easier west side via the Jewell or Caps Ridge trails. Yes, that would leave him on the wrong side of the mountain, away from his car, but it would get him down to where he could work his way back to Pinkham Notch among people and traffic.

The descent into the Great Gulf, however, set up a meeting with an impassable river. Then, as he searched for a crossing, he encountered deep, soft snow and off-trail hiking that can slow progress to feet traveled per hour. In pursuing his alternate route, Mason took on a shortcut that stretched his and his rescuers' trials over days and nights, even as mild temperatures kept them all hopeful. Mason also exposed himself and those searching to real risks in the wallow of the springtime Great Gulf.

Despite breaking through snow and getting soaked in meltwater (but avoiding being swept down into the stream, where he clearly would have died) and not being fully equipped for overnight camping, Mason survived his three nights out, as he searched for a way across the river that blocked him. Admitting to himself, finally, that getting over the river was impossible, Mason then turned up toward Washington again. After slogging up out of the Gulf, he was found some forty-five minutes from the top by one of the teams out looking for him.

Postscript

In the immediate aftermath, everyone, including Major Tim Acerno of NHFG, agreed that once bogged down in the gulf, Mason had "done everything right." He had used his Boy Scout training to make fires, sheltered in a newly purchased bivy sack, and kept his composure. Mason and family expressed his gratitude in words (and, later, with a $1,000 donation) that said he knew he'd put rescuers at risk. But in July, this happy postrescue tableau shattered when NHFG delivered the $25,000 assessment for negligence. Mason and his family opted to fight the bill in court, and a number of SAR organizations from around the country condemned NHFG's action. One prominent rescuer in Colorado, Paul "Woody" Woodward, president of Colorado's Alpine Rescue Team, had this to say: "If it had happened in Colorado, he would have been applauded for being able to survive for three days. New Hampshire is way out on their own on this one."

The omnibus rescue group, the Mountain Rescue Association (MRA), was equally critical. Though western-based, MRA's ninety-plus search and rescue groups include the nearby Vermont State Police and groups from New York State and New Jersey. On August 1, 2009, MRA issued a position statement saying that billing for rescue was dangerous to victim and rescuer alike. All SAR work should be free:

> The Mountain Rescue Association (MRA) with over 90 teams from the United States, Canada, and the United Kingdom—most of which are comprised of expert unpaid professional members—work through or for a local government search and rescue authority. In an effort to give back to the community, defray public agencies' costs and keep taxes down, the MRA teams have been performing the bulk of all search and rescue operations for the past forty-eight years, and those were done without charge to the victim.
>
> The MRA firmly believes that training and education are the keystones in the solution to this issue. We believe that the individual must accept responsibility for his or her actions and that training in proper outdoors skills and for self-rescue might be the quickest and most effective method of resolving most rescue situations.
>
> However, no one should ever be made to feel they must delay in notifying the proper authorities of a search or rescue incident out of fear of possible charges. We ask all outdoors groups and organizations to join us in sending this mountain safety education message.
>
> We recognize that the governmental agencies have a need to address de-

fraying their costs, and we would welcome any opportunity to be involved in discussion of solutions or alternatives to the charge for rescue issue. The expert volunteer teams of MRA are proud to be able to provide search and rescue at NO cost and have NO plans to charge in the future.

Other rumbling objections from the general public pointed even to possible economic penalty for a region imposing such bills on those rescued, even when they had acted with negligence. "I would go elsewhere for my climbing," wrote Laurence Gonzalez on the adventure blog posted by *National Geographic*. In response, a Colorado SAR group member posted this comment:

November 19, 2009, 11:58 a.m.

People that never enjoy the outdoors are often quick to judge the actions of those that do. They sit at their desk and complain about having to pay for someone else's rescue. In reality, they do not pay, the rescuers do. I do. I contribute over 1,000 hours a year to training and missions along with my colleagues. Nobody pays us a penny when we mobilize to the Sierras to find a lost hiker or hunter. The only thing that costs money are the rangers and the helicopters; and as Mr. Gonzales points out, the helicopters fly regardless, and the rangers get paid regardless.

I for one will not be visiting parks and districts where bureaucrats are allowed to charge thousands of dollars for being involved in rescues. We're supposed to be looking out for each other. That's what societies do.

Mark Trevor

Contra Costa SAR

Mountain Rescue Group

Your thoughts go here.

Here are my thoughts:

Embedded assumptions litter these comments, and the word "bureaucrats" drips with scorn; it supposes faceless functionaries lodged at their desks, drumming up reasons to bill the pure-hearted adventurers who actually go out, into the world. But even a little nosing about in the SAR world of New Hampshire brings you to a different reality, where the toll is personal as well as financial. "I have good COs retire early all the time," said Colonel Kevin

Jordan, "in large part because of the grind of search and rescue work. I've had both shoulders rebuilt and knee work also, and my doctor pointed to the repeated work of carrying litters." Throughout my research, I kept bumping into other COs who'd had orthopedic work done. That "grind" can spill from the physical to relational. So many incident reports point to the off-hours nature of search and rescue—the calls often arrive at night, or the effort bleeds into it—which saps COs of sleep and disrupts family life. Add to the physical and relational grinds the emotional toll of seeing tragedy time after time, and you have a human cost hard to sustain. In my conversations with the NHFG conservation officers, I've yet to meet a faceless bureaucrat. But it is also clear that when you mix volunteerism with professional imperatives and the money gets sorted, there's room for grievance and misunderstanding.

In this instance a complicating factor was the behavior of Mason and his family. Yes, Mason was resilient (and weather favored), but the decision making that put him in trouble was poor, even for an adolescent. First, he chose to do this long loop alone without a lot of miles accrued. If he were an über-fit thirty-five-year-old with years of Whites trail experience, that decision might look okay, but Mason was a minor with very minor mountain experience. Here, his parents figure in—they let him go. That jumps to the old standard of "reckless" behavior, I think. As Colonel Jordan recalled, the law enforcement division of NHFG didn't want to let the family off the financial hook, even after the attorney general's office, citing added background information, recommended doing so. The episode seemed so irresponsible.

The upshot of all this: NHFG got bloodied by comment; Mason's family faced a huge bill; and the whole issue of who pays for SAR rose briefly to some prominence. Some resolution followed. When NHFG ultimately followed the attorney general's advice and dropped its effort to bill Scott Mason (citing new and private medical information), the thought of defraying the department's annual SAR deficit through such billing became less probable. Still, the aforementioned Horgan incident, and others, point out that billing for negligence can still be seen as an option.

The answer to whether or not such billing works as a reliable and defensible funding mechanism seems evident: it doesn't. Even as he has "led the charge" to find some fair way of getting hikers and climbers to share in the funding of NHFG's SAR budget, Colonel Kevin Jordan says, "I haven't done a complete analysis, but collecting the money is a lot of work and, when you add in staff time setting up payment plans and working on these bills, plus the work of the attorney general's office in court [that office gets 41 percent of any settlement arrived at in a court case], it's probably close to a wash." That doesn't account for the negative publicity that seems to follow in some billings' wakes.

In fact, the money realized from such penalties is minor: Colonel Jordan sent me these recent figures: "From 2006 to 2014 we have billed a total of sixty-three missions at a total cost of $112,785.00. We have successfully collected approximately $69,603.00 back into the SAR account. We sacrifice 41 percent to the AG's office if they go to collection. We are fairly consistent in a 62 percent success rate of collecting what we bill." That is an average of roughly $8,000 per year recovered, not much of a dent in the annual deficit that runs to more than $100,000.

> If billing for rescues brought on by negligence on the part of the hiker/ climber doesn't offer budget solutions, what does it offer?

A partial answer may lie in the idea of deterrence. If it becomes common knowledge that New Hampshire will charge for rescue only from clearly negligent behavior in its mountains, hikers, climbers, and snow sliders may think twice before attempting such behavior. PVSART's president and Sugar Hill fire chief Allan Clark argues for such billing as a clear deterrent, though he would return the standard for billing to reckless behavior. Clark likes "reckless" as a standard, because it ranks as a criminal charge, meaning it carries both trial and possible penalty beyond a fine. Such a public display and penalty would draw attention. Billing for rescues brought on by reck-lessness or negligence then becomes a form of education: we can learn from others' errors.

That's the theory. But does penalty for negligence alter people's planning and behavior? The answer is unclear; experts on decision making say "some-times," or, famously, "it depends." We are, it turns out, not very rational in our decisions about risk, substituting our own rose-colored narratives for probability-based thinking. Still, we've also seen that a rescue story's drama does focus public attention. If we can learn about risk, it may be from such stories.

Two years ago, NHFG tried a different approach: it created the voluntary Hike Safe card, which the public could buy—$25 for an individual, $35 for a family, per year. Carrying that card would bring you rescue without billing, should you need it. It is a sort of get-out-of-jail-free card, and the funds realized from its sale would help close the annual SAR budget gap. After years of looking for ways to address that gap, this one made a number of people happy, legislators among them. Finally, it seemed, the agency had come up with a way to elicit a share (fair or no) of support for the SAR budget from the hiking public who, it should be recalled, generate roughly 60 percent of NHFG's searches and rescues. To the tune of $75,000, it worked in year one, and a larger sum (now at nearly $120,000) has come in during year 2016. That, in the context of NHFG's SAR budget, is significant money.

The first person to call for help and be able to show the card was Deborah Bloomer, who hurt her ankle on Chocorua in July 2015. The next day, the papers ran a short story, illustrated by a picture of the smiling "victim," sitting on a picnic table at the mountain's base and showing the camera her wrapped ankle and Hike Safe card. Here was free help down, then, a result of one of society's better inventions, the pooling of resources from many to help the few who find trouble.

NHFG found that the card's rules needed tweaking at year one's end, to make it explicit that the carrier wasn't exempt from a charge if he or she acted negligently. In that case, a bill could still be delivered. Also, the definition of family was broadened to include an adult child who must live at home. The Hike Safe card looks primed to live on (see Appendix A for a summary of the educational part of the hikeSafe Program, which is a different card and program).

What still worries Colonel Jordan and others, however, is the possibility that NHFG's SAR budget will grow increasingly reliant on funding that is voluntary, which means that funding could dwindle or run dry. How do you budget for voluntary contributions? Jordan wants to know. How do you buy and replace equipment and provide training? Various nonprofits do this by budgeting only what was raised last year. Once the novelty of the card wanes, will we—the public—keep buying it? It is really a form of suggested annual giving, in that currently SAR is free of charge, unless there is negligence or recklessness on the part of the lost or fallen. Then, billing for expenses is okay, even if you hold a Hike Safe card.

A more reliable, permanent solution to budget needs cited by the great majority of those I talked to would be legislated basic funding of NHFG's search and rescue budget. As much as I admire the patchwork of White Mountain search and rescue and its sense of making do in the face of modest resources, I am puzzled by the New Hampshire legislature's absence of political vision and will in its reluctance to support their work. Perhaps I shouldn't be—it is a famously contentious body in a famously tax-averse state; "Every little tub on its own little bottom" might be inscribed on New Hampshire's state crest (though the Latin could be a challenge).

Supermajorities don't always indicate wisdom, but in the case of those who understand SAR funding, I think they do. Almost every professional or volunteer I spoke with at any length about White Mountain SAR said simply, "The state should fund it from the general fund." Whether legislators decide to draw from the state's hotel and meals tax—a common suggestion, since there is a direct link between mountain recreation and tourism—or some other source, providing adequate resources for SAR is in everyone's interest. It safeguards the rescuers by assuring sound equipment and training; it eliminates labor-intensive confusion over billing (if the state wants to retain it as deterrent penalty for folly, it should be just that, not a funding mechanism); it silences resentment of various other outdoor "users," who feel they and their license fees are paying for "freeloading" mountain hikers and climbers.

If you accept also Chief Clark's recommendation that those rescued because of reckless behavior be billed, you have, I think, the best of both systems. SAR funding is then secure, seen as a public safety function performed by the backcountry equivalents to front-country law enforcement, and you can work with billing as a deterrent and as public education. Any added monies realized from billings could be used to help fund equipment purchases for the volunteer groups that provide for free the majority of the search and rescue's labor force.

What about the Mountain Rescue Association's worry that possible charges will slow someone's call for rescue? The current influx of calls suggests that's a false worry. As Jordan said: "People call when they hit trouble. Everyone's used to picking up a phone when they need something." In fact, a slower finger on the phone keys, on occasion, might be a good thing.

Yes, hiking and other self-powered sports in the hills can be done "on the cheap," but it is also abundantly clear that most of those heading into the hills have bought fuel or supplies, eaten at a restaurant, stayed the night at a motel, or bought boots, shoes, or a hat. Some may even have been wise enough to purchase a light against darkness, should they be delayed. All those purchases contribute to the state's economy and so to the jobs of the thousands who staff its stores, factories, and establishments. Imagine New Hampshire without them.

< 2 0 >

NEW EXTREMES

Superlative Adventure and
Search and Rescue

In May 2016, during a research trip in the Randolph, New Hampshire, area, I had some unexpected free hours in the midst of a "fifty-center," Joe Dodge's term for a blue-sky, light-wind, clear-vision day. Free time equals trail time in the hills, and I thought to follow the Airline for a look around Star Lake and perhaps a trip up Mount Adams's back side. Fitting this into a four-hour envelope suggested moving at a fair pace, which meant also going light: running shoes, shorts, a few synthetic layers, and then a little frisson of pleasure at packing and donning my new Salomon running vest. Enough for this little trip, I thought, even if—Odin forbid—I fell and needed to wait some for aid. I grabbed my poles and set off at a good clip.

I'm fit, and I've run and fast-walked trails for decades, but no passerby is going to mistake me for any shade of youth. So I was a little surprised when, a few miles up, I happened upon a twenty-something who gave me one scan, and said, "Presi-traverse, right?"

"Um, no," I demurred. "Just a few hours free up Adams."

"Oh," he said, and then went on his way.

I mulled over this meeting as I climbed on and quickly figured that the running vest has become such a familiar sight, especially along the range crossings of legend (the Presidential traverse, for example), that these crossings have become usual. What was once the province of a few "extreme" athletes is becoming the terrain of legions of backcountry runners and hurriers.

Any look at the "new" extremes in backcountry adventure must gain perspective from consideration of the old ones. If you follow anthropology's theories back to our most distant ancestors, you find them making their way "out of Africa" with a whole planet full of unknowns before them. Led, supposedly, by their tribes' oddballs, the scouts and shamans, who could see seemingly sideways, or with their eyes shut, they made their way even to the world's Patagonias and Baffin Islands.

Recorded history spills over with floods and currents of further migration across oceans and through risky terra incognita. Songs, poems, and stories follow. So extreme adventure is nothing new. But as noted at the beginning of this book, it took the advent of outdoor recreation, which included mountain adventuring, for people to begin choosing upland immersion in extremes. In recent years that choosing has burgeoned, as traditional plodding by the masses has birthed new generations of extreme outdoor enthusiasts. A long *New York Times* magazine piece on November 1, 2016, was titled "How Much Suffering Can You Take?" It went on to take its readers inside the Quintuple Anvil, a 703-mile, five-day, pain-athon that asks for an Ironman Triathlon on each of those five consecutive days, or strings the segments together into one continuous swim, then bike, then run. The athletes interviewed contended that such a "race" offers a window to one's soul. "What might I see?" I wanted to ask. But no one went beyond that short, dead end of a sentence. Their default response rang familiar and unsatisfying: "If you have to ask, you won't understand." We do have to ask.

On September 18, 2016, ultra-runner Karl Meltzer arrived at Springer Mountain, Georgia, the southern end of the Appalachian Trail. Meltzer was not in need of rescue; that's not why he appears in these pages. Meltzer was, in fact, surrounded by people. Photos got taken, and trail's end burbled with energy; a little party broke out. When he had left from Maine's highpoint, Katahdin, on August 3, some 45 days before, Meltzer had been aiming for such a moment. But it would happen only if he reached Springer Mountain in under 46 days, 8 hours and 7 minutes, the exact time it had taken Scott Jurek to go the other way over the AT in 2015. Meltzer's journey was clocked at 45 days, 22 hours, 38 minutes; he was the new AT speed record holder. That a 2,189-mile trail was being cast as the site for a race of sorts struck many as wild hyperbole—or just plain crazy. But not so for a fast-growing slice of the running populace, who seem not to have met or heard of a "run" they don't want to do. Ultra-runners can't invent long challenges fast enough; it's safe to say there isn't a long-distance footway in the world that isn't being eyed and whose FKT (fastest known time) isn't being parsed by some ultra folk right now. Where once running a marathon proffered Greek myth status, it now consigns you to a mooing herd, or so say some. "Going long" keeps getting longer.

Meltzer and Jurek are also professionals in this ultra world, and they represent just one strand of the surge in extreme adventuring. Ultra trail runners are being joined by fast packers, slack packers, off-trail skiers and boarders, linked-route climbers, high-speed alpinists, mountain racers, and other boundary breakers in motion as yet unheard of. What all these adventurers have in common is exposure to some edge, whether of distance, fitness, physiology, endurance, psychology, or suffering. Along that edge is where life lives sweetest, they say.

Yet, to paraphrase the poet Philip Booth in *Before Sleep*, a series of poems about a psychologist and the edges of the mind, spend all day along the edge, and sometimes you fall in.

Karl Meltzer and Scott Jurek are unlikely to require rescue (though it would be interesting to ask if, during training, either ever has), because their high-profile efforts are accompanied by a supporting cast. But their lesser-known trail cousins, each engaged in the construction of his or her own trail mythos, sometimes in solo pursuit of FKTs, are often on their own. Or they are running in hastily devised races that may not be anymore supervised than they are thought through.

Yitka Winn's fine July 2016 *Trail Runner* article, "The Thin Line," about the death of fifty-seven-year-old Arturo Martinez in the 2016 Ultra Fiord hundred-mile race in southern Chile offers an excellent case in point. Martinez, an experienced trail runner, succumbed to hypothermia along a snowy midsection of the course, and the questions that followed looked at both the race's organization and the mind-sets of ultra-runners. In mid-article, Winn looks deep into those minds:

> Serious accidents and fatalities are not uncommon in the worlds of climbing, mountaineering and backcountry skiing. Such communities are accustomed to grappling with questions of risk, of where responsibility belongs when things go wrong. Entire books are devoted to detailing preventable disasters in the mountains, and the lessons others can glean from them.

For many of us trail runners, though, these conversations are uncharted waters—especially those who arrive to the sport with a background not in wilderness travel, but in endurance. In some ways the very tenets of trail-running's culture fly in the face of the traditional code of caution. Every mountaineer's been taught to be wary of "summit fever." Conversely, many ultrarunners' code is "to endure at all costs; DNF is a dirty word."

We travel light, we push through pain, we chuckle at our body's physical rebellions, joke about stumbling or hallucinating or vomiting. For our stubbornness and triumphs, we're awarded medals and belt buckles. We get labeled inspirations, immortals, machines, kings and queens of the mountains, conquerors of the wild.

And sometimes we are.

But it becomes easy for any of us—runners or race organizers, outdoor veterans or novices, midpackers or elite runners—to forget how thin the line between life and death on the trail really is.

If they should reach breakpoint and tumble, or near the thin line before their time, these lesser-known trail cousins may need help. That proved true for Lelia Vann and Gregory Reck, a Norfolk, Virginia, couple eighty days into their third thru-hike of the Appalachian Trail in June, 2016. Vann (fifty-five) and Reck (sixty-nine) are slack packers, the AT term for hikers who opt for a string of day hikes to complete this long trail, rather than the traditional, carry-your-village-on-your-back thru-hike. In their adherence to and advocacy of the minimalist practices of slack packing, and in their enduring attraction to a long-distance trail, Vann and Reck offer an everyday example of this trend. Few of us can even imagine running one hundred miles through our own local forests, let alone in Patagonia's snows, but many of us can imagine being afoot on Vann and Reck's long trail days. They are not twenty-four-year-olds who have decided on a minimalist life on the edge, supported only by bare or cadged supplies. Nor are they kin to the now-established tradition of light-and-fast alpinists. As Lelia Vann said to me in one of a pair of open and gracious conversations about their ordeal in a June ice storm, "We like this way of hiking because each night there's a hot shower, a clean bed, and a glass of wine." So clearly Vann and Reck are not drawn by suffering. Nor, I'm guessing, are you. But their adoption of the minimalist practice of slack packing gives them membership in this growing group, where, on occasion, extreme practice may meet natural extremes.

> On June 9, after spending the prior night at an inn in nearby Woodstock, New Hampshire, Vann and Reck and two trail friends walked up the Liberty Springs Trail, aiming for AMC's Galehead Hut, nearly fifteen miles away. That's a bracing hike, but nothing extreme. The forecast they received for the area wasn't great—cool, possibly rainy—and the previous day had been abnormally cold up high, with an average temperature of 33 degrees on nearby Mount Washington, though they were not aware of that. But even as they were sometimes willing to "take a zero day," with no hiking mileage, and wait for better weather, the coming day looked dreary but walkable. They had a reservation for the night at Galehead, so they went up.

If they had been privy to the forecast from the Mount Washington Observatory, which told of tough temps and winds on the higher summits, they might have changed their minds. (Both say now that they would have.) Up high, this day promised to dip even below the day before in temperature, and it did, coming in at an average of 26 degrees (17 degrees below the date's norm) atop Washington. There, the winds averaged sixty-six miles per hour, with top gusts blowing through at a hundred miles per hour.

But in the people-heavy summer Whites of the twenty-first century, Vann and Reck were not alone. They had two companions, and Galehead hutmaster Scott Berkley estimated that more than a dozen people crossed the ridge that leads from Lafayette to his hut during these two cold days. Most agreed that the walk had been far from pleasant. The ridge lies lower than Washington; it ranges from 3,500 to 5,200 feet, and reaches Galehead at 3,800 feet, but it, too, featured ice, wind, and low visibility on both days. Still, they all had arrived without drama or mishap.

Slow drama, however, began unfolding later in the morning of June 9, as the foursome crossed the exposed ridge south of Mount Lafayette. Even back in the small trees along the Liberty ridge they'd noticed ice on the pine needles, which Vann supposed was leftover from a cold night. Now, the ice was more pronounced and still forming along the rocks. In a few steep drops, the group had to work off trail around the iced rocks. The wind they were facing blew steadily, with enough force to slow them further. All of

Iced sign at the junction of the Garfield Ridge and Skoocumchuck Trails on June 9, 2016. Photo by John Hansen.

this added up to their being strung out along the ridge, even as Lelia Vann ferried back and forth between the two trail friends who were out front and her husband, who was dropping slowly back. In this fashion they made their way up the south side of Mount Lafayette, still, as it turned out, protected some by its bulk from the north wind.

Once they topped Lafayette and crossed to its north slope, they were near the trail's high point and fully exposed to the wind, estimated to be blowing in at more than fifty miles per hour, with higher gusts. Here, when they needed some speed to get over and down into the trees, away from exposure, Vann and Reck were slowed further, losing touch with their friends and in danger of losing touch with each other. The world went smeary—both Vann and Reck wear glasses, and for the first time in their hiking experiences, their glasses started to ice over. Each tried clearing the lenses, taking the glasses off; nothing helped, and their compromised vision slowed them further.

"I wear bifocals," Reck said in a later interview, "and I was having trouble looking down. I tried taking the glasses off, but that didn't work, either. The sleet and wind were so strong I had to keep looking away. My steps got uncertain. My feet landed harder."

Not far above the juncture with the Skookumchuck Trail, and so still above tree line, Vann and Reck lost the trail. This was nothing unusual in a wind-tossed day with fog as thick as a sock, but that day two extremes began to come together to create emergency. The weather is the obvious one; Vann and Reck's method of hiking is the other. Vann and Reck had chosen, as was common for them, to slack-pack their fifteen-mile route, a decision inexplicable to traditionalists once this incident made the news. Still, its appeal is easy to see: a slack packer takes in a small pack only what's needed for a one- or two-day hike in between the trail's road crossings. Meanwhile, some friend or courier (from the gypsy economy that adheres to the AT) ferries the rest of the slack packer's gear to some road crossing near the next campsite, where the hiker retrieves it and packs for the next segment. Vann and Reck had aimed at a two-day walk, with Galehead Hut and its food and shelter as the midpoint night.

Anyone who has ever walked over a number of days with a full pack knows the way weight becomes a state of mind. Long-distance lore is full of ounce-obsessed walkers, as they try to pare those ounces to avoid feeling like a plodding beast of burden and move forward instead with the airy steps of the free spirit. Vann and Reck are such spirits, believing in this lighter way of going long to the point of becoming slack-packing advocates. Throughout this journey up the AT, the two were preparing to mine their experience for a book on the subject. For those who like to compare weights, a full, multiday pack may run from thirty-five to forty-five pounds, while a slack packer's daypack can weigh in the low teens, including water. Which is really no pack at all. But if you take less with you, it must be exactly the right stuff for the day you walk. And you must have that day figured correctly to stay on its safe side.

After their morning of slogging up-ridge into the cold wind, Vann and Reck were depleted. When the next cairn kept not appearing in the racketing wind, fog, and ice, hypothermia began its infiltration. The Facebook site of the Pemigewasset Valley Search and Rescue Team, one of the groups involved in saving Vann and Reck, describes what happened next: "Without good winter gear, the couple soon realized they were in serious trouble, and they activated a DeLorme Satellite distress signal at about 12:30 p.m., one of the last things they were able to accomplish with their now nonworking hands."

As they shared recollections of those early afternoon hours in separate conversations, both Vann and Reck described a sort of suspended other-scape, where all the markers that keep us located—time, place, distance, vision—were warped or absent. Vann said she kept ranging out from the last cairn and not finding the next. Afraid of getting off trail, where no one would see them, and unsure how far above tree line's relative shelter they were, she kept returning to its last marker. Finally, needing to get relief from the wind and in hope of rewarming themselves, the pair ducked behind a rock, tried to get out extra clothing, and huddled under their ponchos.

"We said, we need a plan B," Reck said, and then they recalled that there was a DeLorme device in Reck's pack. With or without their iced glasses, they couldn't read the screen clearly, but it seemed that their emergency signal had been sent. "We knew we were in real trouble," each said later. Vann recalled that her "feet and legs lost feeling," and later, when she tried standing, she had trouble walking. Reck's hands "wouldn't work." Neither could see. The wind was unrelenting, temperature in the low thirties. They hid behind the rock and waited.

Hypothermia is insidious. It's a cold-handed mechanic that reaches into your mind and begins detaching some wires and reconnecting others. Much of that rewiring slows you down: what once was routine—a step, a decision to look at a map, finding a light—mimics the drawn-out slur of a tape player winding down: O . . . where . . . is . . . that . . . head . . . lamp . . . O . . . O . . . here it is . . . no . . . no . . . that's . . . not it . . . but . . . what . . . what . . . what?

Among hypothermia's early effects is impaired judgment: What . . . should . . . I . . . do . . . well . . . who . . . knows . . . is . . . it . . . getting . . . warmer . . . I . . . think . . . I'll . . . rest . . . a little . . . longer. . . .

In the valley, the DeLorme signal had set a rescue in motion as NHFG summoned both PVSART and AVSAR volunteers and their own conservation officers. But hours would pass before they could reach the site of the rescue call. Attempts to contact the couple failed (both of their phones were on airplane mode to preserve batteries, and, at that point, they hadn't thought they could get service).

"Wolfman" Adam DeWolfe, rescuer, on top of Mount Moosilauke
a few days before he came upon and saved a couple on the Franconia Ridge.
Photo courtesy of Adam DeWolfe.

Serendipity, in the form of a "Wolfman," happened along and bought the pair and rescue teams those needed hours: "The couple was saved," said PVSART's Facebook page, "by a passing AT thru-hiker (Trailname = Wolfman), only the fourth person the couple saw all day, who discovered them [at around 1:00 p.m.] shivering violently and unable to care for themselves. He was able to set up [his one-person] tent above tree line [in the lee of a boulder] and get the two hikers inside it. This action helped to stop further body-temperature loss and buy the time necessary for rescuers to climb the 4.5 miles to provide heat, food, and hot drinks to bring the couple back to life." And then, walk them back down into it.

Thirty-seven-year-old Adam DeWolfe had set out for Katahdin from northern Pennsylvania on the AT some weeks earlier as part of a nine-hundred-mile walk. Earlier that year, he'd done his first distance hike along the Sierras' iconic John Muir Trail and, at a pause point in his life after a decade of work as an environmental consultant, he had come to the AT. On the morning of the ninth, after a cold night at Liberty Spring Shelter, DeWolfe had checked the Mount Washington Observatory's higher summits forecast and pondered crossing the exposed ridge ahead. A self-described "weather geek" and former Eagle Scout with a tendency "to be prepared," he had anticipated a tough weather day, but he had also figured he was capable of walking through it and equipped to do so.

Liberty Spring Shelter is at 3,900 feet, and it wasn't long before DeWolfe saw the same ice Lelia Vann had noticed earlier along the ridge leading north from Mount Liberty. The little tag thermometer on his pack read just above freezing, and the thin rain and mist persisted. It was, as he and others agreed later, textbook hypothermia weather. In a January 2017 conversation, DeWolfe described his ascent into that weather, and in his lucid description one gains a sense of his capabilities: "Gradually, I got into the thick of it," he recalled. "The wind grew stronger, and there was ice on the rocks. As I came over Lafayette and into the full wind, I had to crouch during the gusts." There, on his climb's 5,200-foot highpoint, DeWolfe was aware that he had reached an edge. All along the ridge he had kept track of his gradual immersion in a hard day, contemplating at times a return to Liberty Spring. Atop Lafayette, where he had to knock the ice off to read the trail sign, he knew he was beyond the return and that he needed to press on and down toward the relative shelter of the trees a half-mile or so ahead. "It was also a little exciting to be in such extreme weather," he admitted. At this point, DeWolfe was only minutes from coming upon Lelia Vann and Greg Reck, when the sudden intimacy of their crisis would also become his. But as he crouched and forced his way through the heavy, ice-watered wind, he knew exactly what conditions he was in and how he was faring.

Such an ability to understand what is going on around him and project his way through it marks DeWolfe as someone who can imagine a way forward from a sound understanding of the present. That sounds common; it is not. Especially in complicated, sometimes perilous situations. In their groundbreaking work on decision making and the ways in which we skew it from a statistical optimum, psychologists Danny Kahneman and Amos

Tversky (Kahneman became a Nobel Prize winner for their insights into economic decision making) have this to say: "We often decide that an outcome is extremely unlikely or impossible, because we are unable to imagine any chain of events that could cause it to occur. The defect, often, is our imagination" (Michael Lewis, *The Undoing Project*, 194). All the way along the Franconia Ridge, DeWolfe had been tracking what was happening, his gradual immersion in the walk and its weather, and imagining what could happen. Unlike the famous frog who can't imagine he's being cooked in slowly heating water, DeWolfe could imagine being cooled on this June day that was "more extreme than a lot of what I'd encountered in the winter." He had the imagination to see how it could happen.

A few tenths of a mile away on the Garfield Ridge Trail, Lelia Vann and Greg Reck were suffering from their inability to imagine this day. Both reported later that they'd never in their thousands of trail miles seen anything like it, and neither had ever seen glasses smear over with ice. Literally and figuratively, they were partially blinded. "When I first came upon Lelia and Greg," DeWolfe recalled, "I thought I was seeing a pack someone had left in the trail. They were huddled under their ponchos (their only shelter) behind a trailside rock. When I looked in, Lelia said, 'We need help.'" DeWolfe said he felt he had "walked into a movie scene."

The help Vann and Reck got was lifesaving. "I knew we needed a miracle," Reck recalled. "Wolfman was a miracle."

"Well, I knew I couldn't leave them," said DeWolfe. "Lelia said she couldn't feel her legs or walk. Greg could walk but couldn't see well, and he said his hands wouldn't work. And I also knew we couldn't stay where they were." DeWolfe wasn't sure how far below the trees began, and, of course, he couldn't see tree line in the thick clouds. First, he scouted down-trail a bit and found a big outcropping that offered more shelter; he went back to bring Vann and Reck to that spot. "Even going those few hundred feet was hard," he recalled. DeWolfe supported Vann part of the way down, and she butt-scooted the rest. Reck followed slowly, but it was clear to DeWolfe that walking them down farther at that point was beyond them all. Perhaps, he thought, we can go on later if I can help warm them some.

In the outcrop's shelter, DeWolfe was able to erect his one-person tent's outer shelter, which made use of his poles, and he found large rocks to pin down the tent ropes so it wouldn't fly away or collapse. "He put the tent up around us," recalled Reck. "And all the while, whatever he did, he would explain it to us, and then do it. Looking back, I'm amazed at how methodical and analytical he was. And it didn't take him long. He did things decisively."

"I must have had one hundred pounds of rocks on each rope," DeWolfe said. Inside, he got Vann and Reck on top of his thermal pad and under his sleeping bag, and then DeWolfe got in too. "The thermal pad helped immediately," he said, and I tried to get them to eat some too." Wind-forced, iced rain penetrates even the best gear, and Vann and Reck had been without such gear; they were soaked. Still, in the tent, they were more protected and remained coherent. The trio talked over what to do.

"I knew we couldn't stay there," said DeWolfe, and he set off down to see if he could reach the woods and get a better fix on their location and possibilities. In a short time, he reached the junction of the Skookumchuck Trail, but that descent had not been easy to follow, and DeWolfe was afraid to go beyond. "I was aware that I was out there without my pack and shelter. I couldn't afford to get lost. Even the short climb back to the tent took forever," he said. "When he got back to the tent, he said he'd almost lost his way," Reck recalled.

Back in the tent, they checked Vann and Reck's DeLorme device, and DeWolfe could see it said, "in progress," but what that meant was unclear. Somewhere around 2:00 p.m. DeWolfe said, "We need to call for help, too." He had service for his cell phone, and his 911 call got patched through to NHFG. At 2:30 p.m. NHFG's lt. Jim Kneeland called DeWolfe, who was able to describe where he was, what condition Vann and Reck were in, and his certainty that he could not walk them farther down. Uncertainty that had arrived with the DeLorme signal—were there four or two people, were they at the site of the signal, in what condition?—vanished. DeWolfe, wanting certainty that rescuers wouldn't miss them behind their outcropping in the gale, went back out and formed an arrow with hiking poles, pointing to where his tent was pitched. The trio was able to text Lelia and Greg's two morning companions to learn that they were nearing Galehead and okay. So NHFG knew now that they were going to help three people at one site. As Lt. Kneeland's NHFG incident report said, "I advised them that help was on the way."

NHFG rescuers conferring above tree line on June 9, 2016. Photo by Chris Whiton

At 5:36 p.m., Kneeland got the call from PVSART rescuers that they were with Vann, Reck, and DeWolfe and providing dry warm clothing and hot liquid jello. DeWolfe also remembers the welcome Starburst candies that are a PVSART signature. By 6:30 p.m. rescuers had warmed Vann and Reck to the point where everyone could start down. By 8:45 p.m. everyone had reached the trailhead.

Here's a complicated point in thinking about this story. I've just cited the importance of an imagination that draws upon knowledge to enter the stories we tell ourselves and use as guides. That is our first and best guard against trouble in the backcountry. But when we know extremes, when we know what can go wrong, the imagined stories that follow can also pin us in place to the point where we don't go out at all. It is entirely possible to become fearful to the point of mountain phobia, which can be seen as a sort of upland, airy agoraphobia—and no one who loves the mountains wants to be kept from them by fear. So we also need to resolve to use our imaginations to help rather than hinder our outdoor experiences.

> Other points to ponder rise like cairns in the cold fog. They line a thin trail of safety through tough weather. As ever, we arrive at a need for balance, essential for walking, essential for surviving. To make a "balanced" decision as we step toward and through each hike, we draw upon what we know and what we've heard to fashion a way on that trail, to imagine that day. As we put hikeSafe's ten essentials in our packs, we imagine what each might be used for. As we seek out the most local, detailed forecast, we compare it to

weather we have walked into, adding a shell here or a bivy sack there to match that weather's possible demands. What Lelia Vann and Greg Reck had imagined and chosen to carry simply wasn't a match for the day.

But even imagining all the right gear won't work unless we have made ourselves adept at using it—all of it. We must practice erecting tents, with fashioning splints, with reading maps and using a compass, and with operating any technology we choose to carry. We even need to practice changing batteries in our headlamps. Here, too, Vann and Reck understand their need to do better. Their DeLorme device was, for some time, even on that rugged day, forgotten equipment. When they finally remembered it, they were unsure of how it worked. They thought they'd sent their emergency message, but blurred vision and unfamiliarity with the device made them uncertain. I recall wondering, in the early days of cell phones, just where the button that turned mine on was. The time to suss this out would not be in a screaming gale or under a veil of pain. Devices can ride with us unused for years, but if we choose to carry them, we must know how to work them blindfolded.

DeWolfe does more than save Vann and Reck; he also introduces us to the mountains' other rescuers: the unofficial, often unsung cadre of us, the hiking tribe. Clearly, his ability to meet Vann and Reck's plight with skill marks DeWolfe as among the best of us. He set up a tent in a gale, got the pair inside and set to warming them, or at least staving off further cooling as best he could. All that suggests solid skills and self-possession, not to mention generosity. And it invites each of us to comparison's room . . . or tent: Could I accomplish that?

Who We Are Out There

So what, when you head out for a day in hills, or on a days-long walk, is your duty to your fellow walkers? And is it changing as what some of those fellow travelers do gets more extreme?

I put those questions to a knowledgeable backcountry-traveling friend while talking about rescues. She and her family have a long tradition of weeks-long descents of far northern Canadian rivers, where rescue is unavailable and fellow travelers scarce or absent. On most of their trips, over hundreds of miles, they meet no one, seeing only signs of former native residents' stone encampments and waymarks. They are "out there" in a way few of us can fathom.

So I wondered about their take on responsibility and rescue. Clearly, they assume responsibility for themselves and their decisions. But what about others, perhaps someone encountered along a Maine river or a New Hampshire trail as they train in this more peopled terrain for their tundra paddling and portaging? What did they think of the tale of Vann, Reck, and DeWolfe? This is what my friend wrote:

> Each of us has come upon a fellow runner, paddler, or climber in need of assistance. Much of my family argues strongly that part of being outside is accepting your responsibility to help the fellow adventurer who has fallen off the edge. But I myself am less troubled by the implications of extreme running/hiking, etc. for search and rescue folk, who will figure out some good response in their rescue community, and more troubled by the implications for all the other hikers out on the same trail.
>
> Clearly, the hiker who stopped to save the lives of this couple could have been putting his own life in danger, even though he had packed responsibly. As extreme approaches to motion proliferate, what are the implications for all the other hikers out there? It seems like the rethinking of the commitments traditionalists take on when they head out on trails is in order. What would that look like? Honestly, I find my impulse is to release traditionalists somehow from some of the responsibilities we all usually assume.

Such release "from some of the responsibilities we all usually assume" reminds me of another extreme, that of Himalayan climbing, where a convention is now well established that if you falter in the "death zone"—above 26,000 feet—you are largely on your own. Rescue there is too difficult, so it becomes every one for her- or himself. Mount Everest is littered with bodies of those who fell and then froze on the way up or down. In the perpetual sterility of high cold, they simply lie there, named by passersby for their bright boots, for example; for years they have been walked by, first in life and then in death, by other climbers. It seems an exaggeration, but could the advent of extreme running/hiking/climbing in these low Whites be courting some version of a Himalayan hands-off policy when it comes to rescue?

Returning to the north slope of Lafayette on June 9, amid the wind-wracked ice, imagine you are DeWolfe. Do you walk by? Do you stop briefly? Do you go the full distance? Break out what supplies you have, give what shelter you can, and hunker down then to wait? In doing so, do you join your emergency to theirs?

I talked over Vann and Reck's rescue with Allan Clark, head of PVSART and also chief of the nearby Sugar Hill, New Hampshire, fire department. Chief Clark added this note to the story of rescue: "By the time we got up the 4.5 miles, we knew we might have three cases of hypothermia to worry about." Clearly, DeWolfe's generous, competent response could have brought him near the edge too.

Clark's observation evokes the frequent search and rescue question of how our actions in the hills affect others. Many deeply experienced mountain walkers say that each of us who climbs away into that world owes consideration both to those who are out there with us and to those who may look for us if we are lost or injured. That surely is the stance of Pat Grimm, AT thru-hiker and AMC volunteer hiking instructor, who knows Vann and Reck from hiking sections of the AT with them, and who voices a traditionalist's code of responsibility well. Grimm suggests that the pair's focus on minimizing pack weight left them underprepared to look after themselves. "I always carry the gear to survive a storm or an unplanned night out. We know the risks: weather changes, accidents happen. I don't think I should expect someone else to carry the basics that will save my life up in the mountains," Grimm says.

Those who place primary responsibility with the walker or climber tend to agree. Calling rescuers into dangerous weather is a risk to them, and that risk is clearly illustrated by DeWolfe's getting slowly cold as he worked to help the pair he'd found. That ethos is an argument against the minimalists who set out to go fast and so go light.

I agree . . . to a point. Each of us should feel responsible for those we summon to help us. And we should summon help only when we've exhausted our options for self-rescue, though gauging that can be tricky, especially with the onset of hypothermia's skewed thinking.

But I stop short of assigning wholesale responsibility to those pressing the buttons of need. Search and rescue is also a dance into which rescuers enter freely. Like dancers, rescuers are not obligated to take steps; instead they embrace the choreography, choose the dance. As has been detailed elsewhere, rescuers are free to decline—no, I think I'll sit this one out—even as doing so is not easy. So responsibility also rests with those who respond, who choose to go up into tough weather or terrain, and that responsibility multiplies for those who command the rescuers. A NHFG officer or a snow ranger or a volunteer group leader is always asking, "Should I send rescuers up? Should I call them back? What are their reasonable limits?" Even as such calling back is very rare.

"What rarely gets said," said Allan Clark, harkening back to the Edward Bacon rescue on the same Franconia Ridge (see chapter 18), "was that Jim Kneeland and I had an ongoing debate that night about whether to call the rescuers off the mountain. The weather was so bad we got this close to calling it off." Clark also spoke of the physical cost of working through bad-weather rescues: "What also went unreported was that six of my people got injuries on the Bacon rescue."

Perhaps you also recall an early incident in chapter 2: in it a woman with an injured knee waits on a cool, windy September day along the Gulfside Trail, while her companion seeks help at Madison Hut. As she waits, not one, but two doctors emerge from the fog separately, and each stops to assess her trouble. Both doctors say she should stay put, waiting for help. Then each doctor shoulders his pack and walks off into the fog, which seems to under-line each one's return to his separate world. Yes, neither the weather and nor the injury is immediately life-threatening, but the response of these fellow hikers prompts us to ask: What would I do? Stay? Pass by?

A skein of incident runs through this book, linking Curtis and Ormsbee to Herr and Batzer, and then to Tinkham and Haas, who suggest Matrosova, who precedes Vann and Reck. Because this is a book of walking trouble, they are not, of course, the only incidents related, but they are joined by a sort of exceptionalism—all of them aim up into extremes of weather, bearing with them only the thinnest margins for error; all of them rely on the capable self making no error. Isn't that, we wonder in our valleys and armchairs, the realm of the gods only? Shouldn't we always pack for, count on, our own blundering?

"People don't know how bad it can get," Mike Pelchat said in an interview after the Matrosova search. And that's true, with a few exceptions—those who go out and up after the Herrs and the Haases and the Matrosovas. These rescuers know just how bad it can get, what can happen when we bring extreme efforts into an extreme world.

The New Normal?

As this thinking was "coming into condition," setting up like a snow slope I hoped to climb to some sort of insight, Northface launched a new advertisement, which popped up on my screen, complete with video clips from extremis. The one I watched had an anthem—"miles from nowhere" was its refrain—and in one iteration, it offered this tagline: "The unthinkable is the new normal."

> Perhaps I was freshly susceptible from all my readings and interviews, but as I watched clips of people—young, attractive people—trying for extremes and often peeling off cliffs and climbing walls, or simply peeling away layers from skin in their sometimes teary failed attempts, I thought back to the late Dean Potter. Potter, a wingsuit legend and accomplished climber of edges, was, as reported by White Mountain friends I trust, a very likable guy. He had found rock climbing as a teenager on New Hampshire's Joe English Hill and then accelerated quickly to its top levels on Cathedral and Whitehorse Ledges. His adventures had later taken him to jumping off high places and using a wingsuit to soar through the air. By May of 2015, when Potter and a suited acolyte launched from Yosemite's Taft Point, he had left the little Whites far behind for bigger drops and longer flights.

Potter's last flight plan was reported to hinge on his ability to clear a col in its midsection. Despite his habit of calculating carefully, that didn't happen. Potter and then his follower piled into the col and, the next day, after their bodies had been spotted, search and rescue people went to retrieve them.

There were no wingsuit flyers in the Northface ad, but clearly gravity was the adversary, the force to be mastered, finally. It is an old dream. But is jousting with it so far out there the "new normal"? I look around at mountain-drawn folks I know; I look inside. I get the appeal—limits, who needs them? But then I look also at the litter of emotions left behind when someone lives and dies at these limits; I see the fiery fall of flying too close to the sun of risk. I see the toll on those who retrieve the bodies. That too is unthinkable.

< 21 >

THE EXCEPTION OF AIR

Aircraft have been part of search and rescue in the White Mountains for decades, with a mix of fixed-wing planes and helicopters sometimes searching for those missing or, on occasion, lifting an injured hiker or climber from trouble. As early as 1933, the legendary pilot Wylie Apte was flying from White Mountain Airport (no longer in operation) in search of Joseph Simon, a missing hiker later found dead in the Presidential Range. Helicopters began to appear regularly in 1964, when the AMC used them to transport construction materials for the building of Mizpah Spring Hut. From 1969 to 1995, the White Mountain helicopter legend Joe Brigham flew construction and resupply missions to AMC's huts and, at times, joined a search and rescue operation. Still, until New Hampshire's Army National Guard began flying SAR missions, and the Dartmouth-Hitchcock hospital developed its Advanced Response Team in 1994, SAR flights were rare, exceptions to the usual, foot-found way. That is no longer so, as NHANG and DHART now take to the air often to find or extract the wayward from the way-back.

Even as we would climb into the sky, we are still land based. Seen from the altitude of an eagle, we crawl here and there, make our way slowly to higher ground. But when emergency is the accelerant, we beam requests to satellites and hope for response faster than feet; we look to the sky for answer. If we are lucky, we may see a different sort of bird, a Blackhawk or an American Eurocopter EC135. Its distinctive "chopper" sound of concussed air may presage a carpet ride back to life, as it did for the injured skier discussed in chapter 16.

New Hampshire Army National Guard (NHANG)

Old sayings often tap a few professions for examples of the sort of person you want in charge when challenge arrives. Surgeons figure in these sayings, as do air traffic controllers—we want their precision and attention to detail. So, too, do pilots. It's easy to see why.

In late February 2017, I'm sitting at a table in a spacious, well-lit briefing room at the New Hampshire Army National Guard's air wing, talking with three Blackhawk crew members about flying rescue missions in the Whites. Pilots Dan Jacques and Iain Hamilton and crew chief Greg Gerbig take turns answering my questions, offering clear explanations of how they work, and remembering moments when the mix of mountain terrain, screaming wind, and flying clouds reduced clarity to the focused mind only. Their sentences are straightforward, unadorned. They are matter-of-fact about flying at times in what can only be described as chaos. Each pilot emphasizes the teamwork of flying, the way a crew of four must divvy up the work and then each focus on his part of that work to fly safely and search effectively. Each is confident about the Blackhawk (Lima model) he flies.

There are times, however, when even the formidable power of a Blackhawk flown by experienced pilots can be overmatched. On February 16, 2015, as the urgency of Kate Matrosova's plight deepened, NHFG asked for helicopter assistance. "This is how complicated it can get," recalled Jacques. "I was in Nevada at a training session, and there I was on the phone talking to the NHFG guys and getting together the crew that would fly." That crew would include pilots Hamilton and David Bretton, crew chief Gerbig, and medic Chris Wareing. Hamilton remembered that the air "was a little bumpy initially" as they flew north from Concord. But as they reached the Sandwich Range, the southernmost group of bigger mountains, bumpy became something else: "I think that's the worst turbulence I've flown in in my life," Hamilton said. "We hit one downdraft where I had the helicopter on full climb to gain altitude, and when I looked at the gauge, I saw we were still going down at between 1,000 and 2,000 feet per minute." That's when he looked over and saw Gerbig being lifted as the aircraft dropped. Gerbig was, as all pilots and crew are, strapped into his seat. "I went up slowly," said Gerbig. But I went up all the way to where my head hit the ceiling." Gerbig's slow rise was being propelled by the helicopter's sustained fall. (Note: the manufacturer's specs estimate a Blackhawk's vertical rate of climb at over 3,000 feet per minute in air with temperatures below 70 degrees, which gives us an idea of the immense force of that downdraft.)

Hamilton and Gerbig made it up to Mount Adams, where they "circled around for fifteen minutes," but they couldn't get low enough "to do anything useful," so, with fuel running low, they decided to return to base. In calmer weather, they would have been able to bring the helicopter's FLIR (forward-looking infrared) camera system to bear on the search which, if Matrosova had been alive and generating a heat signal, might have picked her out in the mayhem. But the record from the wind gauge on nearby Mount Washington tells a story of winds gusting to 140 miles per hour that day, creating "the worst turbulence" Hamilton had ever seen.

"Worst," of course, is not typical. A typical search and rescue mission begins with a call from NHFG that technically puts NHANG's pilots and crew to work for the governor of New Hampshire. Depending on the time of the call, a crew can be assembled rapidly, or over some time. During weekdays, the air group is usually fully staffed, so they can be ready to go quickly. But as we have seen, SAR work often takes place during off-hours—on weekends and at night—when gathering a crew takes time, as those on call drive to the hangar in Concord. When assembled, that crew is composed of two pilots, a crew chief, and a medic. Also usually in the aircraft (unless an extra fuel cell is brought on board for a search with an uncertain time frame) is a NHFG conservation officer. One pilot flies, while the other navigates, using mapping programs that include trails, and also coordinates logistics (refueling, for example). As they reach a search or rescue area, the second pilot searches, along with the crew chief and medic. When the crew is working on a "pick," either the medic or the crew chief will be lowered to the injured hiker by the hoist. The cable attached to the hoist is 250 feet long, but the pilots work to hover between 70 and 130 feet over their target. "By keeping the helicopter close to the tree tops, we get the best visual references for our pilots to minimize fore/aft lateral drift," said Hamilton.

A "pick" often gets made with a "forest penetrator," a metal device about the size of a good-sized anchor, with wings that unfold for seating or, if the hiker can't ride up that way, with a litter. "We used to use solid litters," Gerbig said. "But in the wind, even with someone holding on to the tag line (a rope attached to the litter and held by someone on the ground to prevent spinning or skewing of the person being hoisted), the litter could act like a wing and get blown up into the tail rotor. So now we use litters made with mesh that lets the wind through."

Clearly, a lot is going on in such a scene, and tracking it creates a significant mental load for a pilot. "Talking about the mental load," said Hamilton, "one other thing that has always helped me—it's been a saying as long as I can remember flying—is don't make their emergency your emergency." That saying rests on the remarkable record of safety and usefulness NHANG's pilots have compiled while flying SAR missions in the Whites. It also joins them in practice and spirit to their rescue brothers and sisters on the ground, who have learned to resist the rushing that gets them in trouble.

Jacques, Hamilton, and Gerbig can offer any number of examples, but they agree that the mission that demands the most of them is one where they are working close to the clouds. When the winds are up and the clouds are low, Jacques or whoever else is organizing a mission will send his most experienced pilots. New pilots fresh from mountain flight school in Colorado get routine missions—to pick up someone from atop Mount Washington on a clear windless day, for example. The Jacques, Hamiltons and Gerbigs get the howling days, or the days like one in the Dry River wilderness a few winters ago. There, Jacques recalled, they'd been asked to look for two overdue hikers, and they had found them. The tricky part lay in picking the hikers out. To do so, Jacques had to hover right at the cloud deck, while the hikers were hoisted up. "I was hoping the clouds wouldn't drop suddenly," he said. "What if they had?" I asked. "Then, it's about keeping your head, being deliberate," Jacques said. Hamilton added, "if you get sucked into the clouds, it's important to have an exit plan ready, to have studied and know the terrain and where to turn so the land is going down as you climb away."

Having the focus and experience to work and fly so deliberately takes practice, of course, and that's a constant. "You have to understand what your role is; whatever is going on on the ground has already happened," said Jacques. "And that means staying composed and not getting tunnel vision," Hamilton added. "If you can develop that mind-set," Jacques said, "we can teach you the rest." Pilots emerge from flight school with 130–150 hours of flight time; learning "the rest" to do the work NHANG does, Hamilton estimates, requires 400–500 hours. Those additional hours include lots of practice in angled terrain. The pilots favor the area around Mount Carrigain for its steep slopes and distance from most people. There, they can practice holding a steady hover above the trees, dropping a forest penetrator into those trees, and hoisting someone out.

How much open space do they need to avoid snagging the penetrator and person on a tree limb? "It depends on the weather conditions," Hamilton said. "If winds are calm, you can pick someone through a fairly tight hole in the trees. If we are getting blown by the winds a bit, we try and find a hole that will be a little more forgiving. We practice tight picks quite often, and I am sure it would be hard to find a medic who has been hoisted and not bounced off a branch at least once in his lifetime."

Also, given rescue work in all weathers, seasons, and hours, pilots also must practice with night vision goggles (NVGs). Costing about $10,000 a pair, NVGs attach to a pilot's helmet and can be flipped down before his eyes. Looking through them is akin to using binoculars, and the goggles change the dark landscape below to an eerie, neon green, even as they trim a pilot's peripheral vision significantly. Using them requires more specialized practice, and NHANG pilots do that practice on Tuesday and Thursday nights, when residents living on the fringes of the Whites often hear them flying toward the night mountains.

As noted earlier, NHANG flies its SAR missions as training for their deployments around the world. Jacques, Hamilton, and Gerbig have all flown in Afghanistan, and last year they did three months of humanitarian work in Guatemala. How, I wondered, does their Whites training measure up? "The transfer has been good," said Jacques. "I was flying a mission in Afghanistan that had us working on a pick at about 9,000 feet. It didn't dawn on me at first that the other pilot had no mountain experience. When it did, my workload went up more than it would have if he'd had experience here. It's invaluable, the work we do here."

What about the hiker who is the object of "a pick," the person some 70 to 130 feet below at the end of the cable? What do these pilots think of him? "It depends some on how prepared the hiker is," said Gerbig. "Over time, I've gained some more empathy as I've seen how a small oversight can have huge consequences," said Hamilton, while Jacques added, "After a while, when I'm flying for search and rescue, I've come to thinking less about the individual [being rescued] and more about being of service to the guys on the ground, the guys from Mountain Rescue or Fish and Game. If we can make a pick and get someone out of trouble, we save those guys the work and risk of a long carry. I think that's the value of what we do."

Dartmouth-Hitchcock Advanced Response Team (DHART)

Kyle Madigan, director of the Dartmouth-Hitchcock hospital's Advanced Response Team, ducks under the tail section of an American Eurocopter EC135. "Careful," he says, "I've lost a lot of skin from my head bumping into this." I bend down and get a look up into the bay where a litter can be slid in and fastened down quickly; I imagine the litter lifted from gray rocks by many hands and slipped into place. The pilot is still in his seat; the medic will scramble around to the helicopter's side door, where he'll be at the head of the injured hiker; the flight nurse will come in through the other side and flank the person, who is now a patient. The doors ride shut; the rescuers, who have carried the litter to this landing zone, duck instinctively as they step away beyond the circle swung by the rotor blades. When they are clear, the pilot juices the engine, lifts off, and swings the helicopter into a climb that follows the ridge as it declines, and then swings away, bound straight for a nearby hospital. Already, the medic and the nurse have determined what first treatment the injured hiker needs, and that has helped decide which hospital they are aiming for. They'll be there in ten minutes. Back on the mountain in the sudden quiet, the rescuers gather their gear and get ready to walk out; they'll be at the trailhead in two hours.

I straighten and bump my head, which returns me to place. Responding to my request, Madigan says it's fine to take some pictures, and I include a few of the slot in the aircraft where emergency rides, even as I recall Madigan's telling me that search and rescue response is only "1 or 2 percent of our business."

That 1 or 2 percent of roughly fourteen hundred annual flights can be high profile, however, and since they are offered as "a service to the community," these flights fit also into DHART's mission as a team that provides medical transport for Vermont and New Hampshire. In that North Country much of the ground transport is interrupted by mountains. West-east travel, especially, winds slowly along thin roads. Getting someone who needs advanced care to a tertiary-care hospital via these roads can consume time a patient may not have. So DHART's mission is to help save lives by saving time.

That was the case in chapter 16's example of DHART's prompt response to a skier's life-threatening fall down Hillman's Highway in Tuckerman Ravine. Taking over from the snow rangers who had worked to stabilize the skier, DHART's paramedic and flight nurse offered aid, while the pilot flew the sixty-mile hop to the Dartmouth-Hitchcock hospital. "The difference that we offer," says Madigan, "is that we can respond immediately," and that is a result of DHART's 24–7 staffing.

Founded in 1994, DHART got its first call seven minutes after opening on July 1, a clear marker that theirs would be an essential service. More than seventeen thousand subsequent missions have ratified that insight. "Much of what we do for SAR involves searching," says Madigan:

> An example was a search we did three winters ago up in Lyme [New Hampshire]. A man was out snowshoeing or cross-country skiing and he fell and injured himself, and he couldn't get out. So he called 911 on his cell phone. But they were having a difficult time locating him, and it was getting dark. So they called us and they said, "Hey, could you guys go airborne and help us take a look for this gentleman?" So we lifted off—a new technology that we added about ten years ago is night vision goggles—and with the night vision goggles and this gentleman holding his cell phone, we were able to spot him in about five minutes. He didn't even have to have it shining up; it just gave off so much light when the night vision is in use, it's like he's sitting in a room with the light turned on. We hovered over his location and the pilot radioed, "This is the latitude and longitude," and the fire department was able to plug it into their GPS and drive a snow machine right to him.

When they pick up an injured hiker or skier, DHART's helicopters, unlike the Blackhawks, must land. Having a hoist isn't necessary for their primary work, and Madigan says, "that also adds both training and risk," which means most medical transport groups also opt not to have it. DHART's maps do identify some landing zones, near AMC's Lakes of the Clouds or in Tuckerman Ravine, for example, but mostly the pilot gauges what's possible. He may work also with rescuers on the ground, who can help set up a landing spot. Weather is an omnipresent factor, and Madigan says DHART takes special care with how they ask pilots to decide about flying:

> We blind the pilot to all patient information until such time as he accepts the mission. Here's an example: The dispatch would receive a call, let's say from Tuckerman Ravine, saying, we need a DHART helicopter for an injured skier. Then our dispatch would radio a request saying, "DHART 1, scene request, Tuckerman Ravine." The pilot would respond, "Copy that," and then the pilot would do a weather check. We have some computer programs for forecasting and for winds aloft and for weather in that region. The pilot would look all that over. Then the pilot would make a decision whether it's safe to fly in that weather. If it is, the pilot would then respond, "Mission is accepted.'" At that point the medical crew would be given any patient information.

Such a procedure guards against a pilot feeling emotionally compelled to fly because of patient's condition.

Once they are underway, DHART also has a policy summed up in this saying: four to say go, one to say no. All four people involved in receiving a call must agree on flying; once in flight any one of them can say, "I'm uncomfortable with this," and call it off. But that almost never happens, says Madigan, "because our pilots are very good." Those nine pilots, four in Lebanon, four in Manchester, and one a "floater," come from a fifty-fifty mix of military and civilian training, and they are supplied by Metro Aviation of Shreveport, Louisiana, though most have worked exclusively with DHART for years. So they know the territory.

DHART's quick, professional capability, 24–7 availability, and advanced professional skills prompt me to ask Madigan whether he favors professionalization of White Mountain SAR. In answer, he details an early summer rescue he took part in as a medic on Mount Moosilauke. The day before the call came in, an older man ascending the north side slipped on wet rocks and injured himself. No one passed by, and with minimal clothing, the man was forced to stay there overnight. The next morning, three women climbing the mountain happened upon him, and one went to the top and called

911. Untrained in rescue, however, she went back to the man and out of cell phone contact. DHART got the call and responded to the mountaintop. Meanwhile, a thru-hiker came upon the man and the three women, recognized the man's developing hypothermia, and got him into her sleeping bag, and also heated liquids for him. Atop the mountain, a volunteer passerby scouted for the injured man and found him and his rescuers, then led the three-person DHART crew to him. "By the time, we got there, the thru-hiker had him mostly rewarmed."

Still, this small crew of rescuers needed to get the man by litter to the helicopter on the summit. As they worked at this, more fortune visited in the form of a large group of MIT students, who took over the lugging. Soon the injured man was ready to go into the copter. "It was a nice scene there," Madigan remembers. "Everyone was shaking hands with the man, saying 'good luck to you.' Everyone felt good."

"We deal with volunteers on many levels, because many of the rescue squads in the little towns are all volunteers," says Madigan.

> You get in the back of an ambulance and three of the four people have on their Carhartts and their work clothes. There's a lot to be said for volunteerism and the dedication that people put into it. It all comes down to training, whether you're a professional or volunteer. It all comes down to the amount of support and training that you can gather. Wouldn't it be great if everyone had all the support that they needed from whatever those funds are. We respect everybody. Part of what has brought DHART acceptance [in the SAR community] is that we're part of a team. We fly in in a fancy helicopter, and we wear fancy suits, but we're just part of a bigger team. There was some first responder who got there first, and then there was some search and rescue person, and everybody is doing his or her best for that person. And then we just get to take them and work to the best of our ability to get to the next level of care. If we keep it in that frame, where we're all part of this bigger machinery of search and rescue and patient care, that's what keeps everybody humble and keeps everybody wanting to continue doing it.

As I'm leaving DHART's hangar, I recall PVSART's Steve Smith recounting the rescue of a heavyset man on Mount Jefferson and saying, "When the DHART helicopter was able to land, we all cheered."

> I titled this chapter "The Exception of Air" because the current trend toward more and more air support for White Mountain SAR carries with it both exceptional talent and a marked shift from rescue's traditional, land-based crawl. Air power's speed hews closer to the expectations of our communications, which, increasingly, transmit questions and requests from almost any remoteness in the time it takes to draw a breath. In short, answer by air seems a natural companion for the calls for help that arrive that way too. Then there is the lifting power and quick transport that can eliminate hours and miles of litter lugging or hobbling out. The slow winding passage of a string of headlamps over broken terrain gives way to the rapid arrival of winking lights overhead.

Yes, hard weather can scotch hope or promise of rescue by air, and for those days, the slow approaches and carryouts of walkers will always be the first choice. But this section does raise the question, Why not more rescue by air? Why not even more of this exceptional work?

The chapters ahead seek to deepen these questions and offer answers too.

<22>

BACK TO THE FUTURE?

––––

White Mountain SAR in 2020 and Beyond

Often the future begins elsewhere. An idea or a practice gets tried, and as its story spreads, others adopt and adapt it. That, of course, is true also in the SAR world, and a recent story from the forests of nearby New York State is sure to play out in some fashion soon in the Whites.

It's November 2016, upstate New York. The search for a lost hiker hemmed in by a forest fire takes this turn:

> The mission began with ground crews deploying a five-pound quadcopter to scope out the blaze and relay coordinates back to a K-MAX helicopter, which then automatically filled its sling-loaded pail and doused the fire. With that taken care of, the crews then launched a Desert Hawk—a fixed-wing drone small enough to easily fit in the vehicle or even backpack of a first responder— to track down the lost "hiker" using visual and infrared cameras. It passed on that information to another helicopter dubbed SARA which—without a pilot or any control from the ground—took off toward the hiker's position. Using onboard sensors to identify a safe landing site, SARA recovered the hiker and returned to safety. (www.backpacker.com)

And there, in an aircraft-rich depiction, you have it: the future, according to SARA. Not tomorrow, but soon, it seems, once integration into the sky community is made possible by a structure that manages an atmosphere full of winged robots:

> But to transition to domestic roles, they [drones] need to learn to talk to other aircraft, most of which are still piloted by humans. In a combat zone, crowded

skies haven't been an issue (nor are they a problem during forest fires, which normally become no-fly zones). But according to McMillen [Lockheed Martin spokesperson], there are no rules in place for larger systems like K-MAX and SARA over the majority of U.S. airspace, and the technology for dealing with other aircraft during search and rescue or other missions hasn't been integrated into these unmanned systems yet. (www.backpacker.com)

That future may be some years distant, but drones, though illegal for recreational flyers over the White Mountain National Forest, will soon get some exploratory testing by those responsible for search and rescue. It takes little imagination to see how a drone with a camera might provide information for searchers who have received a distress signal from the Great Gulf or Pemigewasset Wilderness. Further along in the future, there will be drones capable of bearing loads and dropping supplies (headlamps!) for stranded hikers. In the fall of 2016, I talked with some Baxter State Park rangers in Maine, who hoped to conduct some drone experiments in support of search and rescue, once they had worked out flight permission with aviation authorities.

If we build it, it will fly. The only question seems to be where.

Adjacent Terrain: How It Looks

We, as a species, are relentlessly comparative, always measuring how we stack up against the other—person, group, outfit, and so on. Some envy-driven unhappiness aside, that's a good thing, because we can learn from those others. Searchers and rescuers are no different; they are always looking at other SAR outfits to see what's new, or what's suddenly gotten old. In that spirit then, those who run search and rescue in the Whites look to adjacent mountains and, given the common problems that come down from all mountains, that adjacency goes beyond the near geographic. Here are three mountain areas—Katahdin in Maine, Rocky Mountain Colorado, and Chamonix, France—where searchers and rescuers bring to their missions sensibilities and practices that sometimes differ markedly from what we have come to think of as "usual" in the White Mountains of New Hampshire.

MAINE'S KATAHDIN AND BAXTER STATE PARK Maine's back-country law bears close resemblance to New Hampshire's. Its wardens from the Department of Inland Fisheries and Wildlife carry responsibilities and powers similar to those of NHFG's conservation officers; each is the most powerful law officer in his state. When someone goes missing or calls for help, Maine's wardens are the legal leaders of the effort to go find or retrieve him or her, even as volunteers provide much of the labor.

Nestled in Maine's expansive backcountry, which dwarfs that of neighboring New Hampshire, lies Baxter State Park. With its wild 209,644 acres, Baxter bears some resemblance in scale to the Whites, though its roughness, hinted at first by the AT crossover Mahoosuc Mountain range, surpasses that of the Whites. Katahdin, like its structure-topped cousin, Washington, is the massif around which the whole montane personality of the park revolves. As New England mountains go, this northern endpoint of the Appalachian Trail is the most challenging of the bunch. As such, it draws a lot of aspiration and attention, even as it is much more remote than its New Hampshire cousins. That attention must be managed and, when upland trouble occurs, it too must be answered by the managers (and volunteers) of the park. That Baxter State Park has a single authority overseeing it, and so a single SAR response, suggests that it can offer a worthwhile comparison for the complex patchwork of the Whites.

Here is what happens if you find trouble in Baxter State Park. The following is a garden-variety rescue, and so it offers easy comparison with many similar efforts in the Whites. What differs is the mission-guided response of authorities.

On June 27, 2014, Justin L., age seventeen, a friend, Rose R., also seventeen, and Justin's grandfather, Miles S., age seventy-five, climbed Katahdin. On the way down, the two younger hikers separated from Miles, so that they could fish at day's end; the three had agreed to this plan. As dusk deepened, Justin and Rose grew concerned when Miles didn't appear. They worried both for Miles and because he had the car keys. Justin approached a Baxter park ranger and asked that he go back up the Hunt Trail to search for Miles.

The ranger replied that, unless they knew that Miles was injured, it was up to the threesome to manage his getting down. Anxious about his grandfather (and anxious also because Rose was too tired to go back up and would have to wait alone outside their car), Justin repacked his gear and went up in search of Miles. He found Miles a mile and a half up the trail, sitting on a rock, benighted. Miles had forgotten to bring a light and, once darkness came on, he had felt it was unsafe to descend any farther, so he sat down to wait. Using Justin's light, the two started down in dark and were met soon by a park ranger, who had been sent up when the rangers had learned that Justin was a minor, something he hadn't told them earlier when he asked for help.

All ended well, but in an article in the *Bangor Daily News*, Justin and his family blasted state park officials for not rescuing Miles. Baxter State Park's published policy, however, argues against such easy summoning, saying that rangers will work to rescue only those who are injured. Getting benighted in benign weather doesn't qualify. Here's how Baxter State Park superintendent Jensen Bissell put it in the article: "We try our best to prepare people. We're going to tell you what you need and advise you as much as we can. Your safety is something we take as our responsibility right up until you get to the trailhead. Then, after that, it's yours. Think about what could happen. Sometimes hikes don't go as you plan," Bissell said.

In the Whites, rescuers tend toward the responsive end of the search and rescue spectrum when hikers are late or lost. But there are also any number of unreported instances of NHFG conservation officers trying to "talk" people down from the hills before they go and get them. Given technology's expanding reach, this discussion is bound to recur, at times loudly.

The *Bangor Daily News* article drew robust comments, many of which sided with the park. Three hundred and sixty-seven responses went up before the comment section was closed (though, as usual with public commentary, the thread degenerated into name-calling and misinformed anti-government/tax screeds).

Baxter's emphasis on self-reliance and its control of the numbers of people admitted to the park have given it something of a Big Brother reputation that runs counter to a more libertarian, freedom-of-the-hills ethos in New Hampshire. Park superintendent Bissell bristles some at this charge. In explanation, he cites Baxter's clear mission, from which all its policies and practices flow. Compress that mission to a single sentence, and it might read like this: Baxter State Park will favor wilderness values over those of humans and their recreation when the two come into conflict. Practically, that puts more responsibility on hikers, climbers, skiers, and other back-country travelers who seek out that wilderness. Figuring out one's way into the wilderness has the flip side of figuring out one's way out.

If you fall into injury via unlucky slippage, rangers and volunteers will come for you, and they will bring great skill to their work. But if you blunder in and are otherwise okay, you will need to blunder back out.

As in most areas of policy and politics, money talks. Percival Baxter, the Maine governor and entrepreneur who financed much of the gathering of the park's first 200,000 acres and then donated them to the people of Maine, knew that. So he left Baxter State Park the gift of its own voice—a $7 million endowment that, along with admission and other fees, makes it financially independent, and subject to its own principles rather than the whims of those in political power at budget time. Recall, then, the NHFG search and rescue budget and its funding dances with the legislature—a different tune entirely.

A December 8–9, 2014, search for an Ontario man, who had gone missing during an attempt to climb Katahdin resulted in an assessed bill for rescue costs, only the third in park history. The hiker and a friend had camped without registering (as required) for a few days prior to the eighth. Under-equipped and alone, the hiker went up on the eighth, was reported missing that evening, and was found as a search got under way on the morning of the ninth in the face of an oncoming storm. That storm and uncertainty about the hiker had led searchers to call in a Blackhawk helicopter from the Army National Guard, in addition to deploying ground searchers.

Baxter Park sent the hiker a bill for $10,000, which really amounted to a fine for the hiker's actions. Park officials called those actions "negligent" and "reckless" in statements, and that impelled them to invoke Park Rule 2.2: "The Baxter State Park Authority may request reimbursement of search and rescue costs in case of reckless hikers."

"Most people don't cross the threshold of true recklessness in our minds," Park Superintendent Jensen Bissell said. "We don't like to do this. It's not something we seek to do. Most of our users are conscientious and thought-ful. People usually have to make two or three really bad decisions to get into serious trouble. But these people made far more than that. We're just really lucky that he survived."

This case, Bissell said to the media, was different.

Baxter Park's decision to pursue these costs rekindled discussion of such charges for negligent backcountry behavior. On January 4, 2015, the *Bangor Daily News* published an editorial with this title: "Lost and Negligent: Should Maine Charge for Search and Rescue?" Yes, the editorial said: "This is a necessary, but difficult, debate. People who have accidents in the woods should be rescued, just as a house fire should be put out no matter the cause. But when people are truly negligent while recreating, it is reasonable to have them bear a price for their rescue."

But the editors went on to suggest adoption of a policy outlined by David Trahan, executive director of the Sportsman's Alliance of Maine:

> He suggests that a system be created whereby people who act irresponsibly, leading to their need to be rescued, would be fined. A three-member board, made up of the head of the Maine Warden Service, a retired judge or attorney and a representative of recreational interests, would be established to determine whether someone was negligent. If they determined negligence—and not just bad luck—was a factor, the panel would then assess a fine. State law would need to be rewritten to require that the fines be paid, with set penalties for not doing so. (*Bangor Daily News*, January 4, 2015)

Referring to the December 2014 search in the *Bangor Daily News* article, Bissell said, "We feel if you're hurt in the park, we're ready, without question, to come to your aid. But it's really hard for me to put rescue crews at risk for people who didn't even care to try to do the right thing."

IN COLORADO'S ROCKIES Coloradans spend a lot of time looking up. At least that's true of those who live west of the eastern third of the state, because that's where the land goes. And that is often where the state's millions of annual visitors (77.7 million in 2015) go, too, spending in 2015 a tuneful $19.1 billion and generating $1.13 billion in state and local taxes. Coloradans are clear about what rises above them and how it lifts their economy. So when it comes to going out looking for visitors (or residents) who haven't come back, they see it as part of the cost of maintaining lands attractive to tourists. Colorado's SAR response, while facing many of the issues common to SAR in the Whites, tends toward a more forgiving or tolerant, cost-of-doing-business attitude. As noted earlier, Coloradans have been prominent among those condemning some of New Hampshire's billing-for-rescue practices.

Unlike New Hampshire, where large-scale government agencies assume legal leadership of backcountry searches and rescues, Colorado's search and rescue falls mostly under the wing of local sheriffs' offices. Their smaller scale and limited staffing mean that nearly all the actual searching and rescuing in the state gets done by volunteers. Those volunteers come from a multiplicity of trained SAR groups, but the only state monies they receive are grants for equipment and training, and that money can be hard to come by at times. Like New Hampshire, Colorado has turned in part to the voluntary funding of a card, the Colorado Outdoor Recreation Search and Rescue (AAU) card, to help meet those costs, but the card goes for only $3, and that yields $2 for SAR costs. In the 2015–16 fiscal year (FY), Colorado's SAR fund gained $74, 802, or 15.3 percent of its $490,428 total influx from sales of the card. It is important to note that the AAU card is a donation, not an insurance card, which could be used to defray expenses for, say, a helicopter rescue.

A breakdown of that FY 2015–16 funding shows surprising similarity to NHFG's resources in their search and rescue budget: hunting licenses contribute 26.5 percent; fishing licenses, 39.4 percent; OHV, snowmobiles, and boats, 15.5 percent; and a small miscellaneous category offers 3.3 percent.

With that budget, administered by Colorado's Department of Local Affairs (DOLA), the state reimbursed local authorities with $60,888.96 for SAR expenses incurred on seventy-four missions; more impressively, they made thirty-three awards to SAR groups, totaling $339,124.25 in monies distributed. Those awards replaced equipment and funded training and new gear.

Yes, Colorado is a much larger state than New Hampshire, and its mountains are more numerous and rise higher, but the disparity in state support for SAR is also eye-catching. Volunteer groups are simply more richly supported, an acknowledgment of their overwhelming importance to statewide SAR. New Hampshire's volunteer SAR groups depend upon individual gratitude and generosity, often funneled through the nonprofit New Hampshire Outdoor Council. New Hampshire's license-sourced SAR allocation—already, as we have seen, underfunded and controversial—partially supports only NHFG's law enforcement division and its work in SAR.

CHAMONIX, FRANCE Doug Mayer, a Randolph resident, RMC and AVSAR veteran, and now trail-running owner of Chamonix-based Run the Alps, talks of helicopters and a typical summer day in Chamonix: "I'm completely used to them by now; everyone is. You can be sitting in a café with friends and the distinctive sound of a helicopter flies right overheard, and no one looks up. If anyone says anything, it's a simple, 'There goes another one. I wonder who fell where?'"

Such familiarity stems from the professionalized mountain rescue scene in the Alps, where the rescue helicopters in a region all sport the same insignia and carry professional rescuers as they go out and up to pluck people from aiguilles or scour glaciers for signs of the lost. Many of those awaiting the copters (given, of course, fair or possible flying weather) have rescue insurance, which comes with membership in a country's Alpine Club, or may be purchased annually for somewhere around fifty euros per year. Carrying this card gets you professional rescue, often by air, at no added charge; the team that comes out for you is partially funded by this insurance pool.

The European gold standard for airborne rescue is Chamonix's Pelotons de Gendarmerie de Haute Montagne (PGHM), whose pilots, medics, and rescuers are among the most able in the world. Often performing many missions in a week, on and around a mountain (Mont Blanc) classed as one of the deadliest anywhere, the PGHM are a fully professional rescue wing of law enforcement. One article estimated that 97 percent of PGHM's missions involve a helicopter. Their reliance on helicopter-transported, highly trained rescuers creates a light and fast (many would add the word "bold" to this mix) ethic very different from the people-intensive rescue scenes in the United States. A typical rescue may pluck an injured climber from a cliff or glacier with a winch and cable, and it may require a pilot, a crew member, and two rescuers, with a medic added if there are health complications.

Neil Brodie's 2010 article in *Climbing*, "Angels of Mont Blanc," described a rescue summoned by two Swiss climbers stranded at day's end on the famous Walker Spur. The PGHM delivered rescuer Jean Claudon to the cliff where, while the helicopter hovered and waited at some distance, a cloud blew in and persisted. Though Claudon had readied the two climbers for evacuation by air, the helicopter pilot couldn't risk being unsighted with his rotors so close to the cliff, and, when his fuel ran low while he was waiting for the cloud to clear, he had to retreat to Chamonix. Now what? Claudon then cajoled and led the climbers up the route's 5.9-rated, loose-rock remainder and then down a complicated 1,000-vertical-meter glacier descent on the other (Italian) side, where the three finally reached clear air and could be picked up and flown back to town. The rescue, deemed a *beau secours*, a beautiful rescue, was, in the end, accomplished by a pilot and one rescuer.

Such an arrangement seems diametrically opposite to New Hampshire's volunteer-rich mosaic; it springs from the Euro-social end of the spectrum that appears distant from the point that the Live Free or Die state inhabits. While few of the New Hampshire SAR people—volunteer or profession-al—I spoke with spent time advocating for a full European-style response, some White Mountain figures do question our system. The veteran White Mountain guide and guide service owner Marc Chauvin is one such voice. In a Facebook posting about the March 13, 2016, sliding accidents and helicopter evacuations on Mount Washington (discussed in detail in chapter 16), Chauvin had this to say:

> Within the current paradigm of mountain rescue in the USA things went really well. What our community needs to discuss is the availability of helicopter rescue with lift capability and a trained crew in mountain rescue. This exists in every other advanced, mountainous country and in some developing countries. We expect and get a respectful analysis of accidents, but shouldn't we also get a respectful analysis of the SAR response? It's time for the mountain community to consider if we are underserved. What would have been the capability of the response had these injuries happened out at sea? Would it have been done with better machinery and with a higher standard of training? Is that appropriate?

Chauvin and most of us know who flies out to find you if you are in trouble at sea: the U.S. Coast Guard, a government wing replete with boats and highly trained search and rescue helicopter crews. Being injured or in trouble out there is truly scary, but the SAR people who come to get you are among the world's best trained and equipped. As a guide who has worked internationally, he knows of the system in Chamonix. Chauvin's comment returns us also to Colonel Jordan's conviction that backcountry SAR is public safety work, and so it should be funded by the public.

Two avenues of change seem possible: the first draws on what we all pay toward the commonweal, taxes; the second draws on a form of insurance pooling by which those of us interested or wary enough buy a share, in the form of a rescue card, that collectively funds a rescue team. "It's so odd that we go out into the mountains to rescue someone," said Jordan. "We carry him out, sometimes over many hours and with many hands, and then, as soon as we slide him into an ambulance, he begins paying for services. What's the difference?"

Chamonix and the Whites have another commonality: both are wild, sometimes risky uplands surrounded by hordes of wealthy, recreation-happy people who are always looking for and pressing against boundaries. In her 2012 article in the *Atlantic* ("Why Is Mont Blanc One of the World's Deadliest Mountains?"), Lane Wallace reflects on the way commercial recreational culture brings hundreds of unqualified climbers to the slopes and glaciers of Mont Blanc every year. Sold by guiding services as a "long walk," the ascent of the 15,870-foot mountain is much more, and trouble often ensues. In a "good" year, an estimated thirty people die in these mountains; a "bad" one sees sixty or more deaths—and that is with the topflight rescue presence available.

In mid-essay, Wallace has an exchange with an officer from the PGHM. She has just looked up at the route her guided group is slated to climb the next day and, given her novice status as a climber, she has decided against the climb:

> I told him I'd decided not to summit. He asked me how many alpine peaks I'd done before this one. I told him none. His eyes got wide only momentarily. Then, wearily, he shook his head.
>
> "You have no business on this mountain unless you have at least six alpine peaks under your belt," he said. "That's why we have so many people killed here." He gestured to the rock face I'd decided not to climb. "We lost three people off that face a couple of weeks ago," he said. "Two novices and a guide. One novice lost his footing and fell, pulling the second guy off, and the guide couldn't hold both of them. So all three fell to their deaths."

Wallace also cites the views of an American guide, Aidan Loehr, who talks about the scene on Mont Blanc: "The fatality rate on Mont Blanc doesn't reflect the inherent, fundamental risks of that mountain," Loehr says. "[That there is] guiding isn't the problem. It's the approach to guiding there that's the problem. It's a combination of the sheer numbers of people on the mountain, the low level of experience of the people climbing the mountain, and the approach of the guides, that's causing the fatality rates on that mountain."

It isn't a stretch, even with their wildly varying heights, to see Mount Washington and Mont Blanc as deadly cousins. Even as Mount Washington's guide culture is much more conservative and attentive to the individual, and so much more life preservative, the throngs that climb its sides and fall or wallow in its folds resemble those on Mont Blanc in number and variability of fitness and experience.

Does a professional rescue presence encourage overextension and overcrowding on the Alps' heights? Or are professional rescuers simply a response to a modern wave of ascenders who, whether rescue is on offer or not, just may swamp the mountains on their own? Should we look to Chamonix as a guide to a better rescue future? Or is such alignment simply a quicker route to mountains swarming with people like ants discovering a sugar bowl?

Given a chance to consider an insurance-based professionalization of SAR in the Whites, a number of those I spoke with said, "I'd consider buying into it." Still, "buying in" would indicate a cultural shift that raises questions about what we want our mountains to be. I'm taken back to Doug Mayer's observation about Chamonix's commonplace copters, and their motoring regularly overhead. Already, the Whites have their share of helicopters at work. The AMC uses them for supplying its huts in the early summer and for transporting materials for backcountry construction. As seen in chapter 21, NHANG and DHART helicopters offer growing support for search and rescue, especially when injuries are deemed dire. How much traffic do we want flying over our wild lands? Are they still wild if they are so overflown?

> All this consideration must soon include SARA, the drone we met at this chapter's beginning. How much of a humming sound do we want just over the next ridge?

There Will Be More

Whatever search and rescue's future structure looks like, it's safe to assume it will be called for more often. Most of the groups engaged in rescue are seeing more and more action from swelling numbers of backcountry visitors of all levels of expertise. These numbers from the NHFG website point to this trend:

Over the past six years (2008–14), NH Fish and Game completed a total of 1,023 reportable Search and Rescue (SAR) missions at a total cost to the Department of $2.1 million. An average of 180 missions were conducted each year. The average cost of each mission was $2,100.

Of the total 1,023 Search and Rescue missions:

609 missions were required for hikers and climbers. This represents approximately 60 percent of all SAR missions.
138 SAR missions were required for hunters, anglers, boaters and OHRV riders, representing approximately 14 percent of all SAR missions.
116 missions were searches for walkaways/runaways. This represents about 12 percent of all SAR missions.
429 SAR missions occurred within the White Mountain National Forest. That means that approximately 43 percent of all SAR missions within the past six years took place on National Forest lands.

"Reportable" is the key word in the first sentence. In addition to the 1,023 missions cited, there are countless phone calls and near missions, where conservation officers work to orient those who can't find their way. In short, especially in the tourist-heavy summer season, SAR work takes up a growing percentage of a CO's time.

A detailed study of search and rescue in Maine's Baxter State Park pointed also to an increase in incidents, rising steadily over the twenty-year period from 1994 to 2014. What further caught the attention of Baxter personnel was an "older demographic" precipitating rescues in the park. Seemingly related to that demographic was the prevalence of fatigue as a contributing factor to problems requiring rescue. Baxter's study also offered a graphic reminder familiar to everyone who climbs—"Going up is voluntary, coming down is mandatory." Their study shows the overwhelming presence of exhaustion during descent in SAR incidents. It's an excellent reminder of the need for vigilance on the way down.

All of that predicts more SAR work in the years ahead. That increase will also deepen search and rescue's effects on our backcountry. A look ahead must consider those effects and who will create them.

< 2 3 >

NEXT GEN

For those alive in a vital present, a succession plan for who will take your place often languishes last on the to-do list. Volunteer search and rescue groups in the Whites have all experienced the sudden arrival of the question of succession. Mountain Rescue Service has found this particularly true as, during the 1980s, 1990s, and 2000s, a core group of around twenty climbers rallied to a number of rescue missions that has now surpassed five hundred. At one point not long ago Rick Wilcox remembered that they looked up and realized that many of them were kissing sixty. They had been so ready to help over these decades that the next generation of MRS volunteers simply was a thin presence. It's hard to form an allegiance and affection for such hard work unless you get its call and feel its saving work and the camaraderie that comes with it. "We need new guys," they said, and that realization launched a drive to develop MRS's next gen.

How do you bring new rescuers into the fold? As Barbara Arnold of AVSAR pointed out earlier, groups use Web platforms and social media to advertise needs and requirements, but mostly, throughout the little towns and tight mountain cultures of the Whites, rescuers still get recruited by word of mouth. Here's a story that shows the route one rescuer took and points to how the MRS culture of excellence that Steve Larson described earlier gets passed on, too.

Justin Preisendorfer, MRS's spokesperson and a current USFS forest ranger, was a young New Hampshire climber in the late 1990s. In a June 2016 interview, Preisendorfer recalled his first serious incident as a rescuer, one that led him to apply to join MRS and the rescue community: "I was working for the AMC at Camp Dodge. It was late summer, maybe August, and a number of us had been out climbing for the day. When we got back, the camp's co-ordinator said, 'Hey Fish and Game is looking for folks to help with a rescue over in Crawford Notch. They said if you have technical gear you should bring it. You guys already have all your stuff in your packs. Pull together some food, some extra headlamp batteries, some water, and jump back in the van. Go for it.'"

Preisendorfer and three companions went for it. "As in 90 percent of incidents, we had bad information from the beginning," he said. "We were told the incident was on Willey's Slide, and we drove by, but there was no one there. But there were a bunch of vehicles back by the Willey House, so we went back there. And they said, yeah, the accident is on Mount Webster. It's up in this gully. So we hiked up."

What Preisendorfer found came as a surprise. Two brothers (and their dog) had decided to go on an adventure and set off up a gully. The gullies of Webster are not terrain for the faint-hearted or inexperienced; the gully the brothers had chosen was the aptly named Landslide Gully. About halfway up, they triggered a small rockslide, which killed one of them, injured the other, and hurt the dog as well.

Preisendorfer recounted the rescue effort and some of its effect on him:

> I'd been on a couple of minor carryouts, where I'd happened to be in the area and said, "Sure, I'll help out." But I'd never been on something of this magnitude. When we got there, they were doing CPR on this guy. The other guy was screaming and asking how his brother was doing. . . . I remember Joe Lentini, who has been on MRS for decades, looked over and pointed at my friend Seth and me. "You and you," he said. "I recognize you, you're climbers. Do you have gear?" We said, "We have gear," and he said, "All right, come with us."
>
> And so our job was to set the [rope] systems and manage a series of lowers for the litter of the brother who was alive. I remember feeling, "This is serious now." We got everything set up, got the guy hooked up, and we're about to go, when Lentini leans over the guy and says, "I know it's difficult, but you've just got to try and relax and be calm. You've got the best climbers in the world here helping you out." And I'm like looking around for them.

Partway through this lowering, the injured man asked Preisendorfer and his friend how his brother was, and a doctor who had climbed up with the rescuers had to tell him his brother had died. "Right then, the guy let out this wail," Preisendorfer recalled. "And a couple of hundred yards away, their dog, who was being walked down by two rescuers, howled in answer.

I remember thinking, "There's no good end to this story, but we can prevent it from becoming worse."

Preisendorfer is part of MRS's answer to the next-gen question. So too is MRS's new president, Steve Dupuis, who was appointed to succeed Rick Wilcox in 2016. Dupuis, a husband, father of four, self-employed stonemason, and a winter season guide, who has also been president of AVSAR (2012–13), joined MRS is 2000. In 2007, he became one of their team leaders, and he has also served on the board of directors for six years. Over these years, he estimates that he's been on a majority of the missions in the central Whites. "My pack's all set in the closet, ready to go," he said during a phone conversation.

Dupuis also knows rescue from the other side of the litter, having received its gift in October 2002. "I took a one-hundred-foot ground fall on Eagle Cliff" (in Franconia Notch), he said. "I broke my back and some ribs and was carried out by NHFG, AVSAR, and the Sugar Hill Fire Department. I had been a rescuer already, and I looked up from the litter and thought, 'I know a lot of people here. And then I thought, 'This is going to cost me a lot of beers.'"

"We go out to help people on what may be the worst day of their lives," Dupuis said, amplifying Preisendorfer's hope of preventing that day from becoming worse. Dupuis also knows that "it's a lot to ask," especially because in addition to rescue's hard work, it often takes place at night and/or in tough weather. MRS publishes its requirements on its website, and they do add up to a big ask:

> Resides in or near the Mount Washington Valley
> A year-round climber who is competent leading/on-sighting 5.9 traditional rock climbs, NEI 4 ice climbs, and moderate alpine terrain
> Comfortable undertaking multiday trips on the harshest days in a winter alpine/backcountry environment
> Wilderness First Responder certification or the equivalent
> Avalanche safety education
> Owns gear for search and rescue work in all seasons (including subzero arctic conditions) including avalanche safety equipment, a clothing layering system, ice and rock climbing hardware, footwear, camping gear, etc. Available 24 hours/day for search and rescue calls.

MRS reviews applications at an annual board meeting, and when we talked, Dupuis and his board had just brought on three new members, all in their late twenties—one a local guide, one a former military man, and one a welder. All are highly capable climbers. Pleased with this new blood, Dupuis also pointed to the ongoing evaluation that new team members receive. "We have a full year of evaluation," he said, "during which experienced members of the team watch how new members perform." Successful completion of that first year brings full membership in the group.

"We're only as good as we train," said Dupuis, and he hopes to make training available monthly for two-plus hours each time. "By training together, we learn our strengths and weaknesses. Some of the older guys may not be great with GPS, but they know rope systems, while some of the younger guys may be great with tech systems. We can improve and adapt, so when we get out there we know what we've got."

That knowing leads also to a phenomenon others have mentioned too. Highly skilled athletes are not without ego. They are, after all, exceptional, and many MRS members have climbed at high levels in the world's hardest terrain. Dupuis notes, however, that "once we get out there, egos seem to evaporate." Instead, rescuers get into a common "flow," where, even in the toughest weather and at extreme angles, people make the right moves, support each other, and rescues "just happen."

The skills rescuers bring with them are rare and in demand, but Dupuis underlines what may be MRS's and other groups' toughest requirement: you must be available at all hours. That requirement asks for sacrifice and it brings with it a sense of common cause among all the rescue groups in the Whites. Out at all hours together, they form deep bonds, which help them go out at all hours.

So locating the next iteration of MRS, or any of the search and rescue groups that serve the Whites, isn't as simple as posting public notice and waiting. MRS and AVSAR and PVSART and others invite application, but then they test their applicants. They know, as recruiters do, that bringing a person onto the team is some of their most important work. Dupuis says he is "not a fan of required or legislated rescue procedures." He believes that "peer-reviewed" work of the sort MRS performs is more effective. In short, Dupuis believes in the team.

Dupuis is also optimistic about search and rescue's future in the Whites. "I have deep respect for New Hampshire Fish and Game," he says. "I can't say enough good about them. The sense of volunteering, of giving back, is also strong in New Hampshire, and we raise money to support our volunteers. We seek grants to replace equipment that gets worn out." Asked about professional rescue coming to the fore in the Whites, Dupuis says he doesn't see it in the immediate future. The combination of what that would cost and the slim resources given over to it by the state makes that possibility remote. "I don't want a paycheck for what I do," he says, echoing a sentiment I've heard throughout my travels and conversations in the region. "There's a tremendous amount of professionalism out there, but people don't need to be compensated for what they do. I think we can go on for quite a long time this way."

WHAT'S AT STAKE

— — — —

How Search and Rescue Shapes Our Mountains

Those engaged in search and rescue in our White Mountains represent the thinnest fraction of all who come to enjoy the freedom of our hills. But despite their small numbers, one can argue that they are among our mountains' primary users and in that use they shape what we seek and what we find there. They are its guides, its most skilled travelers, and most celebrated characters. How they come to our hills and what they do there unites practice and path, and almost everyone else follows along, or walks under the wing of their presence.

Early in this book, we looked at the mountain-altering story of Curtis and Ormsbee, noting the way that their deaths caused deep introspection among the day's leading climbers, helped speckle the uplands with shelters, and offered resolve to those who go out after hikers in trouble. The narrative track we've followed forward has outlined the seams and multihued sections of what has often been called "a patchwork," or, more comfortingly, "a quilt" of rescue. But the practice of that rescue has become anything but patchy— where once it consisted of informal aggregates of whoever was around, it now is a precise and proficient response to robocalls sent out by leaders of groups spaced throughout the Whites. As it deals with the wild sets of variables the mountains and their walkers, runners, skiers, and climbers can create, and even as NHFG, its supervisory agency, is chronically underfunded, White Mountain SAR manages to remain highly efficient. At the same time, White Mountain SAR has stopped short of becoming the fully professional contingent that patrols the Alps. It is a giving practice, supervised by professionals and brought to life by volunteers, who, time after time, suspend the usual and climb up into another world to bring us back when we've fallen.

And there we are, in our gaudy variety, a spectrum of seekers that runs from jokers and clowns to Zen walkers and mystics, with the great middle being average citizens who would feel the touch of wild and, for a day or more, enjoy this extraordinary upland gift of the natural world. But even as we aspire to self-sufficiency in that wild elsewhere, most of us carry the usual here there. We bring along phones and beacons and soundtracks, often just for sending out a modern equivalent to postcards—Don't you wish you were here? Like me? If trouble finds us, or we find it, very few of us resist calling here for help getting out of there.

That someone will answer is the modern equivalent to sun worship—it is there; it gives life; we bow to it. Now it is the assurance that someone will go out there to find or lug us back here that colors in the human character of our wild lands.

Consider then, for a bit, what the Whites and your experience in them would be like if there were no searchers and rescuers available. Back in chapter 15, I quoted from Robert Kruzyna's provocative (and to some extent, tongue-in-cheek) essay from the 1990s arguing for just such an absence. Others, too, have made that argument; it is a sort of libertarian dream. Okay, you've probably not migrated to that point along the spectrum of response, but where do you set up shop along that line?

Does your consideration argue for even a little dialing back of search and rescue? Or do you want your SAR dialed up—fueled and ready to lift off at moment's notice? That's a central question posed by this book. But it's one for each reader and, finally, a collective of mountain-drawn people to answer.

In that spirit, here's my answer: Bans don't work, either of equipment or behavior. Prohibition once seemed a reasonable answer to the ways in which alcohol could alter lives. During the ban, alcohol went right on altering lives, and we—society—had a whole new set of problems of criminal empowerment and debasement of law to deal with. The freedom to wander up into the hills, and the freedom to summon help when those hills deliver difficulty can't be banned or tightly regulated; neither should they be. But what each of us does when we walk up, or what we do when summoned by someone who has stumbled up there, can be measured and done with restraint.

Restraint by both mountain seekers and rescuers seems such a namby-pamby answer: "Be moderate . . . please." Please?

Yet moderation is, in fact, what's called for, in part because it must be spawn of thought; restraint asks each of us to take up residence in rational response, to consider consequences, to think our actions through. Chamonix and its rescue scene, copter-based and professional, offer magnetic stories, drawing both narrative's and heart's compass needles. They seem pure positives. Chamonix's rescuers are similar to those of the Mountain Rescue Service, in that they are guides and climbers of high caliber. But Chamonix's PGHM await your call at any hour in a sparely furnished room right next to a helipad; they can be off to the rescue in minutes. In the Whites, NHFG must gather its rescuers, professional or volunteer, from the disparate scatter of their lives. Yes, they are all "local" to the scene, unlike their high-angle forerunners from the 1950s and '60s and before, but collecting them still takes time.

Time is of the essence, say advocates for professional rescue. The clock's ticking can be a heartbeat running out, a metronome of measured possibility that runs down. Soon.

> There's no denying that. It's simply true.

But if the Whites were to shift to professional, on-call rescue, they would change. Irrevocably, I'd argue. Once organized and fledged, professional rescue will not confine itself to time-sensitive emergencies; it will go out pretty much for any call. Otherwise, how do you justify its expense? Very few professions build in a structure for less use. Surgeons, for example, want to operate; they want to use their fine skills. It's no stretch to liken a pilot who can fly with his rotor blade only feet from a cliff and a rescuer who can be lowered from that helicopter to precise place on that cliff to a surgeon. They all share fine-tuned senses of space, and they revel in using their uncommon skills.

You can, of course, create your own comparisons with other professions. The point is that skills and a career thrive through use. In the early 2000s, as NHFG's Specialized Rescue Team developed and gained confidence, their use of volunteer groups waned. As fewer calls came in, volunteers drifted from rosters. The volunteer enterprise of going out to get your own seemed in danger of atrophy. But as we've seen, NHFG conservation officers have many responsibilities, and as those responsibilities burgeoned, too, volunteers got more calls; the SAR system settled back to its usual mix of responders.

I'm arguing for restraint, which is sometimes slow. I'm arguing against a fully professional response, which is often speedier. "We did what we could with what we have" might be that SAR's motto. How does that stack up against, "We did everything we could?"

How does one argue against doing "everything" to save a life?

At this point, I wish to speak a word for Nature, as Thoreau famously did in his signature essay, "Walking." The other life at stake in this question needs consideration, too. That life doesn't have an individual face and back-story; it is huge, amorphous, and sometimes threatening, and it doesn't vote. But wild Nature is also a savior. It is our oldest home, the one that shaped us, the one that now reminds us who we are. It is the place many of us go to find ourselves, a search as vital as any in this book. A backcountry overflown and lined with the suture sound of helicopters and drones loses quickly its wild nature. Its primary sound, silence or the sotto voce whisper of trees and rocks and air, vanishes. Using more machines in it encourages their further use. When the backcountry becomes infested with our technology, it is no longer itself. We have lost it. Then, I would argue, we too are lost. Restraining our wing-and-rotor brigades helps keep our wild country intact, lets it be itself. That's vital for all life.

Restraint then. By those who would wander and call, and by those who would answer and search. Learned behaviors all. It seems that the future of the Whites may lie in this bumpy, hard-won terrain. For a limits-testing species, that may not be welcome news. But whether restraint lies in our response to a large-scale challenge such as climate change, or a small-scale decision such as whether to call for or provide rescue, it is rooted in human decision making and ethics. There is much that is beyond our control, but within the limits of what we *can* control, restraint may be our greatest asset.

A final thought: not doing something can be seen as passive. I'm not arguing for sleepy response. I'm arguing for *active* restraint. I'm arguing for the sort of vigilance that has us sitting forward and getting up. I'm arguing for a holding back that is as alert as an animal's eyes.

<25>

WHY GO?

- - - -

Saving Others, Saving Yourself

I'm sitting in the back of The Met, a North Conway coffee place, away from the front room's bustle so we can talk uninterruptedly. It's quiet back here, and at my question, it gets even quieter. I ask, "Why do you go? Time after time?"

Alain Comeau, MRS veteran, mountain guide, and trainer of U.S. military special forces, pauses; his face goes almost blank. After an hour of animated stories I expect this pause. I have asked this question of other rescuers many times, and it has always yielded a pause. These months later, I am still provoked by this moment of silence. It's as if Comeau's hesitation and all those preceding it add up to this response: Why wouldn't I go? Who wouldn't?

Every group, every tribe, has it markers of membership, those points of personality and practice that let the world know who their members are. I have come to know the SAR tribe, in part, by this response.

A second response has also been universal throughout my research and conversations: "It could be me out there," or, "It has been me out there." I've heard this even in response to some of the lamest of predicaments, where people have arrived in the mountains, ignorant of even basic understanding of terrain and weather and necessary gear, and then have climbed away into those mountains to compound that ignorance with mishap. Until, finally, they decide to press one of their many buttons and summon help. "Where am I?" they say. Or, "Come get me," and, "Oh, when will you get here?"

"It could be me out there." Well, sure. All rescuers have more than one story of a miscalculation or time when the familiar world dissolved before them, and they were hobbled or lost, in place, in time, or in both. An old saying goes that if you haven't gotten lost in the woods, you haven't been very far into them. Yet it almost never is them out there. SAR people are, as a matter of course, among the most skilled of those drawn to the mountains; they are the guides, climbers, hikers, skiers, runners, and wanderers, who have spent the most time "out there." They have also made it their mission to learn the intricacies of terrain, weather, and self that make "out there" a best place to be. All that knowledge accounts, in large part, for how few end up on the other side of rescue.

And there is pride, born of all that time "out there." In October 2016, I attended the wedding of a former student and her groom, a ranger in Maine's Baxter State Park. At the wedding dinner, I was seated at a table with three of the groom's fellow rangers, and we got to talking about SAR at Baxter. I asked my always-question: Why do you go out? Along with saying simply, "It's part of our job," all three said, "It could be me out there."

"But it almost never is," I said, and waited. The three exchanged looks, and then one said, "Well, yeah. I'd crawl for four days to avoid calling for rescue."

So it could be one of them "out there," but we'll probably never hear of it. I've related one story of rescue by others from a veteran SAR person but heard no others. Close calls, yes. Self-rescue, yes. But only one strapped-into-the-litter carryout.

In addition to the "It could be me response" from rescuers, there is also their implicit reaction: Who wouldn't go? That reaction was printed on Alain Comeau's face. Yet the answer is: most wouldn't and couldn't and don't; only a small number do. Life is full of many more bystanders than it is of those who drop whatever's at hand to go and look for those lost and in trouble. Research suggests that's especially true when the decision to help is considered rather than impulsive. Jumping into a lake to help someone who appears to be in trouble happens in an instant; signing on to a search and rescue team takes application, planning, and a willingness to suspend one's central life in service of another's.

Of course, there's more than a little romance to being a savior. Ask anyone from one of the "helping" professions—nurses, psychologists, teachers, the list is long. My own decades of work as a high school teacher kept me acutely aware of this. On days when students were happy to see me arrive, or when they professed acceptance or gratitude for what I'd offered, I felt buoyed, important; "the horse I rode in on" seemed a knightly one. On flipped days, where I was simply an unwelcome prod or presence, a pallor of mind and spirit sometimes took over. I was a foot-borne straggler.

The "helper" and his or her mental (and spiritual?) integrity are often tied to the progress and success or failure of those they are helping. Many of those who coordinate search and rescue's volunteer groups point to the appeal of being a savior as a draw for those who sign up for the work. They point also to the collision that sometimes occurs between the heroic vision of helping the lost or fallen and the often grinding, scut-work nature and tedium of the work, many citing the litter carry as example. As Barbara Arnold, who controls and tracks membership for AVSAR, told me, "a number of volunteers never return to the work after their first (and only) litter carry." They have met disjunction between heroic imagination and gritty reality.

Another reality, more cloaked from the public eye, also counters the romance of rescue, and here, our limited experience—unless we are EMTs, nurses, doctors, firefighters, or police—keeps our imaginations quiet. It is hard, sometimes graphically disturbing work trying to keep someone alive, and it can be devastating when we do the work—and fail.

> I once heard a description of the heroic (I don't use this word lightly) efforts of a hiking group and later, rescuers, to save a person who had collapsed on the trail miles from the road. When the hiker dropped, good phone reception sent the call out immediately and, when NHFG learned the details, they immediately asked the National Guard for a helicopter, which also was dispatched quickly. Rescuers converging on the scene—in one case running up the trail with medical equipment—found the hiker's group practicing CPR, and that effort had cracked ribs and brought up blood, which had overwhelmed safety masks. The hiker's companions had worked forward despite the blood until relieved by rescuers. The hiker could not be saved, but the rescue attempt from the first moment on was a best effort. It developed with clockwork efficiency and, given the incident's remote location, remarkable speed. The scene described was a hard one, and the room went quiet as the story unfolded.

Such a blood-laved reality runs deeply counter to our often-sanitized imaginations when we think of rescuers (and, perhaps, imagine ourselves) rushing in to help someone who has fallen. In the great majority of rescues, the emergency is much less dire. But the life that runs through us is red, and battering falls and internal ruptures can bring it out into the open.

The quasi-military order and response to this tragedy—real military in the case of the National Guard—suggests further insight into the questions of who goes and why when SAR calls. In the fall of 2016, I read Sebastian Junger's slim but powerful book, *Tribe*. In it Junger considers a question that has plagued society for millennia, and one that seems especially current and poignant now: Why do veterans whom we have sent to war have so much trouble rejoining the society from which they were sent? Why do combat veterans often feel safer and more supported in lethal war zones and more vulnerable and isolated in the seemingly peaceful world most of us inhabit? Is the now commonly recognized PTSD instead a troubled response to modern society by a veteran's psyche?

One answer, Junger suggests, lies in the closeness one feels as a member of a military unit, a platoon, for example, such as the one he lived with, studied, and documented in his film *Restropo*. There, at a remote firebase in Afghanistan's Korengal Valley, Junger and his friend the photographer Tim Hetherington filmed and interviewed the platoon's soldiers, who came under fire daily. They lived in a stripped-down, armored island, within the most dangerous region in their war. They were also a varied lot of Americans—different races, ethnicities, politics, sensitivities—but their devotion to each other was clear and transcendent. They would, as some did, die for each other. But later, in interviews set back in the seeming tranquility of their home country, these veterans often sounded unmoored, haunted by a desire to be back in their unit.

Junger opens *Tribe* with an arresting example from colonial America. Though it's unrecorded in common history books, the early colonies had a problem with colonists leaving for a preferred life with Indian tribes. Junger quotes Benjamin Franklin, who writes in a letter to a friend:

> "When an Indian child has been brought up among us, taught our language and habituated to our customs, [yet] if he goes to see his relations and makes one Indian ramble with them, there is no persuading him ever to return. On the other hand," Franklin continued, "white captives who were liberated from the Indians were almost impossible to keep at home: 'Tho' ransomed by their

friends, and treated with all imaginable tenderness to prevail with them to stay among the English, yet in a short time they become disgusted with our manner of life . . . and take the first opportunity of escaping again into the woods." (3)

Citing prolific research, Junger argues that we have a clear preference, verging on a basic need, for affiliation with small, clearly defined groups—in short, tribes—and modern mobility and globalism have stripped much of such affiliation from our lives. For the warriors of *Restropo* and other veterans, a military unit can answer this need. Membership in a group with a clear purpose and shared goals can, he argues, restore us to health, to full selves. It's not much of a leap to look at the search and rescue groups in the Whites and find such small tribes of purpose, brought together by their shared love of the mountains and their ability to be of use there.

At *Tribe*'s end, Junger offers a postscript that points to what is at stake for each of us:

> While I was researching this book, I read an illuminating work by the anthropologist Christopher Boehm called *Moral Origins*. On page 219, he cites another anthropologist, Eleanor Leacock, who had spent a lot of time with the Cree Indians of northern Canada. Leacock relates a story about how she went on a hunting trip with a Cree named Thomas. Deep in the bush, they encountered two men, strangers, who had run out of food and were extremely hungry. Thomas gave them all his flour and lard, despite the fact that he would have to cut his own trip short as a result. Leacock probed Thomas as to why he did that, and finally he lost patience with her. "Suppose now not give flour and lard," he explained. "Just dead inside."

To be alive inside, to be alive fully, then, we must help the other. Alain Comeau knew this when I asked, "Why go?"

Carrying Weight . . . with Friends

Not long after I read *Tribe*, Lt. Jim Kneeland of NHFG gave me another take on what it means to be alive inside. At the end of a search and rescue meeting, we were talking about his work as an incident commander, a role that often keeps him "in the truck" with his communications gear and maps at or near a trailhead, while those he's directing climb to the rescue. "I miss being on those missions," he said. "The walking together, the carrying, the laughing. Often, the person we're carrying gets laughing, too. It's the camaraderie."

Kneeland went on to point out something I'd noticed but not credited fully: being a conservation officer for NHFG is mostly solitary work. SAR work, which often involves carrying weight with friends, offers the solidarity and relationship of a tribe.

As I mulled this over, an image returned to me: I'm sitting in Gorham's White Mountain Café, waiting to interview NHFG's Sgt. Mark Ober. It's an average winter morning in January of 2016—wan light outside, chill temps—and the café is a warm, coffee-scented refuge, with a dozen people creating a pleasant burble of talk. The doorway darkens as a large figure with a wide-brimmed hat stoops to enter. When he does, people look up, and the room goes quiet. Inside, Ober straightens to just over six uniformed feet; his side-arm is prominent on his hip, and his uniform is immaculate. Pins marking his membership in the Dive Team and the Specialized Search and Rescue Team wink on his chest. He removes his hat, spots me rising, and smiles as we step toward each other. The room exhales, and everyone returns to coffee talk. That pause in the everyday world, that intake of breath, must happen everywhere when a CO steps through a public door. It happened again, in the same place, when Lt. Saunders, a smaller man, but no less trim and distinctive in his Stetson and uniform and similarly armed at the hip, arrived to talk with me in November of the same year. It is a reminder of difference, singularity, separation. In contrast, work with the SAR tribe can offer aid to more than just the victim of accident, providing rescuers a welcome chance to join with others in a group effort that brings everyone closer together.

Going Out to Get Your Own

The sense of tribe is, I imagine, alive and palpable in the gathering and work of all SAR groups; it certainly permeates this whole book. It engenders, too, a spirit of generosity common in the Whites' searchers and rescuers, and that generosity points to the possibility of extended tribes, ones that swell to include those sought and rescued. Even as I have talked with SAR volunteers and professionals about tens of incidents, many occasioned by chuckleheadedness, I've encountered remarkably little finger-pointing judgment. There are exceptions, of course, rescues where the willful or ego-driven endanger others, but they are relatively rare. Much of the time, it's as if engagement with search and rescue expands, temporarily, the membership of the SAR tribe to include those it seeks to rescue. You may be a novice and even head-waggingly dumb in your climb, but once you are in trouble, the "elders" come out to get you.

In the end, we come to this: search and rescue professionals and volunteers—like other tribes—go out and do grinding, sometimes dangerous work in the spirit of shared membership and responsibility. What they get in return is the satisfaction of helping others, the sense of belonging to a greater cause, and the knowledge that they are alive inside.

> POSTSCRIPT: Gratitude—I hope it is clear that rescuers go out often for their own reasons, often as part of a quest to become fully human. They don't go out looking for gratitude from those they help. But of course hearing it voiced is welcome, too. It seems good then to close with a note from someone who was helped. Here are words of thanks, posted on the Pemigewasset Valley Search and Rescue Team's Facebook page in January 2014:

> My name is Peter H., though you may know me better as Callout #15. I want to thank each and every one of you that put your life on hold to come to my assistance on the Old Bridle Path on December 27, 2013. I was overwhelmed and humbled by the generosity and compassion of the 25 volunteers that braved the cold and dark to assist a hiker in need.

> Earlier that day, my hike on Mount Lafayette was interrupted by a twist, a fall, and a crunch. Though I'd never broken a bone before, I knew in an instant that something unfortunate and irreversible had just occurred. From where I landed I was able to trace with my eyes the contour of the ridge I'd need to descend to get back to the trailhead. It would be 3½ miles down a steep, rocky, snow and ice covered trail. I rested for a bit before getting up and trying to walk, but when I did it was obvious that I wouldn't be able to manage the descent on my own.

> I was relieved to discover I had cell phone reception, and dialed 911. They listened as I sheepishly explained my predicament, then patched the call over

to the NH Fish and Game Department. Without a trace of hesitation, I was told that a team of rescuers would come to my assistance. Within forty-five minutes after making that call, I had the good fortune of meeting Jeff and JoAnn Fongemie. Without even discussing it amongst themselves they altered their plans. They spent the next eight hours keeping me company, carrying my pack and assisting the other rescuers. My wait would have been very lonely without them.

It never escaped me just how hard each of you was working to lower me down the trail. You each made me feel like there was no other place that you'd rather be. In just a few short hours, you transported me from a world of darkness, snow, and ice, to the comfort and warmth of an ambulance. I don't believe I've ever been so happy to smell diesel fumes!

I was sad to learn that one of the members of the SAR team sustained an injury during the decent. I hope it was minor and that recovery is quick.

You didn't have to drop everything to come to the mountain. You didn't have to carry all that gear up just to turn around and come right back down. You didn't have to come to my rescue . . . but you did. And for that I am eternally grateful.

Thank you to James Kneeland for providing telephone updates to my wife throughout the afternoon and evening. To all the volunteers of the Mountain Rescue Service, the Pemigewasset Valley Search and Rescue Team, the New Hampshire Fish and Game Department and the U.S. Forest Service: Thank you, thank you, thank you!

This illustration shows both sides of NHFG's advertisement for its Hike Safe card. Created by the NH Legislature, this effort seeks to reduce the annual deficit in the NHFG's SAR budget. The Hike Safe card is unrelated officially to the hikeSafe program, an educational effort developed jointly by the USFS and NHFG. Used by permission of NH Fish and Game.

‹ APPENDIX A ›

THE HIKESAFE PROGRAM

The best rescue is, of course, the one not needed. Self-sufficiency and self-reliance are prized highly in the mountains, but, as these two appendixes make clear, both qualities begin in the resolve and preparation of the mountain wanderer. New Hampshire Fish and Game has joined the U.S. Forest Service in creating and promoting the hikeSafe Program, which has become highly visible throughout the White Mountains. Their educational hikeSafe cards listing hiking's ten essentials and other useful advice are distributed in outlets throughout the mountains.

Note: The hikeSafe card differs from the Hike Safe card described in chapter 19. That card may be purchased for a voluntary contribution that helps defray SAR costs and exempts its holder from charges should he or she need rescue, as long as that rescue is not precipitated by negligence.

< APPENDIX B >

PACK LIKE A RESCUER

Want to pack like a rescuer, perhaps in service of guarding against needing him or her? Many SAR group members have ready-packs so that, when the call comes, they need simply to open the closet, grab the pack, and go—with no rooting about for those gloves or that jacket. Or that headlamp. Such a pack is fuller than Hike Safe's one because this pack's carrier anticipates going to the aid of another.

Here's what the National Association of Search and Rescue (NASAR) says a rescuer's pack needs to contain. The list that follows also contains explanation of the need for many of the items to be packed. In this way, the list offers another lens into the thinking of a rescuer.

Section 1: NASAR Consolidated Pack Guide

NASAR recognizes that SAR responders operate in extremely varied environments. In consideration of local environments, legislation, circumstances, or team standards, NASAR has compiled this Consolidated Pack Guide. This guide is the single publication that documents all NASAR program pack recommendations, and it supersedes all previous pack standards and guidance.

The SAR 24-hour pack is designed to prepare a sole searcher on a field assignment for up to 24 hours with no outside logistical or re-supply assistance. The searcher is expected to wear or carry (layers) clothes/uniform appropriate for the response environment, circumstances, duration and task. It is also expected that the searcher will have the supplies necessary to assist and support an injured victim (or injured searcher) for a portion of the 24-hour assignment.

The recommended equipment falls into several required core capabilities a searcher must be able to perform:

- ＞ Survival / First Aid / Signaling
- ＞ Self-Rescue
- ＞ Hygiene / Personal Items
- ＞ Navigation
- ＞ Communications
- ＞ Light Sources
- ＞ Clothing & Personal Protective Equipment
- ＞ Shelter
- ＞ Food & Hydration
- ＞ Load Bearing / Packs
- ＞ Search

For efficiency, it is recommended that items selected for your 24-hour pack have multiple uses. For example, alcohol wipes can be used as a disinfectant or as a fire starter. Any item that has more than one use helps lighten and consolidate your pack. You can further conserve weight by standardizing the battery used by your communications, lighting and navigation electronics. A lighter pack makes for a more effective search responder.

Setting up your 24-hour pack does not have to be overly expensive. You can save yourself some money by taking advantage of generous pro deals available to NASAR members (e.g. Promotive) or your local team. Most importantly, train with your 24-hour pack in conditions similar to those to which you will respond.

Section 2: Core Capability Item Recommendations

The following tables contain recommended items that may satisfy the requirements for a searcher's core capabilities. Explanation is provided, where applicable, allowing students, instructors and lead evaluators to evaluate equivalent substitutions.

Instructors and lead evaluators are given some latitude in determining needs based on the environment, circumstances, agency requirements, assignment and the searcher's experience.

NASAR expects that safety is always the priority when reviewing items.

Acetaminophen / Aspirin Tablets/ Ibuprofen	For pain management.
Diphenhydramine (Benadryl) Tablets	These can be used to help counteract allergic reactions.
Antiseptic Cleansing Pads	Antiseptic Pads can be used to clean small cuts and scrapes to keep them from getting infected. Alcohol-based pads may sting when you use them, but they can also be used to assist in starting a fire in a survival situation. Iodine-based pads do not sting when you use them, but they have no fire starting capabilities.
Antiseptic Ointment/Cream	These help prevent infection and promote healing of small cuts and abrasions.
Band-Aids, Various Sizes	For wound care.
Candle, Long Burning, Survival Type	For lighting and fire starting, can also be used as a heat source in your shelter.
Cotton Swabs, Non-Sterile	These can be used to help clean small wounds and when soaked in alcohol or Antiseptic Ointment can act as an improvised fire starter.
Duct Tape	The most functional are 3" wide, and can be stored by wrapping it around itself or another pack item like a water bottle or pencil. At a minimum, 10 feet should be carried.
Leaf Bag	A leaf bag makes an expedient raincoat or mini-shelter from the wind and weather for a searcher or subject.
Fire Starting Capability such as Waterproof matches in a protective case or a fire starter that uses a sparking striker	See the NASAR FUNSAR or Freedom of the Hills texts for fire starting options and techniques. Remember, simpler is often your best option.
Moleskin	Moleskin is used to help treat foot blisters.

Gauze Bandage, Roll	First aid.
Safety Pins	Safety pins can be used to repair gear or clothing, as well as to secure slings or bandages.
Splinter Forceps, Tweezers	Removal of stingers or splinters.
Space Blanket / Emergency Reflective Sleeping Bag	Patient or survival shelter.
Hand Sanitizer	In addition to sanitizing, certain types can also be used as a fire starter.
Whistle	Plastic, chamber-based (no ball) whistle is the preferred option. Ball-type whistles can freeze in cold temperatures, rendering the whistle inoperable.
Signal Mirror	Glass mirrors have the best reflective properties, but plastic mirrors are less prone to cracking or breaking in your pack. A mirror that is specifically designed for signaling has a sight window built into it, which is suggested.
Strobe Light/ Other Visual Signal Devices	The surplus government models can be seen for long distances but require a particular battery type. Many newer headlamps and flashlights have a flasher mode built in – a consideration when you buy a light. Laser-based signaling devices are also available. Also, consider small, lightweight signal panels. These are particularly good working with helicopters when you don't want to blind pilot or observers.
Smoke Signal (smoke grenade/ smoke bomb)	Smoke signals are effective signaling devices in the marine environment. In land-based environments, they must be used with extreme care because of the fire hazard potential. In some cases, searchers are not allowed to carry smoke signals or pyrotechnic devices on transport helicopters. The use of a signal mirror is preferred over the use of smoke signals. Signal panels mentioned above as alternative in some circumstances.

Para–Cord / Cordage (50')	For shelter building or repair lashing.
EMT Type Scissors	EMT style scissors are designed to cut through thick fabrics or rope easily.
Sterile Dressings (3 or 4, 4" squares)	First aid.
Water Purification Capability	Several common methods can be used to purify water. The method best for you depends on the local environment and mission. FILTRATION BASED SYSTEMS use a pump and effectively remove suspended solids from dirty water. CHEMICAL SYSTEMS purify the water, but leave the suspended solids in the water. UV SYSTEMS utilize a battery-powered light to kill bacteria but leave the suspended solids. Some systems combine filtration with either UV or chemical methods, providing the best chance for clean water. Spend some time researching what works best in your area and what other members on your team carry. Please refer to Freedom of the Hills for more details on water purification.
Wire Ties / Zip Ties – Several sizes	These can be an aid when building shelters, building splints, closing water containers, repairing a broken zipper or fixing a tent pole.

Carabiners	Meeting or exceeding ASTM F1774 requirements (a locking steel or aluminum carabiner – major axis gate closed 20Kn minimum, minor axis gate closed 7Kn minimum).
Knife or Multi-Tool	A Multi-tool or Swiss army knife is preferred as they have more than one use. Fixed blade knives are less useful than folding blades or a multitool.
Prusik Loops	It is ultimately your responsibility to determine your specific cord requirements for your host rope.
Webbing, 1-inch tubular style, 25ft long.	As this is a life safety item, care must be taken to protect it from chemicals or sunlight exposure. It should also be replaced if overloaded, such as when used to tow a vehicle.

HYGIENE/PERSONAL EQUIPMENT

Personal Medications	Searchers should carry at least 72-hours' worth of personal medications in the event of delay in getting back from an assignment.
Spare Prescription Eyeglasses / Contact Lenses	Personal item.
Sunglasses, 97% UV	Eye protection.
Hand Trowel / Shovel	Used to dig latrine holes for human waste.

Toilet Paper / Feminine Hygiene products	Many outdoor stores sell compact rolls of toilet paper for backpacking. It is important to keep your hygiene products dry. TP and feminine hygiene products can also be used as fire tinder in an emergency, and the latter can also be used as first-aid dressings.
Lip Balm	A lip balm with sunscreen is preferable. Lip balm is just as important in cold weather as it is in hot weather. This can also be used as a tinder accelerant.
Sunscreen	A lotion that has UVA/UVB SPF of 50 is preferred. A higher or lower SPF is a personal preference based on your complexion, environment, and cancer risk.
Insect Repellent	Types and composition vary based on local environmental needs.

NAVIGATION

Compass	A SAR compass should be an orienteering type compass that is graduated in degrees, fluid-filled, has a mirror sighting system, and a clear baseplate.
Pacing Beads/Counter	For measuring distance in the field.
Grid Reader / Map Ruler / Protractor	When working with maps, accuracy is critical. Using a grid reader or map ruler helps you navigate accurately. Should be scaled for use with the maps used most commonly by your AHJ.

GPS	Use of GPS technology has become commonplace in SAR. Many GPS models will work for SAR, and there is a broad range of pricing and features between makes and models. Talk to other members of your team, and see what they carry. Just remember that GPS technology uses batteries and has accuracy issues under certain environmental conditions. Do not allow yourself to become reliant on GPS to the point that your map and compass skills degrade or perish.
Altimeter	Altimeters are typically used in mountainous or hilly terrain and help you in determining how high you are on a slope. There are several styles, with most being barometer based and must be referenced with a known altitude point benchmark. Many GPS units will also display this data.

COMMUNICATION

Radio	Make sure you receive training on its operation, test it before you leave basecamp and have a spare battery.
Cell Phone	Cell phones are commonplace, but cell service is not always reliable in many areas. As battery life may be an issue, consider carrying a backup power source. This backup may also be able to recharge your GPS or some headlamps.

LIGHT SOURCES

Primary Light Source	Your primary light source should be as bright as you can afford, and be hands-free (i.e. a headlamp). You should carry several spare sets of batteries for your primary light. The primary light should be able to be easily moved and manipulated to achieve the greatest effect for searching (moving light source above or below vegetation for example).
Secondary Light Source	Things to consider for the backup light source include common battery size with your other electronic devices, size and weight.
Chemical Light Stick	A white or bright yellow/green light stick can help light the area immediately in front of you. A light stick tied to the end of a 3' para-cord can be swung around in a circle quickly and makes an effective signal at night. A series of light sticks can show an evacuation path for a litter team in the dark.

CLOTHING AND PERSONAL PROTECTIVE EQUIPMENT

Cap / Headgear / Hat	Several hats may be required on a single mission depending on the environment, weather, circumstances, and assignment. Considerations include thermal, rain, sun and eye protection.
Clothing	Appropriate for the environment, weather, circumstances, and assignment. This can be the uniform required by your agency, or team. Be sure to account for weather variations over the next 24 hour period.

Clothing (Extra Set)	Appropriate for the environment, weather, circumstances, and assignment. In the event you, a fellow searcher or the subject is wet, cold, or contaminated, you have options to continue searching, protect someone from the environment, or prevent further contamination. These should be kept in a dry storage bag.
Helmet	Type as determined by your Agency Having Jurisdiction.
Footwear	Choice of footwear is dependent on your environment and mission. You want to select something that protects your foot, fits well, supports your ankle and wears well. You might also want to consider breathability, waterproofness, tread, and the type of sock you are going to wear. Comfort is a paramount concern with footwear. This cannot be overstated.
Gloves	There are different types of gloves you will need to carry: SURGICAL-STYLE GLOVES should be used for triaging and treating victims or collecting evidence. Be considerate of people with latex allergies and use latex-free gloves. LEATHER-STYLE WORK GLOVES protect your hands when searching at night or doing USAR, rescue work, or other rough activities. Many environments feature thick prickly brush which requires gloves day and night. GLOVES THAT PROVIDE PROTECTION and comfort for the environment in which you work.

Eye Protection	Eye protection is a requirement during night searching and will protect the wearer from branches or debris on trail. They should also be worn when working around helicopters where high-speed dust is in the air. Eye protection should meet local safety requirements, can be glasses or goggles, and can be tinted for UV protection (sunglasses).
ANSI/ISEA 207-2010 Compliant Vest	Required when working near traffic and is visible in the wilderness to helicopters, searchers, and hunters.
Socks	Select socks made from wool or synthetic materials that will help wick perspiration away from your feet. They should also provide adequate cushioning based on your mission requirements.
Rainwear	A durable and breathable jacket and pants set with an attached hood are preferred. Gore-Tex or similar material is preferable to plastic or rubber coated materials that can cause overheating. Armpit zipper vents help moisture escape and make the jacket more comfortable.
Trekking Poles	Trekking poles are very useful in many environments, especially when hiking hills. They can double as tracking sticks, a shelter pole or an expedient field splint.
Gaiters	These protect the wearer from thorns, insects, ice, and snow. Make sure you purchase the right gaiters for the mission as snake gaiters are not snow gaiters, etc.
Bandana / Handkerchief	In hot, dry environments, a wet bandana can be used cool your neck. In sunny conditions, a bandana can provide shade. In cold environments, a bandana can be used as a mini-scarf to stay warm. They can also be used as a water filter, signaling device, bandage or sling.

| Zip Lock / Alloksak or other dry bags. | Not only can dry bags be used to keep gear dry, but they can also be used to collect water, keep dirty or contaminated clothes separated from other gear, protect collected evidence, etc. |

SHELTER

Ground Insulation	Depending on the environment, weather, circumstances, and assignment this could be a self-inflating blow-up pad, foam pad, leaf bags stuffed with leaves, etc.
Shelter Material	This can be a tent, bivy or tarp system in some environments. An 8' × 10' piece of waterproof or water resistant material, combined with your paracord and items found in place, should allow you to build a shelter that will protect you from the environment. Inexpensive, lightweight alternatives include disposable Drop Cloths, plastic sheeting or Tyvek.
Leaf Bags	Emergency Shelter material. At least two for sheltering needs.

FOOD AND HYDRATION

| Water Bottle / Canteen / Hydration Bladder | There are many options for carrying water. Some searchers carry hydration bladders that slip into their backpacks, with a drinking tube that comes over their shoulder. Some searchers carry multiple water bottles or other canteens for their water. Personal hydration requirements, as well as local environmental factors, will determine how much water and what style carrier a searcher will carry. |

Sports Drink	Sports drinks like Gatorade or Powerade can enhance water to help replace electrolytes. Avoid mixes with high sugar contents.
Leaf Bags	Emergency Shelter material. At least two for sheltering needs.

LOAD BEARING AND PACKS

Pack	This pack needs to be able to carry all of a searcher's personal items comfortably, while leaving space for any team gear that the mission may require.
Waist/Butt Pack	A full pack may not be required for urban response, as logistical support may be close.
Radio Chest Harness	Radio chest harnesses may also carry your maps, notebook, writing instruments, flagging tape, etc.
Rain Cover (Pack)	To keep your gear dry.

SEARCH EQUIPMENT

Photo Identification	To identify you to an agency or the public if asked.
Pad and Pencil	A searcher should always have a couple of writing instruments and a notebook (preferably waterproof paper) with them at all times.
Tracking Stick – 42" Length	A trekking or a tent pole can be set up as an expedient tracking stick. A 42" length is widely considered to be a minimum length.
Binoculars	Or monocular, to zoom in on distant objects.

Flagging Tape, Fluorescent, 1" thick, 100'	Flagging tape can be used to mark your trail, the areas searched, or an evacuation route for a rescue team.
Measuring Device	Searchers need to be able to measure and compare footprints and strides. Many trackers carry an 18" to 24" small retractable measuring tape or cloth measuring tape. It also can be used for navigation and map work or to provide a scale for photos.

SOURCES AND
FURTHER READING

Appalachia. Boston: Appalachian Mountain Club, semiannual publication begun in
1877.

Booth, Philip. *Before Sleep: Poems*. New York: Viking, 1980.

Braestrup, Kate. *Here If You Need Me: A True Story*. New York: Little, Brown, 2008.

Doherty, Paul T. *Smoke from a Thousand Campfires*. Gorham Hill, NH: P. T. Doherty,
1993.

Howe, Nicholas. *Not without Peril: 150 Years of Misadventure on the Presidential Range
of New Hampshire*. Boston: Appalachian Mountain Club, 2010.

Ilgen, Fred. *The Fatal Hiking Trip*. New York: Fresh Air Club, 1942.

Johnson, Denis. *Seek*. New York: Harper Collins, 2001.

Junger, Sebastian. *Tribe: On Homecoming and Belonging,* New York: Fourth Estate,
2017.

Kahneman, Daniel. *Thinking, Fast and Slow*. New York: Farrar, Straus and Giroux, 2015.

Kick, Peter. *Desperate Steps: Life, Death, and Choices Made in the Mountains of the
Northeast*. Boston: Appalachian Mountain Club, 2015.

Koester, Robert J. *Lost Person Behavior: A Search and Rescue Guide on Where to Look—
for Land, Air, and Water*. Charlottesville, VA: DBS Productions, 2008.

Mayer, Doug, and Rebecca Oreskes. *Mountain Voices: Stories of Life and Adventure in
the White Mountains and Beyond*. Boston: Appalachian Mountain Club, 2012.

Osius, Alison. *Second Ascent: The Story of Hugh Herr*. New York: Laurel, 1993.

Putnam, William Lowell. *Joe Dodge: "One New Hampshire Institution."* Canaan, NH:
Phoenix, 1986.

Ropiek, David. *How Risky Is It Really? Why Our Fears Don't Always Match the Facts*.
New York: McGraw-Hill, 2010.

Smith, Steven D., and Mike Dickerman. *White Mountain Guide: AMC's Comprehen-
sive Guide to Hiking Trails in the White Mountain National Forest*. 29th ed. Boston:
Appalachian Mountain Club, 2012.

Tilburg, Christopher Van. *Mountain Rescue Doctor: Wilderness Medicine in the Extremes of Nature*. New York: St. Martin's, 2007.

Thoreau, Henry David. *The Writings of Henry David Thoreau*. Boston: Houghton
Mifflin, 1906.

Thoreau, Henry David, Edward Hoagland, and J. Parker Huber. *Elevating Ourselves: Thoreau on Mountains*. Boston: Houghton Mifflin, 1999.

Waterman, Laura, and Guy Waterman. *Backwoods Ethics*. Woodstock, VT: Countryman, 1993.

———. *Forest and Crag: A History of Hiking, Trail Blazing, and Adventure in the Northeast Mountains*. Boston: Appalachian Mountain Club, 2003.

———. *Wilderness Ethics: Preserving the Spirit of Wildness*. Woodstock, VT: Countryman, 2014.

INDEX

Page numbers in italics refer to images.
The acronym "SAR" means "search and rescue."

121–24, 156; strategy when caught in, 123; USFS forecasts, necessity of checking, 42, 100, 183

AVSAR. *See* Androscoggin Valley Search and Rescue

Ayres, Philip, 82

Bacon, Edward, 186–91; lawsuit to avoid rescue costs, 190–91; poor judgment of, 188–90; rescue of, 186–88, 191, 224

Baldwin, Lewis, 180–81

Battles, Crispin, 135–36

Batzer, Jeff, 121–24, 156

Baxter, Percival, 240

Baxter State Park (Maine), SAR in, 238–41

Belknap, Jeremy, 63

Berkley, Scott, 212

billing for rescues, 172, 186–91, 191–95, 198–207; debate on, 192–95, 198, 201–7; Maine's policy on, 240–41; number of billed cases, 204; SAR groups' opposition to, 198, 201–2; standard for, 198, 204, 206

Bissell, Jensen, 239–41

Bloomer, Deborah, 205

Bloomsburg College Quest group, rescue of, 38–43; postincident changes to program, 42–43; rescue from Mount Washington, 38–40; sources of trouble for, 41–42

Bourne, Lizzie, 66–67

Bowman, Matt, 14–16, 22, 22, 33, 34

Bretton, David, 227

Brigham, Joe, 226

Brodie, Neil, 243–44

Brown, Chip, 18, 19, 21

bushwhacking, 81

Caggiano, Joe, 79, 95–97

Caldwell, Tommy, 18

Cannon, Joe, 83–84

Cannon Cliff (Franconia Notch), *109*; SAR on, 108–13, 176–78; and SAR improvements, 177–78

CAP. *See* Civil Air Patrol

Carnese, Frank, 95

Carrier, François, 137–38

Carus, Frank, 139, 167–68, 185

caution: as best safety measure, 255–56; during descents, 45; ease of access to trails and, 45–46, 98–99; unfamiliar trails and, 45–46; well-informed, as product of experience, 46

cell phones: calls for help on, 40, 43, 47–48, 186, 219, 232, 233–34, 260, 264–65; and expectations for rapid help, 24, 207, 226, 235; GPS location, potential inaccuracy of, 28; and sense of wilderness, 255; spotty service in mountains, 1–2, 50, 51, 58

Chamonix, France, SAR in, 243–46, 256

Chauvin, Marc, 244–45

Cherim, Mike, 24

Civil Air Patrol (CAP), 24, 27, 28–29, 33

Clark, Allan, 141, 204, 206, 223, 224

cold, extreme, effects of, 21, 26, 30–31. *See also* hypothermia

cold fronts: author's experience of, 79–80; early casualties of, 65–67; SARs due to, 14–35, 38–40, 51–54, 73–78, 108–13, 148–54, 156, 186–91, 212–23, 220; sound made by, 16, 27

Collins, Robert, 110, 112

colonial America, and mountains, 62–63

Colorado, SAR in, 241–43

Columbus Day: park crowds on, 169; SARs on, 170–73

Comeau, Alain, 160, 193–94, 258, 259, 262

conservation: AMC and, 71; creation of National Forest and, 82–84

McCandless, Chris, 18

media coverage: of Matrosova death, 16, 17, 143; of mountain climbing, 17–18; of NHFG role, 174; of SARs, 16, 17–18, 66, 92, 93, 169–73; of SAR system, 131

medical training for hikers, 167

Meltzer, Karl, 209–10

Mont Blanc: deaths on, 245–56; SAR on, 243–44

Moore, Everett, 187

moral responsibility: to aid others, 221–25; to not endanger rescuers, 223–24

Mount Adams, SAR on, 146–47

mountain climbing: and apprenticeship versus training, 118; and appropriate skill level, 41–42; and ease of ascent versus descent, 162, 166–67; ladder of experience in, 117–18, 118–19; media interest in, 17–18; need for special rescue teams in, 108–13; new forms of competition in, 210; North Conway as center for, 113–14; popularity of, and rising death toll, 245–56

Mountain Rescue Association (MRA), 201–2, 206

Mountain Rescue Service (MRS), 115; camaraderie in, 252, 263; expertise of, 25, 119, 128; history of, 114–16, 132; and much-improved rescue capabilities, 177; need for, 108–13; and NHFG, 119–20; recruiting of members, 249–53; role in SAR, 2, 24, 38; SARs by, 25, 26–27, 29, 32, 40, 43, 45, 54, 134–35, 149–54, 176–78, 181, 188, 192, 193, 265; variety in members of, 119–20; as volunteer group, 119

Mountain Voices (Mayer and Oreskes), 116–18, 126, 185

Mount Everest, death zone on, 222

Mount Jackson, billing of hiker rescued on, 192–95

Mount Jefferson, SAR on, 148–54, 156

Mount Katahdin, SAR on, 238–41, 247–48

Mount Lafayette: author's first climb of, 4; SAR on, 51–54, 211–21, 264–65

Mount Madison: as exposed summit, 50; SAR on, 50–51

Mount Moosilauke, SAR on, 233–34

Mount Washington, 38–39; deaths on, 37, 44, 65–67, 73–78; eastern slope, and rock climbers, 113–14; as highest peak in White Mountains, 36; Huntington Ravine, SAR in, 121–24, 156; Lion Head Trail, 43; Oakes Gulf, dangers of, 191; rapid changes in conditions on, 163–64, 165; responsibility for SAR on, 37–38; SARs on, 38–40, 43–46, 137–38, 161–62, 162–63, 163–66, 166–67, 172–73; severity of weather on, 37, 41–42, 76, 78, 90–91, 108; skills needed to climb, 37, 41; summit, facilities on, 37; Thoreau and, 64, 65, 67–68. See also Tuckerman Ravine

Mount Washington Avalanche Center, 19, 42, 100, 164

Mount Washington Observatory (MWObs), 38, 43–44, 49, 86, 89, 93–94

Mount Washington State Park (MWSP), and SAR, 38, 43–44, 130

Mount Washington Volunteer Ski Patrol (MWVSP), 38, 131, 159, 162

Mount Webster, SAR on, 249–51

MRS. See Mountain Rescue Service

Murphy, Heidi, 140–42

MWObs. See Mount Washington Observatory

MWSP. See Mount Washington State Park

Mygatt, Liz, 97

National Association of Search and Rescue (NASAR) pack recommendations, 269–82

Native Americans, in seventeenth
century, 61–62
Nawn, Jake, 135–36
NEK9. *See* New England K9 Search and
Rescue
Neubauer, Paul, 150–51, 152–54
New England K9 Search and Rescue
(NEK9), 136–38
New Hampshire Army National Guard
(NHANG), aerial SAR by, 32, 44, 53,
54, 135, 193, 226–31, 260; and bad-
weather flying, 227–28, 229; cost of, 53–
54, 230; and night vision goggles, 230;
pilots' views on, 230–31; pilot training,
229–30; risk of, 44, 53–54; role in SAR
system, 24, 38, 138; safety record of,
229; typical procedure for, 228–29
New Hampshire Fish and Game. *See* Fish
and Game agency, New Hampshire
(NHFG)
New Hampshire Outdoor Council
(NHOC), 139
NHANG. *See* New Hampshire Army
National Guard
NHFG. *See* Fish and Game agency, New
Hampshire
NHOC. *See* New Hampshire Outdoor
Council
North Conway, NH, as rock climbing
center, 113–14
Not without Peril (Howe), 89, 98–99, 107,
148, 149, 180

Ober, Mark, 2, 23–27, 29, 31, 43–44, 47–49,
58, 132, 263
off-highway recreational vehicles
(OHRVs), regulation of, 169–70,
170–71
Ohler, Bob, 95, 96
Ormsbee, Allan, 73–78
Osius, Alison, 121, 124

pack list: for hikers, 220–21, *266*; for SAR
personnel, 269–82
Parker, Herschel, 75
Parysko, Jacques, 99, 101–2
Pelchat, Mike, 2, 21, 40, 44, 46, 152,
224–25
Pelotons de Gendarmerie de Haute
Montagne (PGHM), 243, 245–56
Pemigewasset Valley, *56, 82*; logging
industry and, 81–83; SAR in, 54–57
Pemigewasset Valley Search and Rescue
Team (PVSART): letter of thanks to,
264–65; member recruitment by, 252;
role in SAR system, 24, 131–32; SARs
by, 54, 57, 187–88, 214, 215, 220; size of,
131; women members of, 140
Perry, John, 111
Pickering, Edward C., 71
police, and SAR, 2, 23, 24, 58, 115, 138–39
Potter, Dean, 225
Powell, Wesley, 113
Preisendorfer, Justin, 33, 34, 131, 249–51
Presidential Range, *38–39*; traverse of, 19,
79–80, 148, 208
Putnam, William, 1, 113
PVSART. *See* Pemigewasset Valley Search
and Rescue Team

Randolph Mountain Club (RMC), 38,
47–49, 50–51, 133–34
Ray, Brad, 159, 160–61, 180–85
Reck, Gregory, 211–21, 222–23
recreation, as concept, 12–13
rescue insurance: in France, 243; and SAR
funding, 245, 246
Restropo (film), 261–62
Rindge, NH, lost boy in, 138
risk-taking: availability of SAR and, 157,
246; by casual hikers, 128–29, 183, 185;
and group decision-making, 165–66;
"Kodak courage" and, 165; popularity

recruiting of new MRS volunteers, 249; on rescue group funding, 139; SARs by, 25, 27, 45, 193; on variety in MRS members, 119–20

wilderness: availability of rescue and, 246, 255–56; emergency shelters and, 80; in myth and legend, 61; shrinking of, 12

Wilkerson, Janet, 29, 30

Wilson, Geoff, 26–27, 29, 177

wind, extreme effects of, 21, 40, *152*

Winkler, Kurt, 177

Winn, Yitka, 210–11

WMSRT. *See* White Mountain Swiftwater Rescue Team

women: as caretakers and hut personnel, 142–43, 144–45; and climbing sports, 72, 140; in SAR groups, 140–45

woods, in winter, ease of losing paths in, 191–92

Woodward, Paul "Woody," 201

World War II surplus gear, and mountain recreation, 99

Wright, Spencer, 113

Wrigley, James, 142, 186

X games, and increase in risky behavior, 174–75